INTERNATIONAL TRADE FINANCE

A PRACTICAL GUIDE

Kwai Wing LUK

City University of Hong Kong Press

First published 1999
Second printing 2001
Printed in Hong Kong

ISBN 962-937-050-6

Published by
City University of Hong Kong Press
Tat Chee Avenue, Kowloon, Hong Kong

Internet: http://www.cityu.edu.hk/upress
E-mail: upress@cityu.edu.hk

INTERNATIONAL
TRADE FINANCE

Contents

Detailed Chapter Contents

Preface

There is very limited published material on international trade finance in Hong Kong. I wrote the book *Foundations of International Trade Finance* for the Hong Kong Institute of Bankers (HKIB) in 1995. Since then I have been urged to write a text book providing in a practical approach to the subject matter for students and banking practitioners.

This book is written primarily for students studying the "Trade Financing" course of study at the City University of Hong Kong. In addition, the book is tailor-made for candidates taking the subject "Banking Practices in Hong Kong" for the HKIB Associateship Examination (Section B). Written in succinct prose and where appropriate in an outline format, the book is a comprehensive treatment of the subject and should prove useful as training material for bankers and lawyers practising in Hong Kong.

In writing the book, I have taken into account the importance of both concept and practice. Risks associated with most trade finance products are discussed. Many examples are given to illustrate the concepts and highlight the practical points. In addition, revision questions are set at the end of each chapter to test the readers' understanding of the subject matter. Reading lists are recommended for most topics so readers can refer to other works for further analysis.

I am much indebted to the following persons for their invaluable advice.

1. Mr. Peter Bentham, a UK training consultant in international trade finance, for his advice on the chapters dealing with "Documentary Credit", "Documentary Collection" and "Banking Facilities and Services for Exporters and Importers".
2. Mr. Joseph S. C. Chan, Training Manager of the Bank of China Group, for his advice on the topics of "Transferable

Credit", "Back-to-Back Credit and Bridge Credit", "Summary of Important Articles of UCP–500", "Techniques in the Examination of Import Documents", and "Points to Note for Exporters upon Receipt of a Documentary Credit".

3. Mr. Marcus Hung, Moderator of "Banking Practices in Hong Kong" of the HKIB Associateship Examination, for his advice on the coverage of the syllabus of the subject examination.

4. Mr. Abdul Latiff Abdul Rahim, a well-known consultant in trade finance, for his advice on the chapters of "Types of Bonds in International Trade" and "Documentary Credit".

5. Mr. T. O. Lee, an international consultant in trade finance, for his advice on the topic "Contractual Relationship of Various Parties in a Documentary Credit Operation".

In addition, I would like to thank the Hong Kong Institute of Bankers for its permission to adapt to the present volume most part of Chapters 2, 3 and 7 of *Foundations of International Trade Finance*.

Last but not least, I am extremely grateful to my colleagues in the City University of Hong Kong Press and Division of Commerce for their full support to me in writing this book. I am particularly indebted to Mr. Edmund Chan for his hard work in editing this book and Dr. Paul Kwong for his valuable editorial advice and patient work in proof reading this book. All omissions and mistakes are, of course, mine.

Kwai Wing LUK
Division of Commerce
City University of Hong Kong
October 1999

Chapter Summaries

The book is divided into two parts. Part I covers basic theory and definition of various instruments in international trade, and the important institutions that have been offering help in promoting exports. Part II provides an in-depth analysis and application of some of the instruments addressed in Part I. As Part II is relatively technical, authentic case materials are used to help readers understand the concepts and practical procedures.

Part I

In international trade, the first and fundamental question is the terms of payment (methods of payment for export sales) to be incorporated in a contract.

Chapter 1 in Illustration

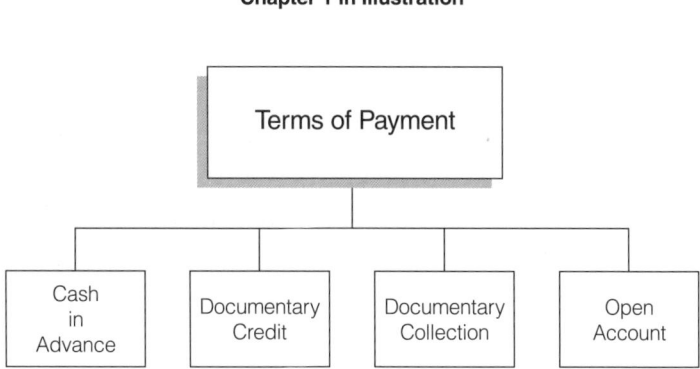

Chapter 1: This chapter describes the components of terms of payment. They are open account, documentary credit, documentary collection, and cash in advance.

Chapter 2 in Illustration

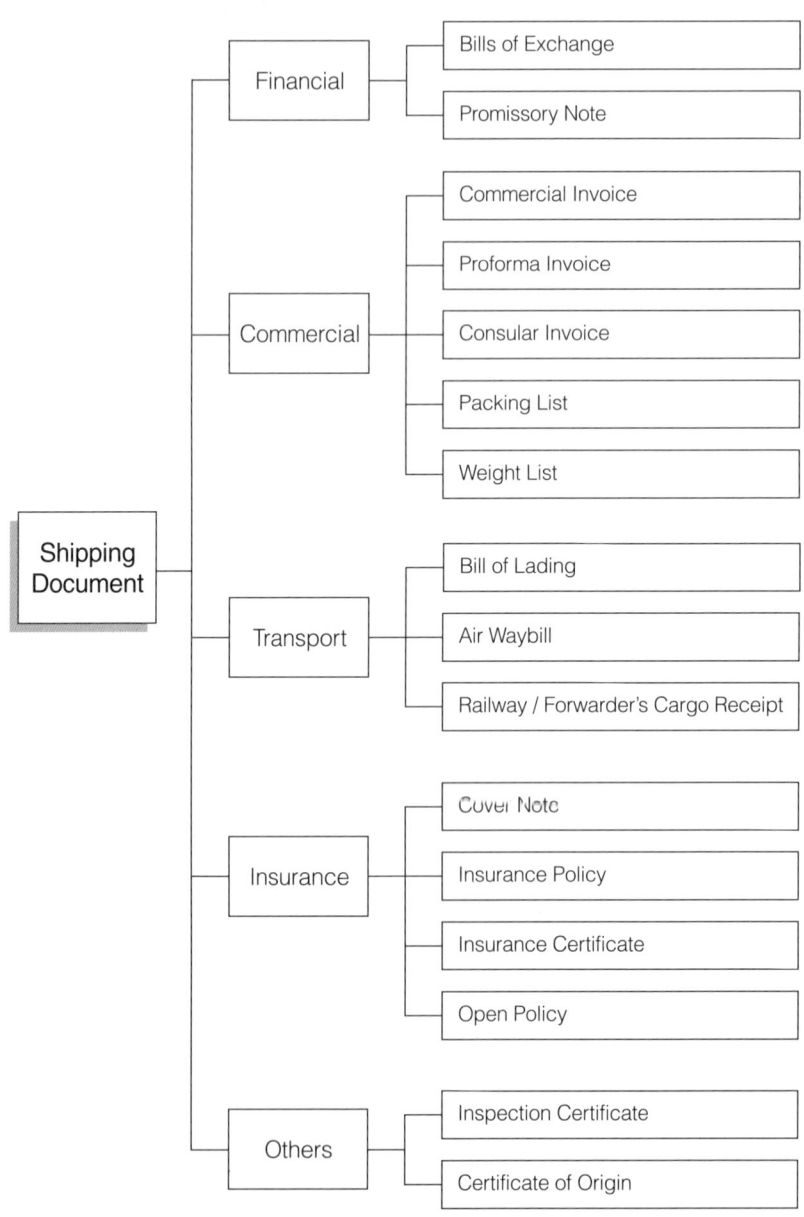

Chapter 3 in Illustration

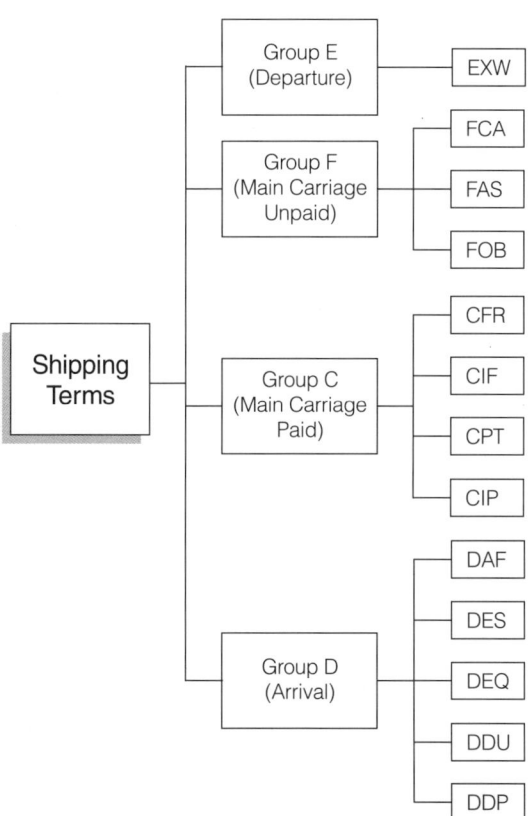

Chapter 2:   Shipping documents are requested to show that the exporter has shipped the goods as agreed. They are prepared either by the exporter or obtained from a third party such as the transport company or the insurance company involved. Examples of shipping documents are financial documents, commercial documents, transport documents, and insurance documents.

Chapter 3:   Shipping terms constitute a part of the sales and purchase contract. They delineate the division of costs and risks between the buyer and the seller, particularly in terms of the cost of the goods, the cost of and risk in carriage, and the party responsible for insurance premium. There are 13 standard shipping terms and that are divided into Group E, Group F, Group C and Group D.

Chapter 4 in Illustration

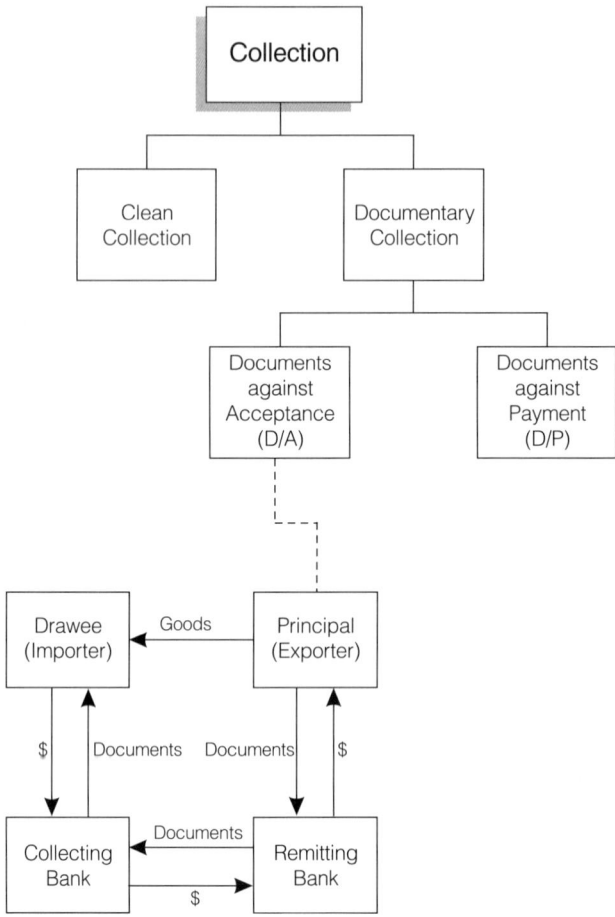

Chapter 4:   The four types of terms of payment in Chapter 1 are described. Collection is one of the four types popularly used in the market and the chapter describes clean collection and documentary collection. Clean collection refers to collection of financial documents without shipping documents. Documentary collection refers to collection of financial documents as well as commercial documents. Documentary collection may refer to collection of commercial documents only. The various parties involved in D/P and D/A are the principal, remitting bank, collecting bank, and the drawee.

Chapter 5 in Illustration

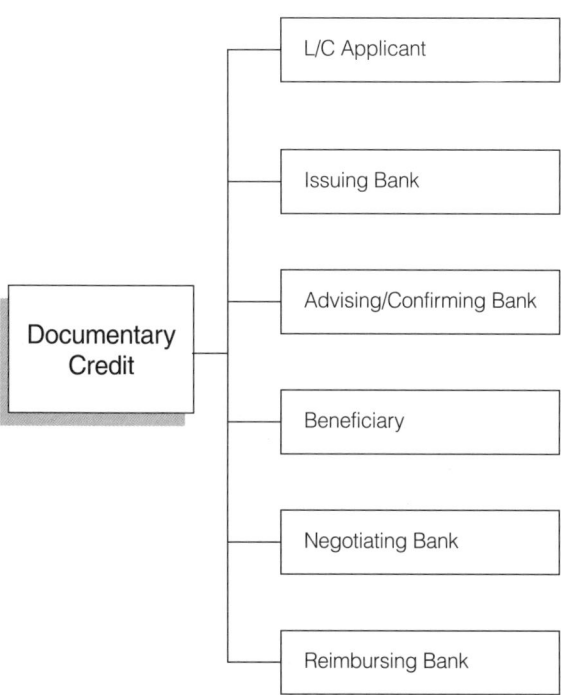

Chapter 5: Documentary credit (D/C) is another term of payment popularly used in international trade. It can be divided into various types of credit which are addressed in Part II in a practical way. The D/C itself is a payment undertaking given by the opening bank in favour of a beneficiary with conditions incorporated in the credit. Various parties are involved in the operation of a simple D/C, namely, the applicant, issuing bank, advising bank/confirming bank, beneficiary, negotiating bank and the reimbursement bank.

Chapter 6: Banks play a crucial role in international trade, particularly in financing. Chapter 6 classifies bank finance into export finance and import finance. Export finance refers to overdrafts, negotiation of export bills, bills discount, bills advance, and usance draft payable at sight basis. Import finance normally refers to loans against imports, trust receipts, shipping guarantees, overdrafts, and documentary credits.

Chapter 6 in Illustration

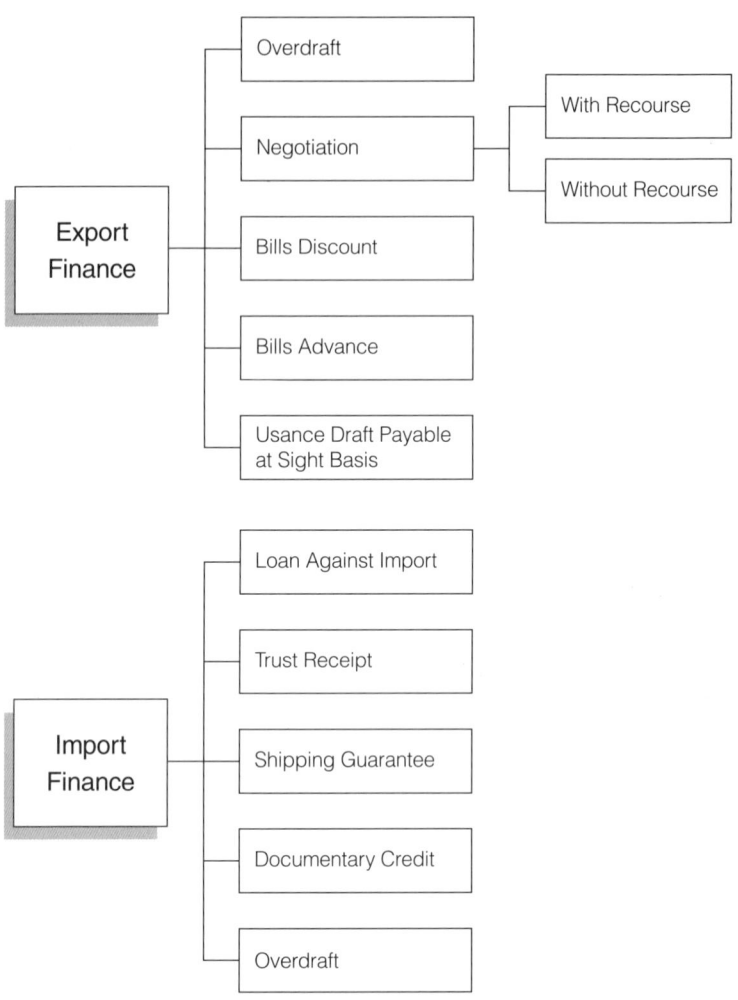

Chapters 7 and 8 in Illustration

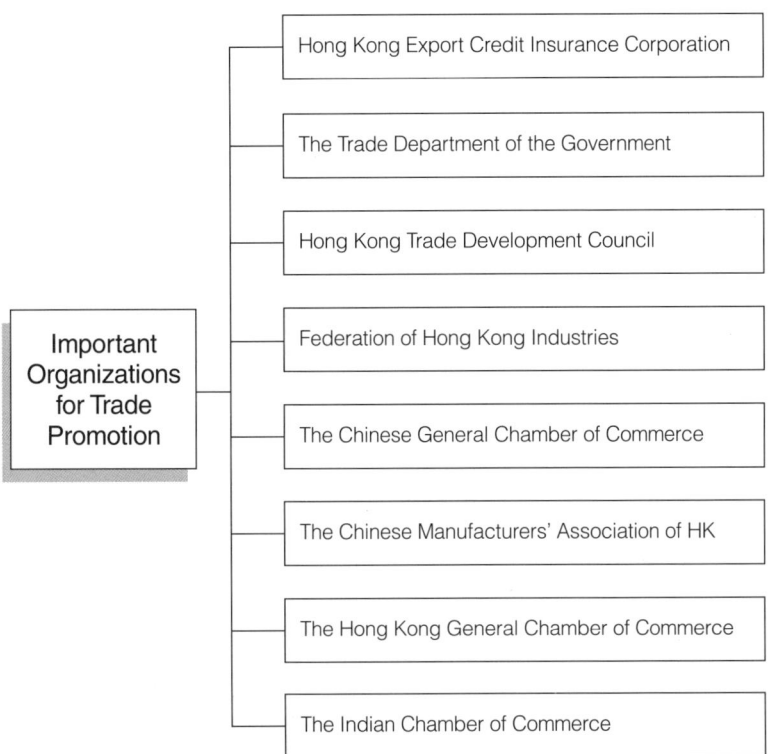

Chapters 7 & 8: Official institutions or semi-official institutions are involved in international trade. They promote Hong Kong products, conduct commercial relations internationally and provide credit information. These important organizations include the Hong Kong Export Credit Insurance Corporation, Trade Department, Trade Development Council, the Hong Kong General Chamber of Commerce, Chinese General Chamber of Commerce, Federation of Hong Kong Industries, Chinese Manufacturers' Association of Hong Kong, and the Indian Chamber of Commerce.

Chapter 9 in Illustration

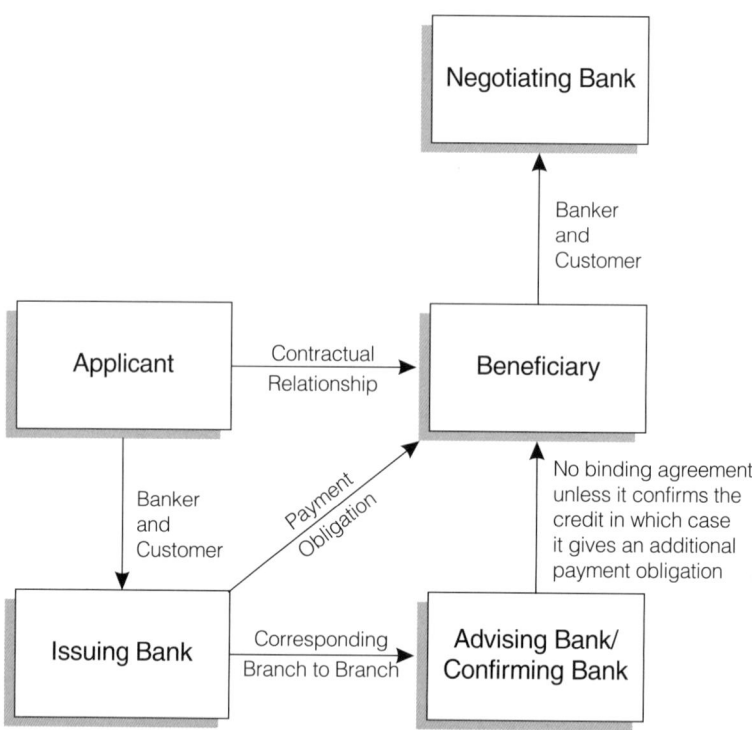

Chapter 9:   As many disputes occur in a D/C transaction, it is important to analyze the contractual relationship among different parties. Lawyers may find this chapter particularly interesting. The following relationships exist in the operation of a D/C:

> Applicant vs Issuing Bank,
> Issuing Bank vs Advising Bank,
> Issuing Bank vs Beneficiary,
> Advising Bank vs Beneficiary,
> Confirming Bank vs Beneficiary,
> Beneficiary vs Negotiating Bank, and
> Applicant vs Beneficiary.

Part II

As mentioned previously, Part II addresses the issues in a practical manner. Many authentic cases are used as illustrations.

Chapters 10, 11, 12 and 13 in Illustration

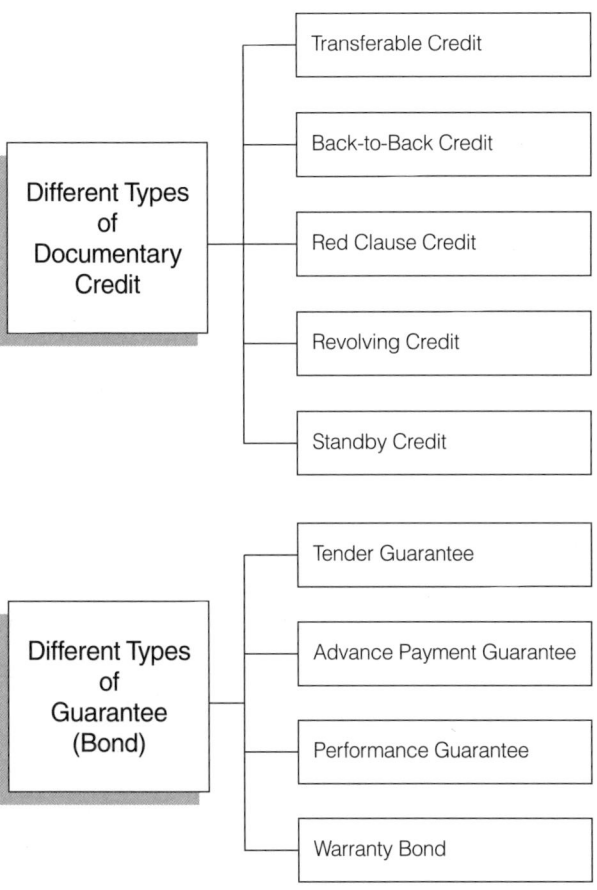

Chapters 10 — 13: The different types of documentary credit are discussed.

Chapters 14, 15 and 16 in Illustration

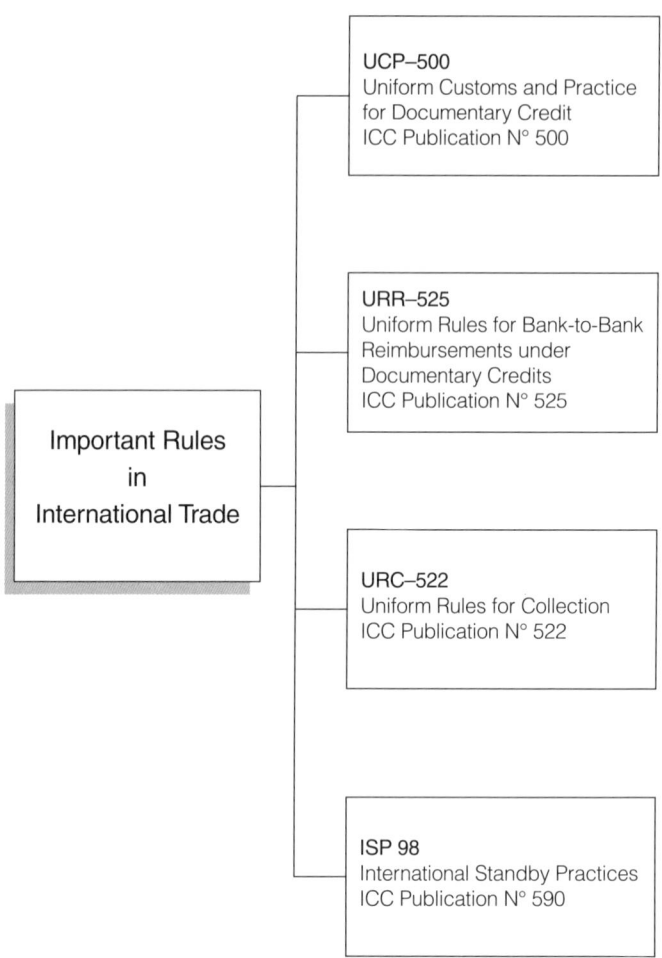

Chapters 14 — 16: Important rules which participants in international trade have to abide by are covered.

Chapter 17 & Appendix: Samples of revision questions and authentic documents used in international trade are displayed respectively.

International Trade Finance

Part I
Principles

1

Terms of Payment in International Trade

❑ Terms of payment in international trade:
   (a) cash in advance, documentary credit (D/C), salient features of a D/C to the beneficiary and applicant
   (b) collection, open account

❑ Different types of documentary credit: red clause credit, revolving credit, transferable credit, back-to-back credit, standby credit, confirmed letter of credit

❑ Advantages and disadvantages of:
   (a) documentary credit to importers and exporters
   (b) collection to importers and exporters

1 Terms of Payment in International Trade

"Terms of payment" refers to the extent to which an exporter would like to be guaranteed payment before he ships the goods to the importer or to a designated place. In general, the lesser the risk to an exporter, the greater the risk to an importer. In other words, to minimize both parties' worries, the importer and the exporter must agree to mutually acceptable payment terms before a contract is agreed. There are basically four terms of payment in international trade. The extent of the risk implied by each term is different for different parties.

These terms of payment are ranked here in ascending order of risk to the exporter. In other words, they are increasingly unfavourable to the exporter but increasingly favourable to the importer:

(a) cash in advance
(b) documentary credit
(c) documentary collection
(d) open account

1.1 Cash in Advance

Under this payment term, an importer is required to pay an exporter prior to delivery. Upon receipt of payment, the exporter delivers the goods to the importer. Cash in advance gives the exporter the greatest protection because payment is received by the exporter either before shipment or upon arrival of the goods. It enables the exporter to avoid tying up his own funds. It is most useful when the importer's country is facing instability such as political uncertainty. Sometimes, exchange controls in the importer's country may cause payment delays or even prohibit funds to move out of the country. If an exporter is facing this kind of country risk, it is advisable for him to insist on trading on this term (see Figure 1.1).

In summary, an exporter may consider trading with this term under the following circumstances:

(a) He is selling the goods which are exclusive to himself in the global market;

Figure 1.1
Cash in Advance

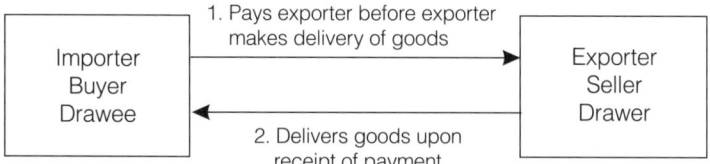

(b) When he is doubtful about the buyer's character and/or ability to pay for the goods; and

(c) When he is exposed to buyer's country risk, arising for example from political and/or economic instability.

1.2 Documentary Credit (D/C)

The meaning of a documentary embodies the following. It is:

(a) a written undertaking given by a bank, known as an issuing bank or opening bank;
(b) to a seller, known as a beneficiary;
(c) at the request and on the instructions of its customer (buyer), known as the D/C applicant;
(d) to pay either at sight or at a specific future date;
(e) a stated sum of money;
(f) against delivery of shipment and submission of stipulated documents and fulfilment of all the terms and conditions in the D/C.

In other words, a documentary credit is a conditional payment instrument made by the issuing bank in favour of a designated beneficiary (or issuing bank and a transferee if transferable). It is especially appropriate in the following circumstances:

(a) When the importer is not well known, the exporter selling on credit terms may wish to have the importer's promise of payment backed by his banker;

Figure 1.2
Diagrammatic Explanation of Various Steps
in the Operation of a Documentary Credit

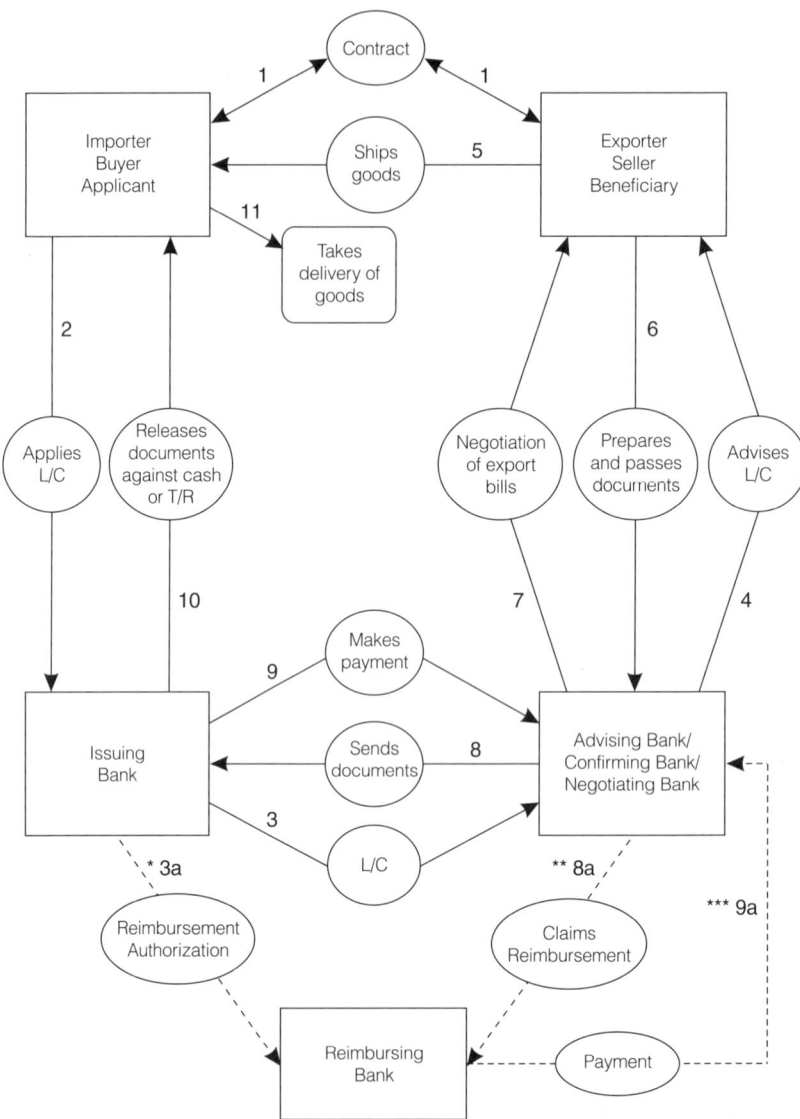

Note: In the case of a reimbursement credit,
1. *   3a } will be involved as well.
   ** 8a }
2. *** 9a   will replace 9.

(b) On the other hand, the importer may not wish to pay the exporter until it is reasonably certain that the merchandise has been shipped in good condition and/or in accordance with his instructions.

A documentary credit, in this case, can satisfy both the exporter and the importer.

1.3 Diagrammatic Explanation of Various Steps in the Operation of a Documentary Credit

Figure 1.2 shows various steps in the operation of documentary credit.

(1) The importer and exporter make a contract before the D/C is issued.

(2) Importer applies for a letter of credit (L/C) from his banker known as the issuing bank. He may have to use his credit lines. If he is a new customer, margin deposit may be required: e.g., 20% deposit on credit amount.

(3) Issuing bank opens the D/C which is channelled through its overseas corresponding bank, known as the advising bank.

(4) Advising bank informs the exporter (the beneficiary) of the arrival of the D/C.

(5) Exporter ships the goods to the importer or other designated place as stipulated in the D/C.

(6) Meanwhile, he prepares his own documents and collects shipping documents or other documents (e.g., insurance policy) from relevant parties. All these documents will be sent to his banker which is acting as the negotiating bank.

(7) Negotiation of export bills happens when the banker agrees to provide him with finance. In this case, he obtains payment immediately upon presentation of the documents. If not, the documents will be sent to the issuing bank for payment or on an approval basis as in the next step.

(8) Documents are sent to the issuing bank (or reimbursement bank which is the bank nominated by the issuing bank to honour reimbursement by the negotiating bank) for reimbursement or payment.

(9) Issuing bank honours its undertaking to pay the negotiating bank on condition that the documents comply with the D/C terms and conditions.

(10) Issuing bank releases documents to importer when the latter makes payment to the former or against the latter's trust receipt facility.

(11) The importer takes delivery of goods upon presentation of the shipping documents.

For an example of a documentary credit, please refer to the Appendix.

1.4 Salient Features of a D/C to the Beneficiary

The main worry for the seller in an export deal is the buyer's default in payment after he has relinquished control over the goods. Assume that the seller receives a documentary credit issued by a reputable bank, that bank stands in the shoes of the buyer to promise to pay him. The promise is in the form of a definite undertaking to pay provided that:

(a) He ships the goods before the latest shipment date.

(b) He prepares documentary support for his shipment. In other words, he is required to submit all the documentary evidence, either gathered from outsiders (e.g., bills of lading, insurance policy) or prepared by himself (e.g., draft, invoice, packing list).

(c) He has fulfilled all terms and conditions as stipulated in the D/C.

As long as he has complied with the instructions in the D/C, the issuing bank (confirming bank, if any) cannot withdraw its undertaking and refuse to pay him. The promise to pay him is enshrined in the "Engagement Clause" which is found in every D/C.

In spite of the above promise, an exporter, upon receipt of a D/C, must make sure that he can subsequently produce all the documents in compliance with credit terms and conditions. Failure to comply with any term, no matter how trivial the inconsistencies may be, constitutes valid grounds for withholding payment. At any time, the exporter must bear in mind that the undertaking given by the issuing bank is conditional. Such conditions are clearly laid down in the Engagement Clause to the effect that the issuing bank engages with drawers and/or bona fide holders that drafts drawn in conformity with the terms of the credit will be duly honoured.

1.5 Salient Features of a D/C to the Applicant

For a beneficiary, it seems that a D/C is relatively more favourable to him compared to a collection. For an applicant, a D/C, meanwhile has much value to him. To a buyer, his utmost concern is the goods, in terms of their quality and arrival time. To ensure that the quality of the goods ordered is up to his standard, he may insert in the D/C a clause calling for an inspection certificate (or even public surveyor's report with loading supervision). He may stipulate in the D/C the latest shipment date to ensure that the goods have been shipped before a stipulated date. Actually, a buyer can, via the issuing bank, add in the D/C any amendment to the terms and conditions which he would like the seller to fulfil before the latter gets paid (provided that the beneficiary accepts such terms).

In spite of the above protection, an applicant should remember that a D/C is a relationship (or contractual relationship as some lawyers said) made between the issuing bank and the beneficiary. According to Uniform Customs and Practice for Documentary Credit (UCP–500), a D/C is separated from the underlying sales and purchase contract made between the buyer and seller. This concept remains unchanged even if any reference whatsoever to such a contract is included in the D/C. Therefore, any disputes in the contract cannot invalidate the definite undertaking of the issuing bank to pay the beneficiary if documents presented comply with the terms and conditions of the D/C. In the worst scenario, even when an exporter has shipped inferior goods, the issuing bank is still obliged to pay the beneficiary if documents presented conform to the D/C. In this awkward situation, there is little the issuing bank can do to help the applicant as, according to Article No. 4, UCP–500, banks deals with documents, and not with goods and services.

Unless the applicant is granted an injunction to restrain the issuing bank from paying the beneficiary in the above case, the opening bank has to pay the seller. However, injunctions of this type are rarely granted by the court. In *Hamzeh Malas & Sons v British Imex Industries Limited*, an injunction was refused. In *Discount Records Limited v Barclays Bank Limited*, it was held that judge tends to be slow to interfere with banker's documentary credit. Both cases reveal that there is little inclination on the part of the courts to interfere in D/C transactions. This is quite understandable as D/C is an instrument to facilitate trade, not to police trade.

1.6 Collection: Introduction

In recent years, collection has become a popular method of payment, particularly in the United states, and there is a growing trend that collection may replace D/C. Collection is a method of settlement of payment by a buyer through bank channels at comparatively low cost and little risk. It is called "collection" because the seller uses the bank system to collect payment from the buyer. Unlike in D/C cases, a bank handling collection is acting as the agent for its customers. In processing collections, banks do not guarantee that the buyer will pay.

The payment instrument in a documentary collection is usually a bill of exchange drawn by the exporter (seller) on the importer (buyer).

Two types of bill of exchange can be drawn:

(a) Sight bill — a bill of exchange drawn by the drawer (exporter) at sight for immediate payment.

(b) Term bill — (usance bill) a bill of exchange drawn by the drawer (exporter) and providing time for the drawee to pay at a fixed or determinable future date, such as 30 days sight.

There are two types of collection (see Figures 1.3 and 1.4). The first type is documentary collection, which means collection of:

(a) financial documents and commercial documents; or

(b) commercial documents only.

Figure 1.3
Documentary Collections: Documents against Payment (D/P)

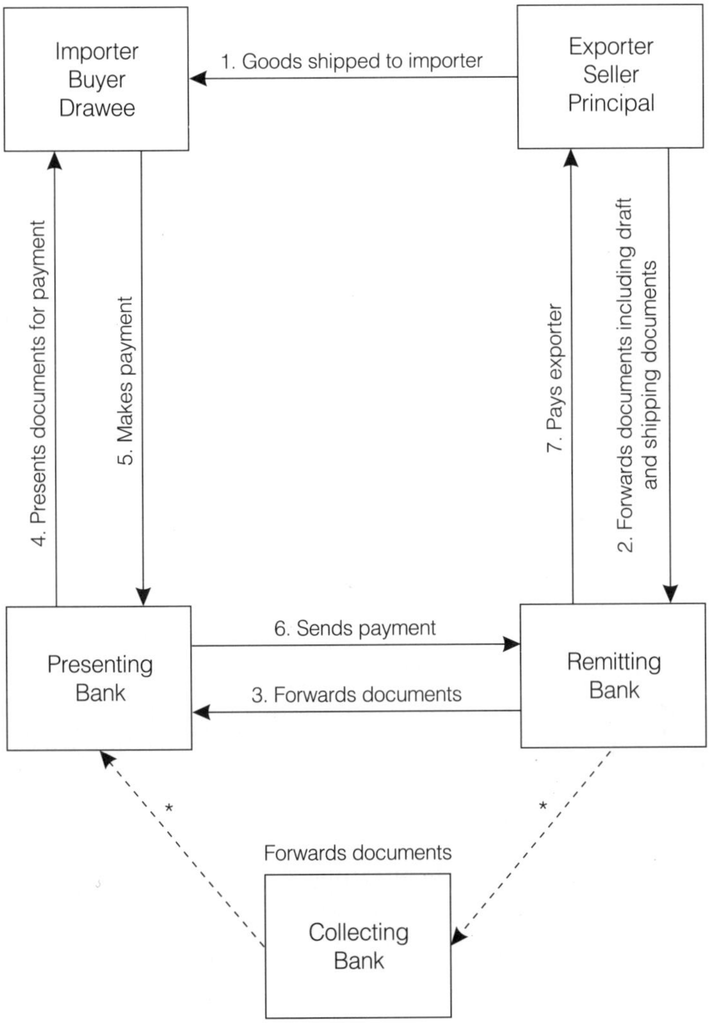

Importer Buyer Drawee
Exporter Seller Principal

1. Goods shipped to importer

4. Presents documents for payment

5. Makes payment

7. Pays exporter

2. Forwards documents including draft and shipping documents

Presenting Bank
Remitting Bank

6. Sends payment

3. Forwards documents

Collecting Bank

Forwards documents

*

*

*   As an alternative to step 3

Figure 1.4
Documentary Collections: Documents against Acceptance (D/A)

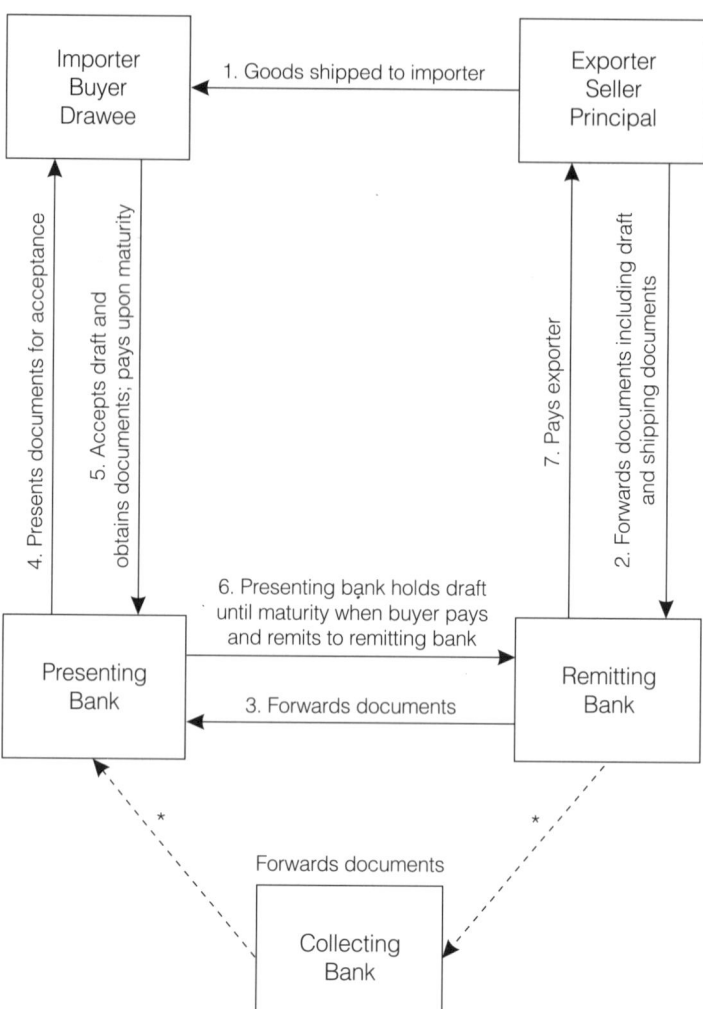

*   As an alternative to step 3

The second type is clean collection. This consists of one or more bills of exchange or promissory notes, for obtaining cash. Clean collection requires no other commercial documents to be attached. In other words, all shipping documents except financial documents are sent direct to the buyer or accompanied the goods. Financial documents such as drafts will be submitted to the remitting bank for obtaining cash (see Figure 1.5).

1.7 Reasons for the Growth of Collection

(a) Collection provides an alternative payment method which can satisfy both the importer and the exporter by means of reducing their worries.

For example, in a potential deal, payment in advance which is favourable to the exporter may not be accepted by the importer. Meanwhile, open account which is favourable to the importer may not be accepted by the exporter. As a compromise, the best alternative is collection which can satisfy both the importer and exporter in terms of:

(1) minimizing the importer's main worry of failure to receive goods after payment, as in payment in advance;

(2) minimizing exporter's worry of buyer's default on payment while he has lost control of the goods, as in open account.

In collection, banks act as the agents for the exporter to collect payment from the importer. Only after having collected payment (D/P, documents against payment) or been guaranteed to pay upon maturity (D/A, documents against acceptance) will the collecting bank release the documents to the importer to enable him take delivery of the goods.

(b) Collection charges are comparatively cheaper for both parties.

(c) Importers prefer to use this method as no credit line is required.

Figure 1.5
Clean Collections

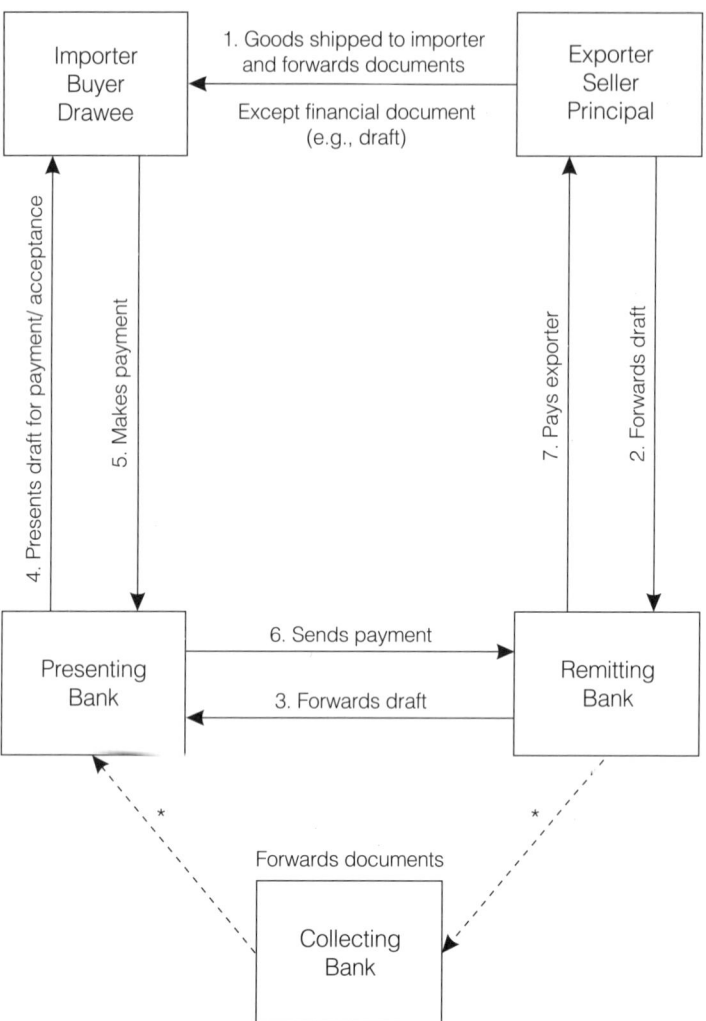

*   As an alternative to step 3

Figures 1.3–1.5 show various steps in the operation of a collection.

(1) The exporter ships the goods to the importer according to contract or importer's instructions.
(2) The exporter presents the documents to his banker (known as the remitting bank) for onward forwarding.
(3) The remitting bank forwards documents to its overseas corresponding bank (known as the presenting bank) according to the instruction of the exporter in the collection order.

   The bank actually making presentation of the documents to the importer is known as the presenting bank. In most cases, the remitting bank forwards documents to the presenting bank which will further present the documents to the importer. In exceptional cases, (for example, the remitting bank has no corresponding relationship with the presenting bank designated by the principal), the remitting bank may forward the documents to another bank in the buyer's country, such as its overseas branch, which is known as the collecting bank as shown by the dotted arrows in the above diagrams. The collecting bank then forwards the documents to the designated presenting bank.

(4) The presenting bank informs the importer of the arrival of the documents and instructs him to make payment or acceptance according to the instructions of the collection order, against the release of documents.
(5) The importer makes payment (under D/P, see Figure 1.3) or accepts draft and pays upon maturity (under D/A, see Figure 1.4) depending on the instructions of the collection order.
(6) The presenting bank sends payment to remitting bank immediately (under D/P) or upon maturity (under D/A).
(7) The remitting bank pays the exporter.

Figure 1.6
Open Account

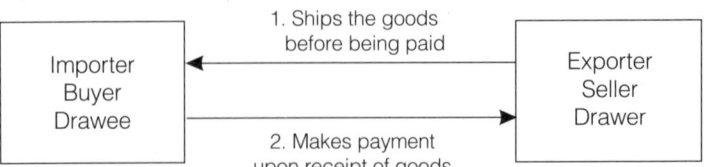

1.8 Open Account

This has become an increasingly important payment method recently in which the exporter ships the goods first and bills the importer later. Upon receipt of goods, the importer pays the exporter by means of telegraphic transfer or sending a demand draft (see Figure 1.6).

These terms are arranged between the buyer and the seller in advance, but the seller has little evidence of the importer's obligation to pay a certain amount at a certain date. This payment method is, therefore, risky for the exporter. Although this payment method bears a higher risk for sellers, open account sales have greatly expanded due to:

(a) major increase in international trade,

(b) improvement in credit information about importers, and

(c) sellers eager to increase export volume.

In most cases, the exporter may accept this relatively unfavourable payment term for the following reasons:

(a) In the domestic and/or global market, the exporter encounters keen competition. In order to be more competitive, the goods have to be sold with the most attractive payment terms to potential buyers.

(b) The market is a buyer's market. The buyers choose to do business only with those sellers trading on open account terms. In order to enlarge export volumes, exporters are given no other choice but to accept or change to accept this unfavourable term.

2 Different Types of Documentary Credit

2.1 Red Clause Credit

A red clause credit is the type of credit with a special clause inserted by the issuing bank at the request of an applicant, which authorizes the advising or confirming bank (advancing bank) to make advances to the beneficiary before presentation of the documents. This constitutes pre-shipment finance in the form of a loan from the advising/confirming bank to the beneficiary. The advancing bank is guaranteed by the issuing bank to be reimbursed for the principal amount plus interest in case the beneficiary subsequently fails to submit documents. The issuing bank has the right of recourse on the D/C applicant.

The credit specifies the amount of the advance to be given to the beneficiary, which can be in the form of a percentage or a fixed sum.

Finance is given against an undertaking from the beneficiary certifying that he promises to ship goods and submit documents to the advising bank which has provided him with finance.

Possible risks in issuing a red clause D/C include:

(a) Exporter may use the advance for other purposes;
(b) Documents presented by the exporter may have discrepancies unacceptable to the importer.

2.2 Revolving Credit

A revolving credit is a D/C which provides for the amount of the credit to be renewed (sometimes known as reinstated) or topped up automatically after use without the need for the applicant to renew the credit every time.

It can be revolved with respect to either:

(a) time, or
(b) amount (e.g., total value of the credit)

A revolving credit "with respect to time" can be cumulative or non-cumulative. A cumulative revolving credit allows any unused credit amount unused during a previous period, usually a month, to be carried forward to the next month. A non-cumulative revolving credit, on the other hand, provides for a maximum amount of credit to be drawn each month. If the exporter fails to draw down for a particular month, the amount in that month (full amount or any utilized balance) will be cancelled automatically.

A revolving credit "with respect to amount" allows the credit amount to be renewed as soon as the exporter presents his shipping documents and uses up the credit amount. As the issuing bank theoretically may incur unlimited liability, this type of revolving credit is rarely seen (refer to Chapter 12, section 5 for details).

Normal circumstances for issuing a revolving credit are if an importer is trading with an overseas exporter and buying the same goods on a regular basis, with the same terms and conditions and at the same unit price, he can issue one revolving credit to this exporter instead of having to issue a separate credit with the same terms and conditions for every shipment. This will save the time and trouble of having to apply for many credits.

2.3 Transferable Credit

A transferable credit is a D/C which can be transferred in whole or in part by the original beneficiary to one or more "second beneficiaries". It is normally used when the first beneficiary does not supply the goods himself, but acts as a middleman between the supplier and the ultimate buyer. Its characteristics are as follows:

(a) A transferable credit must be an irrevocable credit.
(b) A transferable credit can only be transferred once. It cannot be transferred from the "second beneficiary" to a "third beneficiary/beneficiaries". However, it can be transferred to more than one "second beneficiary".
(c) The bank charges in respect of the transfer are payable by the first beneficiary unless specifically instructed otherwise.
(d) The transfer must be in accordance with the terms and conditions of the original credit, except that:

     (1) the name and address of the first beneficiary may be substituted for the name and address of the applicant for the credit;

     (2) the amount of the credit (and the unit price) may be reduced, to allow the first beneficiary to take his profit;

     (3) the expiry date of the credit and shipment date may be shortened.

From an applicant's (original D/C) point of view, a transferable credit exposes him to the additional risks as follows:

(a) He has to deal with an unknown supplier — the integrity of the second beneficiary is not known.

(b) Quality of merchandise is not assured.

(c) Amendments may not be advised to this ultimate supplier, so documents will never comply with D/C terms even though second beneficiary presents documents in compliance with the transferable credit (refer to Chapter 10 for details).

2.4 Back-to-Back Credit

When a beneficiary receives a D/C which is not transferable and he cannot furnish the goods himself, he may arrange with his banker to issue a second credit, known as a "back-to-back credit" to a supplier to supply the goods.

As the two credits cover the same goods, the back-to-back credit must be issued with identical terms to the master credit except that the credit amount, and unit price if any, are smaller. The expiry date of the back-to-back credit is earlier while the latest shipment date may have to be advanced.

The bank issuing the back-to-back credit will obtain repayment through the master credit which is deposited with the bank issuing the back-to-back credit. Also, the bank must try to maintain control of the documents and hold them after payment to the supplier, pending receipt of its customer's invoices, and then present the document itself for payment under the master credit in favour of his customer (refer to Chapter 11 for details).

2.5 Standby Credit

A standby credit is a guarantee type of documentary credit. It may take several forms such as pure loan form, bid bond and performance guarantee form, etc. The situation described below is a pure loan type standby credit.

A standby credit is opened on the request of the customer at the risk of the issuing bank, in favour of a correspondent bank in a foreign country to provide a foreign customer with banking facilities under certain terms and conditions.

On receipt of the D/C, the correspondent bank notifies the foreign customer, stating that a credit line is available to him and at his disposal until the expiry date as stipulated.

At the expiry date, the bank is authorized to draw under the credit for repayment of debts in the event of failure of the foreign customer to make good his payment. A signed statement from the correspondent bank is required to certify the sum unpaid in case of default by the overseas customer.

A standby credit can also be in another form with the same effect as a guarantee against the default in payment of the applicant (refer to Chapter 12, section 7 and Chapter 13, section 6 for details).

2.6 Confirmed Letter of Credit

If a letter of credit is confirmed by a bank (the advising bank), this means that, in addition to the definite undertaking of the issuing bank to honour the beneficiary's draft, the advising bank is instructed to add its promise to pay the beneficiary. Such confirmation by the advising bank not only confirms the undertaking of the issuing bank but also constitutes an additional promise on the part of the advising bank (which becomes a confirming bank).

This confirmation added by the advising bank is requested by the D/C issuing bank which, again, acts at the request of the D/C applicant. In fact, the confirmation request is not made by the applicant, but comes from the beneficiary who may have doubts about the credit worthiness of the issuing bank, or worry about the economic/political stability of the applicant's country.

When the confirming bank has honoured its obligation under the terms of the D/C, it has a right of recourse against the issuing bank.

In practice, the issuing bank must have arranged a line of confirmed credit with the advising bank before opening a confirmed D/C for its customers.

Recently, Hong Kong has seen a particular form of credit confirmation known as "silent confirmation". This confirmation on the credit is added by the advising bank or the beneficiary's banker without instructions from the D/C issuing bank or any prior agreement between the D/C issuing bank and the advising bank/beneficiary's banker.

Such unilateral confirmation by the "confirming bank" without recognition by and knowledge of the issuing bank is not subject to Article 9b, UCP–500 and is made solely at the risk of the "confirming bank".

This type of special confirmation is common among D/C issued by the state-owned banks in China whose policy may not allow the issue of confirmed D/C. It is, however, an open secret that their D/C are silently confirmed by the advising bank/exporter's banker in Hong Kong at the request of the exporter.

3 Advantages and Disadvantages of Documentary Credit and Collection to Importers and Exporters

3.1 Advantages of D/C to an Importer

(a) An importer can be assured that the exporter has complied with certain terms and conditions as specified in the D/C before payment.

(b) He can insist on shipment of goods within a certain time by stipulating a latest shipment date.

(c) He can obtain expert advice from his banker as to the D/C terms.

(d) He can ask for financial assistance from his banker, such as in the form of a trust receipt.

(e) Protection is offered by the Uniform Customs and Practices for Documentary Credits (UCP–500).

3.2 Disadvantages of D/C to an Importer

(a) Since banks deal in documents only, goods may not be necessarily the same as those specified in the credit.

(b) Issuing banks are obliged to pay even though the condition of the goods may be poor.

(c) D/C charges are relatively costly (3% on the first US$ 50,000).

(d) A line of credit or application is necessary before an importer can open a D/C, which may cause extra inconvenience and is time-consuming.

3.3 Advantages of D/C to an Exporter

(a) The risk of non-payment is lower provided he complies with D/C terms and condition.

(b) It is a safe method through which to obtain prompt payment after shipment.

(c) The exporter may obtain expert advice from his banker.

(d) Also, the exporter can seek financial assistance from his banker before the buyer makes payment, in the form of negotiation of export bills, export bills advance, etc.

3.4 Disadvantages of D/C to an Exporter

(a) It is comparatively costly.

(b) Sometimes, the terms and conditions cannot be fulfilled, such as unreasonable shipment date and expiry date and addition of D/C clause "restriction of a designated vessel to be informed by D/C amendment".

(c) The goods must be shipped before payment can be received, so it is not 100% safe.

3.5 Advantages of Collection to an Importer

(a) For clean collections, buyers can take possession of the goods before payment.

(b) For D/A collections, the buyer can inspect and sell the goods before payment.

(c) Term bills provide the buyer with a period of credit from the exporter. Hence, his liquidity can be improved.

3.6 Disadvantages of Collection to an Importer

(a) If he defaults on an accepted bill of exchange (notwithstanding the poor condition of the goods), legal action can be taken against him.

(b) If he refuses to accept or pay a bill, protest by the exporter against non-acceptance or non-payment can be taken by the exporter, which can damage the reputation of the importer.

3.7 Advantages of Collection to an Exporter

(a) It is cheaper than D/C.

(b) A presenting bank may have influence over the foreign buyer and thus be more able to collect the payment than if terms were open account.

(c) Exporters may obtain immediate payment by negotiation of the bill or applying for bank advance.

(d) Exporters can retain control over the goods under D/P.

(e) Compared to open account, an exporter trading on collection basis can apply for bills advance from its banker including clean collection or documentary collection.

3.8 Disadvantages of Collection to an Exporter

(a) Loss of control over goods under D/A.

(b) No guarantee that the buyer will pay because presenting banks are to collect the payment only.

(c) In case of delays or difficulties, an exporter has to bear all the costs arising, such as demurrage charges in the importer's country.

(d) He has to bear buyer's credit risk and country risk.

Revision Questions

1. An exporter known as City I/E Company has been supplying electrical appliances to Vietnam for several years, payment of which is always effected in Hong Kong Dollars by documentary collection. Recently, the company is unwilling to continue to trade on collection terms because payment has been delayed twice by the Vietnam importer. On the other hand, the importer is unwilling to accept "payment in advance" terms.

    Required:

    (a) Define the most suitable method of payment for export sales you would suggest to City I/E Company. Identify the parties involved in this method.

    (b) If City I/E Company is worried that funds may be restricted in moving out of Vietnam as a result of the Asian financial crisis, what other arrangements in addition to (a) would you suggest to your customer so that the chance of "unpaid" bills can be minimized? Explain the characteristics of the instrument.

2. Your customer, City I/E Ltd, is trading actively as a middleman in Hong Kong. It has arranged for a shipment of computer hardware from the U.S.A. to China. The US supplier has insisted on the issuance of a documentary credit as a prerequisite for the trade. As the banker for City I/E Ltd, you wish to offer help.

    Required:

    (a) What types of documentary credit (D/C) can be arranged and issued in favour of the US supplier?

    (b) With reference to the relevant articles of UCP–500, describe the characteristics of one type of the D/Cs you have identified in (a) above.

3. An exporter known as City Company has been supplying technological products to a Chinese buyer for several years, payment of which has always been effected by documentary credit. Recently, the company received a complaint from the

Chinese importer for the increasing commission charged and time involved in this method of payment. On the other hand, City Company is not prepared to accept "open account" terms.

Required:

(a) What are the other methods of payment in export sales available in the market? Describe briefly each method.

(b) Explain the risks of moving away from documentary credit payment terms to open account terms, from the viewpoint of City Company.

4. What is a confirmed credit?

5. State the circumstances under which a back-to-back credit is most appropriate.

6. What additional risks may an original D/C applicant be exposed to with respect to a transferable credit?

Further Reading

1. Charles del Busto, *ICC Guide to Documentary Credit Operations*, International Chamber of Commerce, Chapter 2.

2. Lakshman, *ICC Guide to Collection Operations*, International Chamber of Commerce.

3. James G. Byrnes, *ISP 98 The Official Commentary on the International Standby Practices*, Institute of International Banking Law and Practices, Inc.

2

Shipping Documents
in International Trade

- ❑ Financial documents:
  bill of exchange, promissory note

- ❑ Commercial documents:
  commercial invoice, pro-forma
  invoice, consular invoice, packing list,
  weight list

- ❑ Transportation documents:
  bill of lading and its types, air waybill,
  sea waybill, parcel post, railway cargo
  receipt, forwarder's cargo receipt

- ❑ Insurance documents:
  cover note, insurance policy and
  insurance certificate

- ❑ Other documents:
  quality inspection certificate, public
  surveyor's report, certificate of origin

1 Financial Documents

1.1 Bill of Exchange

According to Hong Kong's S3 Bills of Exchange Ordinance (cap. 19), a bill of exchange is defined as:

(a) an unconditional order in writing;

(b) addressed by one person (the drawer, exporter);

(c) to another (the drawee, importer or issuing bank);

(d) signed by the person giving it (the drawer);

(e) requiring the person to whom it is addressed (the drawee);

(f) to pay;

(g) on demand, or at a fixed or determinable future date;

(h) a certain sum of money;

(i) to, or to the order of, a specified person, or to bearer (payee).

Hence, a bill of exchange is a means of demanding payment used in international trade. It is issued by the drawer (seller) and addressed to drawee (buyer or issuing bank).

A bill of exchange can be either a sight bill or term bill. A term bill is also known as a usance bill, or tenor bill. A sight bill is a bill against which payment must be made by the drawee at sight of the bill. A term bill, on the other hand, allows payment to be made by the drawee at a later date, which can be as few as 10 days, or as many as 365 days after sight. It is quite common to see term bills with "30 days after sight", "60 days after sight", (normally written as 30 days sight, 60 days sight) and so on.

A term bill may read as "60 days after date" which means the bill will expire 60 days after the **date of issue** of the bill. It is paid only at maturity date. A tenor bill, in effect, is a credit period given to the importer at the expense of the exporter.

1.2 Promissory Note

According to S.89(1) Bills of Exchange Ordinance (cap. 19):

"A promissory note is an unconditional promise in writing made by one person to another signed by the issuer, engaging to pay, on demand or at a fixed or determinable future time, a sum certain in money to, or to the order of, a specified person or to bearer."

A promissory note is a promise from the issuer to another that he himself will pay. Common types of promissory note are IOUs and banknotes. In international trade, a promissory note is made by the importer who engages to pay the exporter at a determinable future date a certain sum of money. Upon collection, a collecting bank may be instructed to release documents against the buyer's creation of a promissory note. It should be noted that bills of exchange are more widely used in collection.

2 Commercial Documents

2.1 Commercial Invoice

A commercial invoice is an accounting document issued by the exporter in order to demand payment for goods sold to importers. The contents of a standard commercial invoice should at least consist of:

(a) name and address of the seller;

(b) name and address of the buyer;

(c) date of issue of the document;

(d) invoice number or seller's reference number;

(e) the description of goods, quantity, unit price (if any) and total value;

(f) the trade terms (e.g., CIF Hong Kong, CFR Hong Kong).

Sometimes, a buyer may request the seller to add a statement in the invoice to protect his interests. For example, a D/C may contain the following requirement: "Invoice to certify that the goods shipped are in good condition". This statement serves the same function as if the D/C were calling for a "Beneficiary Certificate" to this effect. It is quite common to observe this practice in D/C issued in Hong Kong in favour of beneficiaries in China, or vice versa.

2.2 Pro-forma Invoice

A pro-forma invoice is different from a commercial invoice. It serves as a price quotation by a seller to a buyer. It is important to note that with the use of a pro-forma invoice, the buyer and seller have not entered into a binding contract. A pro-forma invoice serves the following functions:

(a) The overseas buyer might need a pro-forma invoice with which to apply for an import licence or the foreign exchange to pay for the goods, in which case it serves as a price quotation.

(b) It can be used by an exporter to tender for an export contract.

2.3 Consular Invoice

This is a commercial invoice prepared in a form printed in the exporter's country by the consulate of the buyer's country. It is then stamped by the consulate. The purpose of a consular invoice is to confirm the details of the shipment in order to help the government of the buyer's country to control the volume of imports (e.g., to prevent the "dumping" of goods).

In some countries, traders may prefer to use a "legalized invoice" which serves a similar function as a consular invoice. Here, the document must be legalized by the country's embassy or consulate in the seller's country for which usually a fee may be charged.

2.4 Packing List

The packing list provides details of the packing of the goods and increases convenience for the buyer in taking delivery. This is a useful document as regards imports of goods with different sizes and colours. Where a D/C calls for a packing list, an exporter must be careful that the weights and measurements in the packing list correspond precisely with those appeared in the bill of lading. Meanwhile, he has to ensure that all the details shown are consistent with other shipping documents.

2.5 Weight List (Weight Note)

This is a document issued by the exporter declaring the weight of the goods. It should be noted that this declared weight must be consistent with the weight shown on other documents. In particular, if a D/C calls for a weight list, a seller must be aware that he is expected to present a document with a declaration of weights corresponding to those entered on the bill of lading.

3 Transport Documents

3.1 Bill of Lading

A bill of lading is a transportation document for goods shipped by sea. It is issued by shipping companies or their agents, usually in the form of an ocean bill of lading (marine bill of lading). A bill of lading serves three separate functions:

(a) It is evidence of a contract made between the shipping company and either the exporter or the foreign buyer to transport the goods by sea.

(b) It is an official receipt for the goods taken on board the ship, and provides some details about the condition of the goods received by the shipping company, e.g., "one case broken", "shipper's load and count", "said to contain ten pallets".

(c) A bill of lading is also a **document of title** which means that the company named on the bill of lading has the right to possess the goods. Originally, the title belongs to the shipper (i.e., exporter). When the shipper endorses the title, the negotiating bank or the issuing bank or the buyer may become entitled to the bill of lading depending on the circumstances of the case (i.e., depending on the name of the endorsee). Indeed, the goods will only be released by the shipping company at the port of destination to the party who presents a signed original of the bill of lading.

There are six types of bill of lading:

(a) Liner bill of lading — This is a bill of lading for carriage by vessels on scheduled journeys which have a reserved berth at their destination. Hence, scheduled departure of the ship is certain.

(b) Marine bill of lading — This type of bill of lading is issued by a shipping company when the goods are transported from one port to another port by ship. A marine bill of lading is also known as an ocean bill of lading.

(c) Multimodal transport bill of lading — Most consignments of goods have to be carried by more than one mode of transport, and a multimodal transport bill of lading is a transportation document for the movement of goods from start to finish. It acts as a document of title for the entire journey of the goods including every stage of that journey (e.g., one mode is by land, followed by another by sea). Formerly it was known as a combined transport bill of lading.

The issuer of a multimodal transport bill of lading accepts responsibility for the carriage of the goods from beginning to end and accepts liability for loss or damage to the goods, on whichever stage it might occur.

(d) Short form bill of lading — A short form bill of lading is a bill of lading which does not contain the shipping company's conditions and terms of carriage. In other words, the "small print" on the reverse side of a standard bill of lading is not shown the conditions of carriage and must be referred to elsewhere, for example, on a "master document", or a copy of the carrier's standard conditions, which are obtainable at the carrier's offices.

A short form bill of lading is acceptable according to Article 23 a, v of UCP–500.

(e) Charter party bill of lading — This is a bill of lading issued by the hirer of a vessel to the exporter. This arises when a trading company (known as the hirer) hires a vessel from a shipowner, and there is spare space available for the storage of extra cargo. This hirer may enter into a contract of carriage with the exporter and issue to this exporter a charter party bill of lading. The terms of the bill of lading are subject to the contract of hire between the shipowner and the hirer. Because of the legal complexity and possible conflict of carriage terms between the two contracts, this type of bill of lading is not accepted by banks and UCP–500 unless specifically authorized otherwise.

(f) Forwarder's bill of lading — This type of bill of lading evidences a contract of carriage and a receipt for the goods by the forwarder who will arrange to have the goods transported by a shipping company. Such a bill of lading is not accepted by UCP–500 unless the freight forwarder issuing such a bill of lading:

(1) acts as the carrier or multimodal transport operator and fulfils other requirements of Article 30 UCP–500;

(2) acts as a named agent for and on behalf of the carrier or multimodal transport operator;

(3) unless specifically authorized otherwise.

3.2 Air Waybill

An air waybill is a waybill for goods transported by air. It is a contract of carriage and a receipt by the airline for goods received into custody. These two functions are the same as in a bill of lading.

However, it is *not* a document of title. The airline will hand the goods to the consignee at the airport of destination without asking the consignee to submit the original copy of the air waybill. So, if a D/C calls for an air waybill with applicant to be shown as the consignee, the bank has lost title to the goods. The issuing bank should, therefore, take additional security from the applicant, e.g., earmark the trust receipt facility before the issue of the D/C.

It should be noted that, according to Article 37 a, iii UCP–500, the date of issuance of the air waybill is deemed to be the date of shipment. Where a D/C specifically requires an actual flight date to be shown on the air waybill, then, the flight date is deemed to be the date of shipment.

3.3 Sea Waybill

A sea waybill is a waybill for goods transported by sea. It differs from a bill of lading in that it is not negotiable and is therefore not a document of title. The shipping company will release the goods to the named consignee upon proof of identity. It is normally used when the seller is trading on open account terms. The importer will find a sea waybill allows for more convenience and minimum formality in taking delivery of the goods. In particular, the importer does not have to wait for the original sea waybill to be submitted to the transport company in order for him to take delivery of the goods.

3.4 Parcel Post (Postal Receipt)

This is a post office receipt for goods sent through the post office. The receipt provides details and evidence of the despatch of goods. It is not a document of title as is a bill of lading. The goods will be sent directly to the person named in the receipt. So, if a D/C calls for a postal receipt as a transport document, with importer as the consignee, the bank will lose control over the goods.

3.5 Railway Cargo Receipt

This is a transportation document which allows a railway company to release the goods to the consignee upon proof of identity. A railway cargo receipt serves similar functions as a bill of lading, e.g., (a) evidence of contract, (b) official receipt, (c) document of title.

3.6 Forwarder's Cargo Receipt

This is a transportation document in which the forwarding agent company is instructed to release the goods to the consignee named in the cargo receipt. In Hong Kong, even though the bank is shown as the consignee and the importer as the "notify party", some unscrupulous forwarders release the goods to the importer against the latter's indemnity. So, the bank has in effect lost control over the goods.

4 Insurance Documents

In order to protect against the risks of loss and damage to the goods during transit, it is necessary to arrange adequate insurance cover from the time the goods leave the factory to the time buyer takes delivery. Depending on the trade terms, either the buyer or the seller may arrange and procure insurance. For example, under CIF (cost, insurance, freight) terms, the seller must procure and pay the insurance premium. In a FOB (free on board) sale, it is the buyer who is obliged to arrange and pay the premium. A standard insurance document should contain the following details:

(a) Name of insurer;
(b) Name of insured (beneficiary under the insurance cover);
(c) Types of risks and insured value;
(d) Description of goods;
(e) Whether claims are payable at destination or other places.

In most cases, the seller is shown as the insured party. Endorsement by the insured is necessary so that the right to claim under the policy is subsequently transferred to the buyer. Depending on each case, an insurance document can be:

(a) Cover note — this is issued by an insurance broker to provide notice that steps are being taken to issue an insurance policy or certificate. Hence, it is not a legally valid insurance document and in D/C transactions is not acceptable by UCP–500.

(b) Insurance policy — it gives full details of the risks covered, and is evidence of a contract of insurance between the insurance company (insurer) and the customer (insured). It is used for single consignments.

(c) Open policy — in doing business, a seller may have to ship goods on a regular basis. To insure against damage or loss to the goods, he may have to purchase an insurance policy whenever he ships the goods. This is inconvenient for the seller. Instead of purchasing several successive insurance policies, he can take out an open policy.

An open policy allows the seller under one policy to cover all shipments (up to a limit per shipment) under the same terms and conditions in a given period of time.

Under open policy cover, the seller (the insured) must advise the insurance company of all the details of each shipment by entering the details of the goods in an Insurance Certificate. When the seller has taken out an open policy, he is authorized to issue an Insurance Certificate (a pre-printed form designed and given by the insurance company).

(d) Insurance certificate — this shows the value and details of the shipment, and the risks covered. It is a standard form prepared by the insurance company, filled in and signed by the exporter. Then the certificate will be countersigned by the insurance company. It is normally used together with an open policy. The certificate describes, among other information, the shipping details and makes reference to the open policy.

Whatever forms of insurance document are used, it should have the following characteristics:

(a) The cover should be effective at least from the date the journey starts (It should be noted that the issue date of a policy may not be the effective date of the policy).

(b) The currency and amount of cover should be sufficient. The documents should be signed as required.

(c) The goods should be described on the documents to enable such goods to be identified. The party to whom, and the place from which, claims are to be made payable should be acceptable to the seller or the buyer, depending upon who is to take out the insurance cover. [1]

Risks covered by an insurance policy are often provided on the basis of "Institute Cargo Clauses" provided by the Institute of London Underwriters. These clauses include:

(a) Institute Cargo Clause (A), e.g., All risks;
(b) Institute Cargo Clause (B), e.g., With Average (WA);
(c) Institute Cargo Clause (C), e.g., Free from Particular Average (FPA).

Institute Cargo Clauses (A) is widely used in shipment of manufactured goods, new machinery, garments, electrical goods and packaged commodities. It covers the following risks:

(a) all risks of physical loss of or damage to goods;
(b) general average — goods sacrificed or expenditure incurred to save the entire shipment. For example, suppose there is a fire on the ship and some of the cargo is damaged by the water used to put out a fire. An insured whose goods are unharmed may be expected to contribute to that loss, and if so the insurance policy will cover this.

It should be noted that in Institute Cargo Clauses (A), the following risks are not covered:

(a) wilful misconduct of the Insured;
(b) ordinary leakage, loss in weight, wear and tear;
(c) insufficiency or unsuitability of packing;
(d) inherent vice;
(e) delay;
(f) insolvency or financial default of owner or charterer of vessel;
(g) unseaworthiness of vessel if known;
(h) war and strikes;
(i) nuclear fission.

Institute Cargo Clauses (B) is widely used in shipment of wheat, cement, glass sheets, and used machinery. It covers the following risks:

(a) fire or explosion;
(b) vessel being stranded, sunk or capsized;
(c) overturning or derailment of the land conveyance;

(d) collision of vessel or conveyance;

(e) general average;

(f) jettison or washing overboard;

(g) earthquake, volcanic eruption or lightning;

(h) entry of sea, lake or river water into vessel or craft hold in which the goods are located;

(i) total loss of package during loading onto or unloading from vessel or craft;

(j) discharge of goods at port of distress.

It should be noted that in Institute Cargo Clauses (B), the risks not covered are the same as Institute Cargo (A), plus deliberate damage.

Institute Cargo Clauses (C) is widely used to cover the shipment of steel, timber, loose grains. It covers the following risks:

(a) fire or explosion;

(b) vessel being stranded, sunk or capsized;

(c) overturning or derailment of land conveyance;

(d) collision of vessel or conveyance;

(e) general average;

(f) jettison;

(g) discharge of goods at port of distress.

In Institute Cargo Clauses (C), the risks not covered are the same as Institute Cargo (B).

It is worth pointing out that Institute Cargo Clauses A, B or C do not cover war or strike. To insure against the risk of loss from war or strike, an insured must cover Institute War Clauses (Cargo) and Institute Strike Clauses (Cargo) respectively as per the following:

> Institute War Clauses (Cargo) — this insurance covers loss of or damage to the goods caused by war, civil commotion, revolution, rebellion, capture or detainment, mines, torpedoes or bombs.

> Institute Strike Clauses (Cargo) — this insurance covers loss of or damage to the goods caused by strikers, locked-out

workmen, or persons taking part in labour disturbances, terrorists, riots or civil commotions.[2]

5 Other Documents

(a) If a buyer would like to see the quality of the goods up to his satisfaction or a specified standard, he may ask for an independent party to inspect the quality of the goods before despatch. This independent person would then issue a **third party quality inspection certificate**.

(b) A **supplier's quality inspection certificate** is a signed declaration by the supplier to the effect that the goods have been inspected before despatch and are of a quality in accordance with the contract of sale. As this inspection certificate is issued by the supplier, this assurance is sometimes doubtful. Hence, a third party inspection certificate gives better assurance of the quality and standard of the goods. In addition, a **Public Surveyor's Report** serves the best assurance of the quality of the goods. A Public Surveyor is deemed to be an independent party whose judgement is assumed to be impartial.

(c) A **certificate of origin** is a document required by the authorities of the importing country. This document serves as evidence of the country from which the goods originated. The reasons for calling for a certificate of origin may include the following circumstances:

(1) The importing country may forbid goods to be imported from some countries because of political reasons. Here, the purpose of the certificate of origin is to show that the goods imported are not from a prohibited country.

(2) That the goods originate from a well-known country may have added value to the goods and increased the marketability of the products.

(3) That the goods imported from friendly countries may be exempted from import duty or enjoy preferential rates of duty.

In Hong Kong, various organizations are authorized to issue certificates of origin, e.g., The Hong Kong General Chamber of Commerce, the Trade Department, Federation of Hong Kong Industries, Chinese Chamber of Commerce, Chinese Manufacturers' Association of Hong Kong and the Indian Chamber of Commerce.

Notes

1. Lakshman Y. Wickremeratne, *ICC Guide to Collection Operations*, International Chamber of Commerce.

2. HSBC, *The ABC Guide to Trade Services*.

Revision Questions

1. What is a sea waybill? Explain why an importer may prefer the use of a sea waybill to a bill of lading.
2. Are the functions of a pro-forma invoice similar to those of a commercial invoice?
3. State the main functions of a bill of lading.
4. Which types of bill of lading are not accepted by issuing banks?
5. Under what conditions is a forwarder's bill of lading acceptable to bankers.
6. State the reasons why a Public Surveyor's Report gives better assurance of the quality of the goods than a supplier's inspection certificate.
7. Explain the use of a Certificate of Origin.
8. What is the use of a Consular Invoice? Are there any differences between a Consular Invoice and a legalized invoice?

Further Reading

1. Charles del Busto, *ICC Guide to Documentary Credit Operations*, International Chamber of Commerce, Chapter 5.
2. Lakshman Y. Wickremeratne, *ICC Guide to Collection Operations*, International Chamber of Commerce, Chapter 6.

3

Shipping Terms Used in International Trade

❑ Meaning of shipping terms

❑ Purpose of shipping terms

❑ Common shipping terms and their abbreviations

❑ Division of costs, risks and responsibilities under Incoterms

❑ Summary of I.C.C. Incoterms 1990

❑ Summary of mode of transport and the appropriate Incoterms 1990

❑ Variants in Incoterms

❑ Limitations in Incoterms

❑ Incoterms 2000

1   Meaning of Shipping Terms

Shipping terms (Incoterms) explain the division of costs and risks between the buyer and the seller. Specifically, they divide the responsibilities between both parties with respect to:

(a) Carriage of the goods from seller to buyer: who is to pay freight charges;

(b) Export and import formalities, including export and import clearance, duties;

(c) Who is to arrange and purchase insurance;

(d) Who should pay the costs of loading and unloading of the goods;

(e) The risks of loss of or damage to the goods.

Shipping terms constitute a part of the sales and purchase contract in which quantity, unit price, and contract amount are agreed between seller and buyer They specifically deal with the questions relating to the delivery of the goods. Shipping terms are also known as Incoterms, trade terms, or shipment terms.

2   Purpose of Incoterms (Shipping Terms)

"INCOTERMS" stand for international commercial terms They provide a set of international rules for the interpretation of the trade terms used in international trade contracts by indicating the responsibilities of the exporter and the importer.

Incoterms are established to overcome the difficulties faced by importers and exporters concerning the problems as to the laws of which country will be applicable to their contracts, as well as the difficulties arising from diversity in interpretation, and unclear division of responsibilities between the exporter and importer during the carriage of the goods.

A point worthy to note is that if there are special provisions in the individual contract between trading parties, they will override the provisions in the rules. Traders may adopt Incoterms as the general

Figure 3.1
Diagram for Shipping Terms

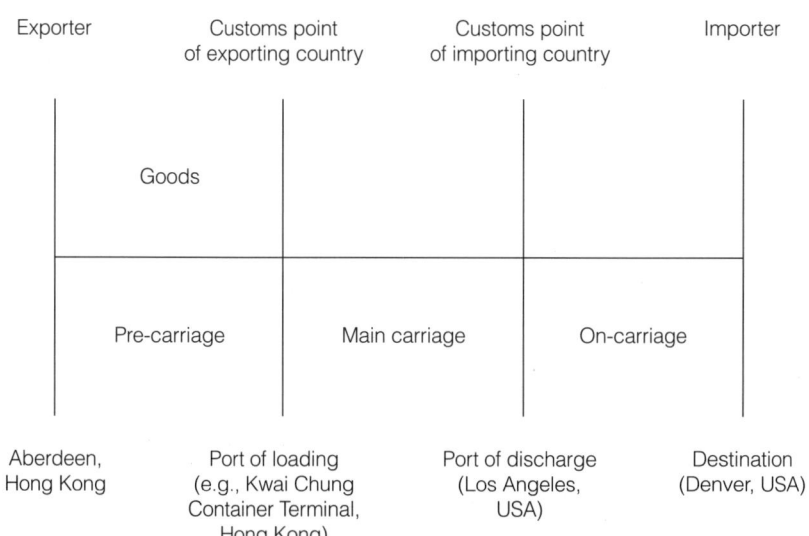

basis of their contract and specify particular variations of them so as to meet their particular requirements.

Before we go into details of every shipping term, let us examine each step during the carriage of goods from one place to another. Figure 3.1 will help to illustrate this.

In this example, a supplier in Hong Kong is exporting goods from Aberdeen, Hong Kong to Denver, USA. The pre-carriage refers to the transportation of the goods from Aberdeen Hong Kong to Kwai Chung Container Terminal. The main carriage refers to the voyage from Kwai Chung Container port to the port of destination, Los Angeles. The on-carriage transportation from the Port of Los Angeles to Denver extends and here is an inland transportation sector.

Under EXW (see Section 3.1 for details), the importer takes delivery of the goods from the exporter's warehouse and hence, he is responsible for all carriage charges. The exporter does not pay any transportation charges.

Under FAS and FOB (see Sections 3.2, 3.3 for details), the pre-carriage charge incurred in the country/city of export is borne by the exporter. In this case, this is the charge involved in bringing the goods from Aberdeen to Kwai Chung Container Terminal.

After the goods are delivered alongside the ship (FAS) or on board (FOB) the ship, any transportation charges relating to the main carriage and on-carriage are to be borne by the importer In this example, these are the charges incurred in bringing the goods from Kwai Chung Container port to Los Angeles, USA plus the inland charge in the USA involved in bringing the goods from Los Angeles to the final destination in Denver.

Under CFR and CIF terms (see Sections 3.4 and 3.5 for details), in addition to the pre-carriage charge, the exporter is also responsible for the main carriage charge. In this example, this is the carriage charge incurred in bringing the goods from Kwai Chung Terminal Port, Hong Kong to Los Angeles, USA. However, the on-carriage charge beyond the port of discharge is to be borne by the importer unless the D/C stipulates that the unloading charge and charges involved in bringing the goods to their final destination are included.

3 Common Shipping Terms and Their Abbreviations

The following six Incoterms (from Sections 3.1 to 3.6) are ranked in order of increasing responsibilities for the exporter. In other words, the first Incoterm, EXW, means the minimum obligation for the exporter and thus, maximum responsibilities on the part of the importer. This is followed by the second term, "Free alongside ship", in which the exporter is required to deliver the goods alongside a ship instead of simply making the goods available at his factory, as in EXW. The last Incoterm, DDP, means most responsibilities are placed on the exporter.

3.1 Ex Works (EXW)

The seller fulfils his obligation:

(a) when he has made the goods available at his own premises to the buyer; or

(b) he may be required to place the goods at the disposal of the buyer at the named place of delivery and notify the buyer;

(c) he is not obliged to load the goods or clear the goods for export unless specifically instructed in Incoterm variants (which are explained later in this chapter);

(d) this Incoterm imposes minimum obligation on the part of the exporter.

The buyer must:

(a) take delivery from the exporter's factory and pay all the costs, this imposes the maximum obligation on the importer;

(b) obtain any export and import licence and carry out all customs formalities necessary for the exportation and importation of the goods;

(c) bear all risks and pay all costs, duties and taxes;

(d) take delivery of the goods.

3.2 Free Alongside Ship (FAS)

The seller fulfils his obligation when:

(a) he has arranged to deliver the goods alongside the ship at the port of loading named in the contract, for example;

> "FAS Kwai Chung Terminal, Hong Kong" would mean that the goods must be delivered free alongside the ship at Kwai Chung Terminal, Hong Kong;

(b) notifies the buyer about the shipment;

(c) provides the usual transport documents;

(d) he is not required to arrange an export licence nor pay any export tax, if any (a major change from Incoterms 1990 to Incoterms 2000 is that a seller is required to arrange an export license and to pay export tax).

The buyer must:

(a) obtain any export and import licence and carry out all customs formalities for the exportation and importation of the goods, bear all risks, pay insurance and pay all costs, duties and taxes;

(b) nominate the carrier, arrange contract for the carriage and pay the freight charge.

3.3 Free on Board (FOB)

Under FOB terms, the goods are placed on board a ship by the seller at a port of shipment named in the sales contract. The risk of loss of or damage to the goods is transferred from the seller to the buyer when the goods pass over the ship's rail. Insurance is to be covered by the buyer.

The seller fulfils his obligation when:

(a) he has delivered the goods on board a named vessel;

(b) he has obtained any export licence and carried out customs formalities required for the exportation of the goods including payment of all costs, duties and taxes;

(c) he has provided a "Freight Collect" transport document.

The buyer must:

(a) obtain any import licence and carry out all customs formalities for the importation of the goods including payment of all costs, duties and taxes;

(b) bear all risks of loss or damage to the goods when the goods pass over the ship's rail;

(c) arrange and pay for insurance, although he is under no obligation to do so.

(d) arrange contract for the carriage;

(e) take delivery of the goods;

(f) pay unloading costs.

3.4 Cost and Freight (CFR, previously known as C & F)

The seller must pay the cost and freight necessary to bring the goods to the named destination. The risk of loss of or damage to the goods, as well as of any cost increases, is transferred from the seller to the buyer when the goods pass over the ship's rail at the port of shipment. Insurance is to be covered by the buyer.

The seller fulfils his obligation when he has:

(a) obtained any export licence and carry out all customs formalities required for the exportation of the goods including payment of all costs, duties and taxes;

(b) delivered the goods on board the vessel;

(c) arranged a contract for the carriage, paid the freight charges and provided a "freight prepaid" transport document.

The buyer must:

(a) obtain any import licence and carry out all customs formalities required for the importation of the goods including payment of all costs, duties and taxes;

(b) bear all risks of loss of or damage to the goods when the goods pass over the ship's rail;

(c) arrange and pay for insurance;

(d) accept delivery of the goods;

(e) pay any unloading costs when they are not included in the freight charges.

3.5 Cost, Insurance, Freight (CIF)

This term is basically the same as CFR but in addition, the exporter has to procure marine insurance against the risk of loss of or damage to the goods during carriage. The seller contracts with the insurer and pays the insurance premium. Hence, an insurance policy or certificate will be submitted.

"Freight Prepaid" or other similar words will appear in the transport documents.

The seller must:

(a) as under CFR terms, provide a "Freight Prepaid" transport document, and pay all costs necessary for exportation of the goods including license fees and export taxes;

(b)   obtain cargo insurance and provide insurance cover.

The buyer's responsibilities are as for CFR above, except that insurance is covered by the seller.

3.6 Delivered Duty Paid (DDP......named place of destination)

Under this term, the exporter must obtain any export and import licences and carry out all customs formalities for the exportation and importation of the goods including payment of all costs, duties and taxes, arrange the contract for the carriage, place the goods at the disposal of the buyer, and provide the transport document.

The importer must accept the usual transport document and take delivery of the goods.

DDP, in total contrast with EXW, means maximum obligation on the part of the exporter and minimum responsibilities for the importer.

The following three Incoterms, once relatively unpopular in Hong Kong, have now become common. This is due to the increasing use of multimodal transport worldwide, with Hong Kong being no exception.

3.7 Free Carrier (FCA......named place)

This trade term is based on air transport or multimodal transport. The separation responsibilities between the seller and buyer are similar to the situation under FOB terms (see Section 3.3).

The seller must :

(a)   obtain any export licence and carry out all customs formalities for the exportation of the goods including payment of all costs, duties and taxes;
(b)   deliver the goods into the custody of the carrier and notify the buyer;
(c)   provide the usual transport document;
(d)   he is not required to pay freight charges.

The buyer must:

(a) obtain any import licence and carry out customs formalities for the importation of the goods;
(b) bear all risks and pay all costs, duties and taxes;
(c) nominate carrier and arrange contract for the carriage;
(d) pay the freight charges;
(e) take delivery of the goods.

3.8 Carriage Paid To (CPT......named place)

Under CPT terms, the seller must:

(a) obtain any export licence and carry out all official/customs formalities for the exportation of the goods including payment of all costs, duties and taxes;
(b) contract for the carriage and pay the freight charges;
(c) deliver the goods into the custody of the first carrier;
(d) provide the usual transport document.

The buyer must:

(a) obtain any import licence and carry out all customs formalities for the importation of the goods including payment of all costs, duties and taxes;
(b) bear all risks of loss or damage to the goods when the goods have been delivered to the first carrier;
(c) accept delivery of the goods from the carrier.

3.9 Carriage and Insurance Paid To (CIP......named place)

Here, the seller's obligations are identical to CPT above. In addition, the seller must:

(a) arrange cargo insurance and provide evidence of insurance cover;
(b) pay the insurance premium.

The buyer's responsibilities are identical to CPT above except that insurance is covered by the exporter.

The following four shipping terms are used mainly in continental Europe and North America. They are rarely used in Hong Kong.

3.10 Delivered At Frontier (DAF......named place)

The seller fulfils his obligation to deliver when:

(a) he has made the goods available and cleared them for export at the named point and place at the frontier but before the customs border of the adjoining country;

(b) he has provided transport documents to enable the buyer to take delivery at the frontier.

The buyer must:

(a) provide import clearance;

(b) pay for on-carriage, if any;

(c) take delivery of goods at the named point and place at the frontier.

Frontier may include exporter's country. It is necessary that "frontier" should be precisely defined by naming the exact point and place so that the responsibility between the buyer and the seller is clearly divided.

3.11 Delivered EX Ship (DES......named port of destination)

The seller fulfils his obligation to deliver when:

(a) he has made the goods available on board the ship at the port of destination;

(b) he has provided shipping documents to enable buyer to take delivery of goods;

(c) he is not required to clear the goods for import at the named place of destination but has to bear all costs and risks in bringing the goods to the named port of shipment.

The buyer must:

(a) be responsible for import clearance;

(b) pay unloading costs, if any;

(c) take delivery of goods at the named port of destination.

3.12 Delivered EX Quay (Duty Paid......named port of destination)

The seller fulfils his obligation when:

(a) he has made the goods available on the quay (i.e., wharf) at the named port of destination;

(b) he is not obliged to clear the goods for import; (uner Incoterm 2000)

(c) he is required to bear all costs and risks incurred in delivering the goods to the named port of destination (become obsolete under Incoterms 2000);

(d) he has provided transport documents to enable buyer to take delivery of goods at the named port of destination.

The buyer:

(a) must take delivery of goods at the named port of destination;

(b) has minimal responsibility.[1]

3.13 Delivered Duty Unpaid (......named place of destination)

The seller fulfils his obligation when:

(a) he has made the goods available at the named place in the importing country;

(b) cleared the goods for exportation but not for importation;

(c) he has borne all the costs and risks in delivering the goods at the named place of the importing country;

(d) he has provided the transport document to enable the buyer to take delivery of the goods.

The buyer must:

(a) clear the goods for import;

(b) take delivery of the goods at the named place of destination.

4 Division of Costs, Risks and Responsibilities under Incoterms

The above Incoterms with respect to the buyer's and seller's responsibilities are written in a simplified manner, as in most standard textbooks. According to International Chamber of Commerce (I.C.C.), Incoterms should allocate costs, risks and responsibilities between the seller and buyer in ten numbered articles, "A" for seller's responsibilities and "B" for the buyer's responsibilities:[2]

A — Seller's responsibilities

A1 Provision of goods in conformity with the contract
A2 Licences, authorizations and formalities
A3 Contract of carriage and insurance
A4 Delivery
A5 Transfer of risks
A6 Division of Costs
A7 Notice to the buyer
A8 Proof of delivery, transport document or equivalent E-message
A9 Checking–packaging–marking
A10 Other obligations.

B — Buyer's responsibilities

B1 Payment of the price
B2 Licences, authorizations and formalities
B3 Contract of carriage
B4 Taking delivery
B5 Transfer of risks
B6 Division of Costs
B7 Notice to the seller
B8 Proof of delivery, transport document or equivalent E-message
B9 Inspection of goods
B10 Other obligations.

5 Summary of ICC Incoterms 1990

There are 13 standard Incoterms in the 1990 version as shown in the following sequences.

Group E Departure:	EXW	Ex Works
Group F Main carriage unpaid:	FCA	Free Carrier
	FAS	Free Alongside Ship
	FOB	Free on Board
Group C Main carriage paid:	CFR	Cost and Freight
	CIF	Cost, Insurance and Freight
	CPT	Carriage Paid To
	CIP	Carriage and Insurance Paid To
Group D Arrival:	DAF	Delivered At Frontier
	DES	Delivered EX Ship
	DEQ	Delivered EX Quay
	DDU	Delivered Duty Unpaid
	DDP	Delivered Duty Paid

6   Summary of Mode of Transport and the Appropriate Incoterms 1990 [3]

Any Mode of Transport including Multimodal	EXW	Ex Works (......named place)
	FCA	Free Carrier (......named place)
	CPT	Carriage Paid to (named place of destination)
	CIP	Carriage and Insurance Paid to (named place of destination)
	DAF	Delivered At Frontier (.....named place)
	DDU	Delivered Duty Unpaid (......named place of destinaton)
	DDP	Delivered Duty Paid (......named place of destination)
Air Transport	FCA	Free Carrier (......named place)
Rail Transport	FCA	Free Carrier (......named place)
Sea and Inland Waterway	FAS	Free Alongside Ship (named port of shipment)
	FOB	Free On Board (named port of destination)
	CFR	Cost and Freight (named port of destination)
	CIF	Cost, Insurance and Freight (named port of destination)
	DES	Delivered EX Ship (named port of destination)
	DEQ	Delivered EX Quay (......named port of destination)

7 Variants in Incoterms

The above Incoterms were designed by the International Chamber of Commerce in 1990 and are not tailor-made for every trader. Sometimes, they may be useful only when used with some variations. For example, EX Works Loaded may be used instead of EX Works to allow a seller and a buyer more flexibility Under EX Works Loaded: in addition to making the goods available at his own premises, an exporter is required to load the goods on vehicles.

Meanwhile, under EX Works Cleared, an exporter is required to clear the goods for export. These variants may be quite useful to the buyer when he is not familiar with the customs formalities of the exporting country. EXW Cleared is used when the buyer would like the seller to clear the goods for export for him at the latter's expense. Other variants in standard terms such as FAS Cleared, DDU Cleared, DDP VAT Unpaid are also used in the market.[4]

8 Limitations in Incoterms

Incoterms deal with the issue of whether the seller has an obligation to the buyer (or vice versa) with respect to:

(a) insurance cover;
(b) freight payment, etc.

Such unilateral obligations imposed on one party only may be detrimental to the other party. For example, under CFR terms, a seller is not obliged to purchase insurance and provide evidence of insurance cover. It is the buyer's responsibility to procure insurance. The buyer, on the other hand, has no obligation to the seller to take out insurance. If the buyer has not procured insurance, either inadvertently or deliberately, the seller's goods which are in transit may be put at risk at his own cost. If the buyer is unable to pay for the goods which, unfortunately, suffer damage, the seller has to bear the loss. Obviously, something needs to be done in the new version of Incoterms. This will make it prudent for the buyer to take certain measures on his own behalf, even though he (the buyer) has no obligation under the

Incoterm to do so in relation to the other party (the seller). Hence, the seller is protected even though he has no obligation under the Incoterm to do so in relation to the buyer.

9 Incoterms 2000

Incoterms 1990 have been used as the standard shipping terms in the last decade. Since its introduction, there have been some changes in the delivery process. Clearer identification of the obligation of either the seller or the buyer is necessary (particularly the point of delivery instead of the place of delivery), in view of the changing mode of transportation. At the time of writing, it is learned that Incoterms 2000 will come into force on 1 January 2000. According to the latest information released by the I.C.C., major changes in the new Incoterms 2000 include the emphasis on the importance of the parties domiciled at their own country to be responsible for import or export formalities. In other words, it is important and more realistic for exporters to arrange export clearance and to pay export duties. Meanwhile, it is more realistic for importers to arrange import formality. Under FAS — Incoterms 2000, exporters are required to arrange export clearance formalities. Under DEQ — Incoterms 2000, exporters are not required to clear the goods for imports nor to pay import duty. Readers are reminded to keep pace with the changes by referring to this latest version.[5]

Notes

1. Under Incoterms 2000, the buyer has an obligation to clear the goods for import and to pay import tax, if any.

2. Jan Rambert, *Guide to Incoterms 1990*, ICC Publishing SA.

3. International Chamber of Commerce, *Incoterms 1990*.

4. Although I.C.C. does not formally recognize variants in Incoterms (this is understandable as there are many variants used in the market and more and more may be introduced by traders to suit their needs), **FAS under Incoterms 2000 is more or less the same as the variant — FAS cleared. Under FAS (the new Incoterms), sellers are required to perform export custom clearance.**

5. Jan Rambert, *Incoterms 2000*, International Chamber of Commerce, to be published.

Revision Questions

1. People's Ltd., a valuable customer, purchases goods from suppliers in the UK. They have been using documentary credits and trading under FOB terms for most of the transactions. Today, the shipping manager of People's Ltd., Mr John Wong, calls to see you and asks you what transport and insurance documents a UK exporter should produce if they wish to use the following terms:

    (a) FCA Heathrow Airport
    (b) FAS Oslo
    (c) CIF Hong Kong

    Required:

    (a) State, in note form, the full name of these Incoterms and how you would deal with Mr. Wong's request.

    (b) State whether the importer or the exporter should pay for marine insurance under the following Incoterms:
    DAF, CFR, EXW, DDP, FOB, CIP.

    *Question from HKIB Banking Practice in Hong Kong, May 1998.

2. What do you understand by "Variants in Incoterms"?

3. What are the differences between DDP and DDU?

4. How does DDU differ from CIP terms?

5. What do you understand by EXW Loaded?

6. Have you found out any "grey areas" with respect to responsibility which Incoterms do not cover and which you want to be specifically dealt with in future versions of Incoterms?

Further Reading

1. Guillermo Jimenez, *ICC Guide to Export-Import Basics*, International Chamber of Commerce, Chapter 4.
2. Jan Ramberg, *ICC Guide to Incoterms 2000*, International Chamber of Commerce.

Documentary Collection

- ❏ Parties to a collection
- ❏ Direct and indirect collection
- ❏ Bank considerations in remitting bills (outward collection) and in collecting bills (inward collection)
- ❏ Procedures for presenting documents to buyer against payment, acceptance, or other terms
- ❏ Procedures for dealing with goods consigned to the collecting bank
- ❏ Procedures for the protection of goods in the event of dishonour
- ❏ Note and protest
- ❏ Case-of-Need

1 Parties to a Collection

1.1 Principal

This is the customer who entrusts the operation of collection to his bank. As well as being the exporter, he is the seller who initiates the collection process. In other words, he is the principal party who gives instructions to subsequent parties to act upon. He is also known as the drawer as he is the party who issues a bill of exchange drawn on the overseas buyer. By means of drawing a set of bills of exchange, a drawer is legally demanding payment from a drawee (buyer).

1.2 Remitting Bank

This is the bank to which the principal has entrusted the operation of the collection. In other words, it is the exporter's bank which sends the collection in accordance with the instructions of the principal party. Hence, the remitting bank is accountable to the principal with regard to a collection activity, although it is also protected by URC (Uniform Rules for Collection N° 522) Articles 11, 13 and 14.

1.3 Collecting Bank

This is any bank, other than the remitting bank, involved in processing the collection. This is the agent bank between the remitting and presenting banks. Very often, a collecting bank is used when the documents cannot be sent direct from the remitting bank to the presenting bank because of political reasons. Also, if a remitting bank has no corresponding banking relationship with a presenting bank and this presenting bank is the bank specifically instructed by the exporter to present documents, (in fact, it is the overseas buyer who asks the seller for this arrangement) the remitting bank will look for a corresponding bank (**collecting bank**) through which documents can be passed on to the presenting bank for onward presentation to the buyer. Hence, a collecting bank in most cases can be a bank in the buyer's country/seller's country/third country with a corresponding relationship with the remitting bank. Its main role is to pass on documents to the presenting bank for onward presentation to the buyer. It receives instructions from the remitting bank and is accountable to the remitting bank.

1.4 Presenting Bank

This refers to the bank making presentation to the drawee. In other words, it is the bank which actually presents documents to buyers for payment or acceptance. In most cases, the collecting bank also acts as the presenting bank in which case the collecting bank has a corresponding relationship with the remitting bank and the drawee has an account relationship with the collecting bank. Where a collecting bank has no banker–customer relationship with the drawee, it may have to send the collection to the buyer's bank in which case the buyer's bank becomes the presenting bank. A presenting bank is accountable to the instructing party which may be a remitting bank or collecting bank.

1.5 Drawee

This is the party to whom presentation is to be made, according to the collection instruction. He is the ultimate party in the collection process. He is the party who has to pay the bill or accept and pay the bill upon maturity. In return, he obtains shipping documents which enable him to take delivery of the goods.

In the collection process, we have identified various parties. Various relationships exist between the parties and these depend on each stage of the collection process. In all cases, the following relationships exist:

(a) Principal vs Remitting bank;
(b) Remitting bank vs Collecting bank;
(c) Collecting bank vs Presenting bank.

Of the above three kinds of relationship, the former party can be known as the "instructing party" and the latter as "instructed party". An "instructing party" must give clear instructions to the "instructed party" to be acted upon. Meanwhile, an "instructed party" must act strictly in accordance with the instructions of the "instructing party" and must not act outside the instructions.

Building on these types of relationship, the basis is the contract made between the buyer and the seller. In a collection, this is the contract made between Principal and Drawee.

2 Collection Instruction

A collection instruction is an application form from the customer to the remitting bank which contains detailed instructions as to how to collect the proceeds. Instructions in a collection instruction should be clear and concise and a remitting bank can only act on the instructions and in accordance with the Uniform Rules for Collection. A collection instruction is in a standard form designed by the bank, to be filled in by its customer so that the remitting bank can act strictly in accordance with the customer's instruction.

Based on the instructions of the collection instruction, a remitting bank forwards the same instructions to an overseas collecting bank by means of a new issue of its own covering letter (also known as covering schedule). Among all the information, a collection order should contain at least the following instructions:

(a) Details of remitting bank and of principal including full name, postal and SWIFT addresses, telex, telephone, facsimile numbers and reference, if any.

(b) Name of the bank to which the collection should be sent. Sometimes, the principal gives instructions to the remitting bank to forward documents to a nominated bank known as the presenting bank; this nominated presenting bank is usually requested by the drawee and is the drawee's bank. In most cases, a collecting bank is not specified by the principal and the remitting bank selects a collecting bank of its own choice.

(c) The name and address of the drawee and telex, facsimile, telephone numbers.

(d) The number of each type of document.

(e) Whether the documents are to be released on D/P or D/A terms.

(f) Whether payment or acceptance may be deferred pending arrival of goods. It is customary in some countries for drawees to defer payment or acceptance until the goods have arrived. Therefore, it is necessary to give clear instructions to the presenting bank to act upon.

(g) Instructions on collection of interest, charges and expenses.

(h) Whether to store the goods and insure the goods in case of dishonour.

(i) Whether to protest in case of dishonour.

(j) Advice of acceptance. Where the bill is a term bill, a principal would like to be advised of acceptance and the date of maturity and payment.

(k) Name, address and power of the case-of-need in case of dishonour.

(l) Amount and currency to be collected and the way in which the proceeds of the collection are to be remitted.

3 Direct Collection and Indirect Collection

3.1 Direct Collection

In some countries, it is customary for exporters to send their collections direct to the overseas collecting bank, bypassing a remitting bank. The collecting bank will act as an agent of the exporter to collect the proceeds. In this type of collection, the collecting bank should make sure that instructions as to how to remit the proceeds are included in the collection order and a collecting bank should remit the proceeds to the exporter's bankers.

From the exporter's point of view, he can save in bank charges and possibly in time. However, he lacks the professional advice and follow-up action of the remitting bank. So, a direct collection is only suitable for experienced exporters who trade with trustworthy importers. Otherwise, the saving in charges and time may not be sufficiently compensated by the possible loss in payment by the drawee.

In recent years, there has been a growing trend to see more direct collections, particularly sent from US principals. Upon receipt of a direct collection, a collecting bank may be ready to present the bill if the drawee is known to him (or a good bank–customer relationship is established between the collecting bank and the drawee). However, most banks are unwilling to act as collecting banks if the documents are sent from an unknown party addressed to an unknown drawee for acceptance/payment. The norm is that, in dealing with a collection, they must at least know one party well, either the instructing party (remitting bank or principal) or the drawee (his customer).

3.2 Indirect Collection

For a clean collection, goods are delivered by the principal to the drawee's premises or a place as designated by the drawee. Commercial documents (including bills of lading, commercial invoice etc.) are sent direct by the principal to the drawee or accompany the goods. Financial documents (usually bills of exchange) are submitted by the principal to the remitting bank which, in turn, will forward the bills to the collecting bank for payment or acceptance.

The advantage of a clean collection over open account is that, with the help of a collecting bank, the presentation of a bill of exchange can remind the buyer to pay/accept a draft and pay upon maturity. Also, there is an additional protection under the Bills of Exchange Ordinance. Despite the fact that a principal has lost control over the goods under a clean collection, this type of term of payment may be relatively less risky than open account for the exporter.

For documentary collection, goods are delivered by the principal to the drawee's country or a place designated by the drawee. Financial documents and commercial documents are submitted by the principal to the remitting bank. Banks may be instructed to release documents against immediate payment. This type of collection is known as "document against payment" (D/P). Where a bill of exchange is the financial document, it is a sight bill. In this type of collection, the drawee must make immediate payment to the collecting bank in order to obtain shipping documents to take delivery of goods.

If the collecting bank is instructed to release documents against immediate acceptance of a bill of exchange, this type of collection is referred to as "documents against acceptance" (D/A). Where a bill of exchange is the financial document, it will be a term bill. In this type of collection, the drawee can take the shipping documents against acceptance of the draft and undertake to pay upon maturity.

4 Bank Considerations in Remitting Bill (Outward Collection)

A remitting bank is a bank handling outward collections (O/C). When a principal hands in an application for collection, there are many steps which a remitting bank has to take before sending an instruction to the overseas corresponding bank for collecting the proceeds. On the one hand, the remitting bank has to act strictly in accordance with the principal's instruction. On the other hand, it has to comply with the Uniform Rules for Collections and take into account the need of being practical.

Upon receipt of a set of documents for collection, the remitting bank must :

(a) check that the customer has a bill account with it and is trustworthy;

(b) check that the number of documents appears to be the same as listed in the collection order. Although the remitting bank has no further responsibility to examine the contents of the documents, it is recommended that in order not to delay the collection process and, in particular, to demonstrate its professional service, it should at least take the following extra steps:

(1) ensure that the bill of exchange is duly signed and endorsed;

(2) ensure that the amount of the bill of exchange is the same as the invoice and collection order;

(3) ensure that a full set (unless otherwise specified by the principal) of bills of lading and insurance policy (if any) are submitted and duly signed and endorsed.

(c) exercise professionalism to remind its customers of any special documentary requirements in the drawee's country, e.g., consular invoice, certificate of origin(in practice, this may be difficult);

(d) advise the principal the need on protest in some countries;

(e) choose a collecting bank at its own discretion or according to the principal's special instruction.

After that, the remitting bank will issue its own "collection covering letter" in accordance with its customers' instructions and in compliance with the Uniform Rules for Collection.

5 Bank Considerations in Collecting Bills (Inward Collection)

A collecting bank is a bank handling inward collections (I/C). It is acting in an agency capacity for a remitting bank. As an instructed party, a collecting bank must act in accordance with the instructions of the instructing party (remitting bank). Therefore, a collecting bank must make sure that the documents received are accompanied by a collection instruction with clear instructions.

Even if a bank–customer relationship exists between the collecting bank (acting as presenting bank) and drawee, the collecting bank owes a duty of agency to the remitting bank. If there is any variation in instructions respectively given from the remitting bank and the drawee, a collecting bank should act strictly in accordance with instructions of the remitting bank. In case of any queries, a collecting bank (instructed party) should go back to the remitting bank (instructing party) to seek instruction.

Upon receipt of a set of inward collection documents, a collecting bank must:

(a) ask itself if it wishes to handle the collection. Sometimes, it may not wish to handle the collection because the collection instruction was sent from an unknown bank/exporter or the collecting bank finds it difficult to collect bank charges because of a deterioration in drawee's credit standing;

(b) verify the signature(s) of the collecting covering letter (in practice, most collecting banks do not need to do this) if it agrees to handle the documents, and that the documents received appear to be as listed in the collection instruction. However, it takes no further responsibility to examine the documents. If documents appear not to be as listed, a collecting bank must inform the remitting bank without delay;

(c) examine the collection instructions. Inform the instructing party for any instructions which it cannot follow, if any;

(d) inform the importer of the arrival of collection documents. Deliver documents against payment or acceptance according to the collection instructions. Act strictly in accordance with the instructions of the collection instruction for other terms.

6 Roles and Responsibilities of a Collecting Bank

A collecting bank acts as an agent of the remitting bank. Therefore, it should act strictly in accordance with the instructions given in the remitting bank's collection instruction. Its main role is to present the bill to the importer either for payment/acceptance or against other terms. However, as an instructed party, it does not guarantee payment of the bills. If the bill is paid by the buyer, it should immediately remit the proceeds to the instructing party, the remitting bank. If the bill is accepted, it should advise the fate of the bill to the remitting bank according to the collection instruction. If the bill is unpaid/unaccepted, it may have to arrange storage and insurance for the goods as instructed in the collection instruction.

Sometime, a collecting bank is instructed to protest on behalf of the remitting bank in case the bill is dishonoured. Whether protest is required depends on whether protest is specifically instructed in the remitting bank's collection instruction. Whenever a collecting bank has taken action in connection to the storage, insurance for the goods or protest, it must immediately advise the remitting bank of the details of the action taken. If there are any unclear instructions or queries in the collection instruction, it should seek further instructions from the instructing party, e.g., the remitting bank, before taking any action. A collecting bank, in any circumstances, acts as an agent only. It must act in good faith and exercise reasonable care.

7   Procedures for Presenting Documents to Buyer against Payment/Acceptance/ Other Terms

Upon receipt of an inward collection, a collecting bank will act in accordance with the instructions of the collection. The first and most important instruction which should be noticed is whether documents are released against payment or acceptance.

7.1   Documents against Payment (D/P)

If it is a D/P collection, the collecting bank should only release documents against payment of the sight draft, and the payment must be immediately available for remittance to the instructing party. If payment is refused or the drawee makes an excuse to make immediate payment, a collecting bank should not release the original documents to buyer. Even if security is deposited with the bank by the buyer against examination of original documents, the collecting bank should not release documents unless full payment is made. A collecting bank should always remember that it is responsible to the remitting bank and is an agent of that bank. Upon receipt of payment, a collecting bank should remit the proceeds to the instructing party without delay.

7.2   Documents against Payment with a Tenor Draft (D/P Usance)

Sometimes, the movement of documents from a remitting bank to a collecting bank is faster than the movement of goods from the seller's country to the buyer's country. It may happen if documents and goods are respectively mailed and shipped from Europe to Hong Kong. Normally, it takes one week or so for documents to arrive in Hong

Kong whereas goods do not arrive by vessel for three or more weeks. A buyer may be unwilling to pay if he is required to make payment immediately upon presentation of a draft which may be long before the arrival of goods. In that case, a buyer may ask for a D/P with a tenor draft as the term of payment, e.g., D/P 30 days. Under this term of payment, the buyer is not obliged to pay until the maturity date which is 30 days after presentation of documents. Hence, the buyer can wait for the arrival of goods during this 30 day period. However, this is not encouraged in URC–522, Article 7A.

Documents cannot be released to the buyer unless full payment is made at any time during this period of 30 days. Depending on the arrival day of the goods and the buyer's urgent need for the goods, he may make an early payment in order to take delivery of the goods. In other words, he may make payment on day one immediately after acceptance of the documents, in return for a set of shipping documents. He may make payment on, say, day 15 (assuming that this is the day when the shipment arrives) in return for a set of shipping documents. He is, however, obliged to pay on day 30 after the day of acceptance of the draft regardless of whether the goods have arrived or not. The amount collected by the presenting bank must be remitted to the instructing party without delay.

7.3 Documents against Acceptance (D/A)

In the case of a D/A collection, the collecting bank is instructed to release documents against the acceptance of a tenor draft. If the drawee refuses to accept the draft, the collecting bank should not release the documents and should inform the instructing party without delay. The collecting bank fulfils its obligation when it obtains the acceptance of the draft and delivers the documents to the drawee. Then, it should advise the remitting bank of the due date and retain the draft until maturity. Upon maturity, it should remit the proceeds to the remitting bank to the debit of its customer's account/cheque or cash.

Should the drawee refuse to honour payment upon maturity, a collecting bank may have to take further action in accordance with the collecting schedule such as:

(a) advise non-payment;

(b) protest for non-payment if requested;

(c) contact the case-of-need if requested;

(d) store and insure the goods if requested.

7.4 Documents Released against Other Terms and Conditions

Sometimes, a collecting bank is instructed to release documents against a promissory note or letter of undertaking issued by the drawee. A promissory note is a promise issued and signed by the importer to pay at an agreed future date. In the case of a letter of undertaking, it is most probable that this document is used to replace a draft to exempt the transaction from stamp duty in some countries. The collecting bank fulfils its obligation when the documents are released to the drawee against the receipt of a promissory note or letter of undertaking or other conditions as per the collecting instruction. Sometimes, a collecting bank may be instructed to release documents against "free of payment" in which case, the collecting bank fulfils its obligation when it releases the documents against a receipt for the goods issued by the drawee. No payment will be collected in this type of collection.

8 Advice of Fate

In almost all collection instructions, the need for a collecting bank to advise the maturity date of a usance document for non-payment or non-acceptance is specified as one of the instructions. Therefore, a collecting bank must always keep the remitting bank informed of the progress (the Fate) of the bill. According to the instructions given in the remitting schedule, a collecting bank may have to advise the remitting bank by telex or by mail or other means.

If a D/A bill is accepted by the buyer, the collecting bank may be instructed to send an advice of fate to the remitting bank stating that the bill is accepted giving the maturity date of the bill. If the bill is dishonoured either for payment or acceptance, the collecting bank should endeavour to ascertain the reasons for this. It may be instructed to protest the bill, contact the case-of-need, warehouse and insure the goods under advice to the remitting bank. The collecting bank is obliged to keep the remitting bank informed of the details of all action taken.

9 Procedures for Dealing with Goods Consigned to the Collecting Bank

Sometimes, an exporter would like to consign the goods to or to the order of a collecting bank. The exporter may feel that if the goods are consigned to a bank, the bank instead of the importer, will absolutely retain control over the goods. Unless the importer has paid for or signified his acceptance on the bills of exchange, he cannot get the documents and the possession of the goods. This is what an exporter normally thinks. As a matter of fact, it may be risky for an exporter to have this arrangement because, according to URC–522, goods should not be consigned to a collecting bank without prior agreement on the part of that bank. If a collecting bank is informed by a transportation company of the arrival of goods and asked to take delivery of them, it is up to the collecting bank to take them or not. Normally, a collecting bank should take the following action:

(a) Inform its customer about the arrival of goods. Decide whether it would be prepared to help its customer or not. If its customer does not want the goods or if the goods do not belong to its customer, then, inform the transportation company that it is not prepared to take delivery of the goods. Meanwhile, ask the transportation company to refer the matter back to the instructing party, which is normally the remitting bank.

Even if the customer wants its assistance, there is no obligation on the collecting bank to take any steps to protect the interests of its customer and the goods which remain at the risk of the instructing party.

However, if the collecting bank decides to be involved in this transaction and in particular to help its customer, it must confirm immediately with its customer whether he really wants the bank to assist him to take delivery of the goods and then seek its customer's instructions.

(b) When the bank assists in the delivery process, it must make it clear that once its customer has taken delivery of the goods, he cannot refuse to pay for the relevant documents which will subsequently arrive. In addition, the customer is liable to pay for all the charges and takes the risk in connection with the delivery.

(c) In helping its customer to take delivery, a collecting bank needs to know the value of the goods and have the same amount of cash/security from its customer. It may ask for a photocopy of an invoice sent from the seller to its customer, or it may send a telex to the remitting bank enquiring the exact value of the goods. If it requests the deposit of a security simply based on the customer's declaration, it may run the risk of taking insufficient security to cover the value of the goods. Some unscrupulous customers know that they do not have enough cash balance or a Trust Receipt facility. When the goods arrive, they declare a smaller value and take delivery of the goods against T/R or deposit of cash. When documents subsequently arrive, the bank may find that the amount in the documents is many time larger than that of the declared value of the goods. Therefore, caution has to be taken to guard against unscrupulous customers.

(d) The bank will create a suspense account (Marginal Deposit Account) pending arrival of documents for settlement.

One point to note is that as mentioned above, a collecting bank has no obligation to take any action in respect of the goods in a collection. It even does not have to take action to protect the goods, including storage and insurance, even when specific instructions are given by the sending party to do so. Besides, the collecting bank, under URC–522, is not obliged to inform the sending party about its refusal to take delivery (in practice, the collecting bank will inform the sending party). However, if the collecting bank has taken action in connection with the goods, whether instructed or not, it is obliged to inform the instructing party of all the details. But the collecting bank is not responsible for the acts of any third parties in connection with the protection of the goods. This third party may be the warehousing company.

10 Procedures for the Protection of Goods in the Event of Dishonour

When the remitting covering schedule requests that goods should be stored and insured in the event of dishonour, the collecting bank will only take such action if they agree to do so. A collecting bank is not obliged to do so according to URC–522. When the collecting bank takes action to protect and insure the good, it will, in most cases, choose a warehousing company and insurance company with whom it is familiar. The collecting bank must inform the remitting bank of the details in connection to warehousing and insurance. However, the collecting bank is not liable to nor responsible for any third parties entrusted with the protection and custody of the goods. If the collecting bank is unwilling or unable to take actions to protect the goods, it is not obliged to inform the remitting bank according to URC–522 (even if specific instructions are given to do so). It is, however, a customary practice for the collecting bank to advise the remitting bank that it is unable or unwilling to take action to protect the goods.

11 Note and Protest in the Event of Dishonour

According to the Bills of Exchange Ordinance, noting and protesting involves handing the bill to a notary public who represents the bill. If the bill is again dishonoured, the notary public notes on the bill the date, a reference to his register, the noting charges and his initial. Noting is cheaper than the formal protest and its main purpose is to extend the time in which a protest can be made. Protest is a formal declaration by a notary public at the request of the holder that the bill has been dishonoured and that the holder intends to recover all the expenses to which he may be put in consequence of it.

If a bill is dishonoured either for non-payment or non-acceptance, a collecting bank will have to protest the bills when specifically instructed to do so in the collection instruction. Regarding protest, particular care must be taken to ensure that such protest be made immediately. Usually, the in-house solicitor of the bank acts on behalf of the collecting bank in effecting protest. The bill may be noted on the day of its dishonour and must be effected not later than the next business day. Otherwise, all signatories are free from liability on the bill. Therefore, a collecting bank must be careful to act strictly in accordance with the instructions of the remitting bank regarding protest. In case of any difficulty in protest, a collecting bank must immediately contact the remitting bank for instructions.

12 Case-of-Need

An exporter may be familiar with a trustworthy party in the buyer's country who is willing to act for him to protect his interest in case of dishonour or problems. The party normally stationed in the buyer's country entrusted by the exporter as his agent is known as the "case-of-need". The role of a case-of-need is to liaise with the collecting bank and the drawee should the need arise. Sometimes, he may even have to assist the seller in finding a new buyer and clearing, storing and insuring the goods. To appoint a case-of-need who is stipulated in the collection instruction may be useful if the overseas buyer refuses to honour his commitment. Where such an agent is stipulated, the extent of his power should be clearly stated. In the absence of a clear indication, the collecting bank will not accept any instructions from the case-of-need. Therefore, if an exporter has 100% trust in the overseas agent, it is wise for him to indicate in the collection instruction that his agent, the case-of-need, has full power and that the collecting bank may follow the agent's instructions as if the instructions were given by the exporter himself.

Revision Questions

1. Compare and contrast clean collection and documentary collection.

2. What are the differences between direct collection and indirect collection?

3. What special considerations would you take upon receipt of an indirect collection?

4. Explain the roles and responsibilities of a remitting bank.

5. Explain the roles and responsibilities of a collecting bank.

6. What are the differences between D/P sight and D/P 30 days sight?

7. You have received a set of documents under inward collection. You have found that this is a D/A 90 days sight documentary collection. You quite understand that you are acting as an instructed party.

   (a) Give a full explanation of the term D/A 90 days after sight.

   (b) What are the procedures you would take to fulfil your role as a collecting bank? Briefly explain the procedures.

8. You have received a set of documents under inward collection. As an efficient banker, you immediately inform the drawee customer to effect payment in return for the documents since the terms are Documents against Payment. However, the drawee requests you to send the documents to him for inspection before effecting payment as there have been numerous reported cases of forged documents recently.

   Would you accept the drawee's request? Give reasons for your answer.

9. Your customer, City Import and Export Limited, has imported goods from the U.K. into Hong Kong on collection basis for the past two years.

   What is your position under Current International Rules regarding each of the following collection instructions with reference to your roles and responsibilities?

(a) Failure of the collection order to indicate whether the documents are to be released against payment or acceptance while the collection order contains a bill of exchange payable at a future date.

(b) In a Documents against Acceptance deal, the drawee offers to effect partial payment upon maturity.

(c) The drawee refuses to pay the charges as claimed by the remitting bank.

(d) The collection order states that collection charges are for account of the drawee who refuses to pay such charges.

(e) The bill of exchange had been accepted by an officer of the drawee company who, however, was not authorized to sign for the company.

(f) The collection stipulates "Case-of-need Consultant Limited" as the case-of-need, without stating further details.

10. Your customer, City Plastic Company Ltd., imports goods from the Far East on collection basis. Today, you received a collection schedule from the Bank of China, Shanghai Branch. Among other instructions, you found the following instructions:

(a) Goods consigned to your bank without your prior notice and authority.

(b) Kevin Luk, Director of Case of Need Company, as the "case-of-need" without stating further details.

(c) 3/3 bills of lading as listed in the remitting schedule whereas only 2/3 bills of lading plus 1 non-negotiable copy were found.

What is your position under Uniform Rules for Collection N° 522 with respect to each of the above instructions?

11. You are working in the Import Bills Department of Tai Fung Bank in Central. Today, you have received from ABC Bank in Germany documents for collection consisting of:

(a) Sight draft signed by Top Hamburg Inc. for DM 50,000 and drawn on your customer XYZ Ltd.

(b)   Invoice showing value of goods as DM 50,000 CIF Hong Kong.

(c)   Insurance certificate.

(d)   Full set of bills of lading evidencing shipment of goods from Hamburg to Hong Kong.

The instructions stated in the collection order are to release documents against payment of sight draft. Upon presentation, your customer offers you DM 25,000 cash.

Required:

Identify all parties involved and state what action you should take in response to this offer. Quote relevant Articles of ICC Publication N° 522.

Banking Practice in Hong Kong, HKIB Associateship Examinations, May 1998.

12. Your customer, Fitty Shoes Ltd., are wholesale importers of shoes. The company has been established for 10 years and has been importing shoes from Italy and the Far East.

Most of the suppliers consign shoes to Fitty Shoes Ltd on sight bill for collection payment terms. Today, your branch has received documents relating to an inward bill for USD 80,000 D/P. The documents included draft, 2 invoices, 2 inspection certificates, a full set of bills of lading evidencing 2,000 pairs of shoes shipped from Florence on 30 September 1998 consigned to order and blank endorsed.

Required:

(a)   List the instructions that might be contained in the remittance schedule enclosed with the inward documentary collection your bank has received from the Italian remitting bank. State relevant articles of URC for each of the instructions.

(b)   Identify financial documents and commercial documents of this transactions. State relevant articles of URC.

(c)   Referring to documents mentioned in this transaction, explain the difference between clean collection and documentary collection. State relevant articles of URC.

Further Reading

Lakshman Y. Wickremeratne, *ICC Guide to Collection Operations*, International Chamber of Commerce.

5

Documentary Credit

- ❏ Parties to a documentary credit (D/C)
- ❏ Revocable and irrevocable credits
- ❏ Issue, amend and principal contents of a D/C
- ❏ Liability of issuing bank in various forms of D/C
- ❏ Bank considerations in issuing a D/C and in examination of import documents
- ❏ Standard for examination of documents
- ❏ Techniques and procedures in checking import documents
- ❏ Reimbursement under a D/C
- ❏ Procedures in handling irregular import documents
- ❏ Notes for exporter upon receipt of a D/C
- ❏ Bank considerations in examination and negotiation of export documents
- ❏ Discrepancies and indemnities
- ❏ DOCDEX and CDCS

1 Parties to a Documentary Credit (D/C)

1.1 D/C Applicant

A credit starts with an applicant who requests his banker to open a D/C for him after a contract has been agreed. An applicant is the buyer and is also referred to as importer. He instructs his banker to give an undertaking to pay the seller against the latter's submission of documents strictly in compliance with the applicant's instructions in the credit. In this connection, he undertakes to reimburse his banker when payments are made under the credit.

1.2 Issuing Bank

It is the bank which issues the D/C on behalf of its customer. Upon issue of a D/C, an issuing bank undertakes to pay the beneficiary against the latter's presentation of shipping documents in compliance with the credit terms and conditions. In other words, an issuing bank stands in the shoes of a buyer to give a conditional undertaking to pay a seller. This undertaking will be conditional upon the seller complying with the stipulations of the credit.

1.3 Advising Bank

This refers to the bank which, upon receipt of the D/C from the issuing bank, advises it to the seller who is known as the beneficiary. Its role is to inform the seller that a D/C has been issued in his favour after authentication. An advising bank takes no further responsibility and, in particular, has no obligation to make payment to the beneficiary. However, it must take reasonable care to authenticate the credit which it advises. If it cannot establish the apparent authenticity of the credit or if it elects not to advise the credit, its duty is to advise the instructing party — the issuing bank without delay.

1.4 Beneficiary

This is the party in whose favour the D/C is issued. A beneficiary is the seller and is also referred to as an exporter. He is assured of being paid by the issuing bank on condition that he has fulfilled all the terms and conditions as stipulated in the D/C.

If he fails to comply with the terms, the issuing bank is exempt from making payment. The only remedy available to the exporter is for him to persuade the buyer to accept all the irregularities and obtain the buyer's instruction to the issuing bank to pay him despite all the discrepancies. This can be confirmed by means of sending a cable to the issuing bank via the negotiating bank. Alternatively, this can be done when his bank sends the documents to the issuing bank for presentation to the applicant for acceptance of discrepancies and payment (see Section 15 for details).

1.5 Confirming Bank

Sometimes, an advising bank is requested by the issuing bank to add an additional commitment to pay the beneficiary. If it agrees to the request, this advising bank will take a dual role. In addition to being an advising bank, it assumes a secondary role as that of the confirming bank to give a payment undertaking to the beneficiary. In other words, the undertaking by the confirming bank is additional to the undertaking of the issuing bank.

This undertaking remains unchanged irrespective of whether the issuing bank, due to some reason, has changed its mind. From an exporter's point of view, he has two banks separately to give him payment undertakings. This can relieve him of the risks of being unpaid arising from either the issuing bank or the applicant's country, as the issuing bank may go into liquidation and the applicant's country may impose foreign exchange control or other constraints on the transaction.

1.6 Negotiating Bank

This refers to the bank which purchases the exporter's documents submitted to it under a D/C. The process where the bank purchases the documents is known as negotiation. A negotiating bank may be specifically instructed by the issuing bank as the negotiating bank, in which case it is known as the restricted negotiating bank. If a D/C is available with any bank by negotiation, then any bank is authorized to effect negotiation, in which case it is known as the freely negotiating bank (in a non-restricted negotiation). When the documents submitted comply fully with the D/C terms and conditions, the negotiating bank may purchase (referred to as negotiate) the exporter's draft and documents. It will credit the exporter's account pending reimbursement from the issuing bank. Negotiation may be on a "with-recourse" or "non-recourse" (without recourse) basis depending on different cases. With recourse means the negotiating bank has a right of recourse to the exporter with respect to the finance. Without recourse means the negotiating bank has no right of recourse to the exporter with respect to the finance. In other words, the negotiating bank cannot ask for a refund from the beneficiary in a non-recourse negotiation. After negotiation, it will send the drafts and documents to the issuing bank for reimbursement.

Negotiation is on a with-recourse basis if:

(a) the issuing bank fails to pay, accept and/or pay the bill for reasons other than the discrepancies being found in the documents, e.g., the issuing bank fails to pay because of liquidation.

Negotiation is on a non-recourse basis if:

(a) the negotiating bank has added confirmation to the credit beside being a negotiating bank, or;
(b) the negotiating bank fails to spot discrepancies which are found by the issuing bank.

1.7 Reimbursing Bank

This is the bank nominated by the issuing bank to honour claims made under the D/C by the negotiating bank. Normally, a reimbursing bank is situated in a different country from that of the issuing bank and the negotiating bank when the credit is in terms of the currency of the reimbursement bank. For example, a Hong Kong bank issues a D/C denominated in US dollars in favour of a beneficiary in Singapore. The D/C is available in Singapore with any bank by negotiation and is reimbursed for example in City Bank, New York. In this case, City Bank, New York, is nominated by the issuing bank in Hong Kong as the reimbursing bank which, upon receipt of a claim from the negotiating bank in Singapore, will pay that bank to the debit of the Hong Kong bank's US-dollar account held with it. A reimbursing bank can be the issuing bank itself when the reimbursement instruction in the D/C is: "upon receipt of documents which are strictly in compliance with credit terms and conditions, the issuing bank will pay the negotiating bank in accordance with their instruction", in which case, the issuing bank becomes the reimbursing bank.

The above banks are the major parties in a D/C operation. On some occasions, a **paying bank** may be involved in a D/C in which case the paying bank is the bank nominated by the issuing bank to make payment to the beneficiary. An **accepting bank** may also be involved in a D/C in which case it is the bank nominated by the issuing bank to accept drafts drawn by the beneficiary providing the shipping documents comply with the credit terms and conditions. Despite the various names of a bank in a D/C operation, a bank may perform more than one of the above roles with different names. For example, an advising bank may be the confirming bank and the negotiating bank in a credit when the advising bank adds its confirmation to the credit and negotiation under the credit is restricted to this advising bank.

2 Revocable and Irrevocable Credits

Documentary credits are of two types, revocable credits and irrevocable credits. A revocable credit can be cancelled or amended at any time without prior notice to the beneficiary. Therefore, it gives no undertaking to the exporter that he will be paid even if he is able to submit a full set of compliant documents. However, if an exporter has shipped goods and submitted a set of compliant documents before the receipt of a notice of cancellation from the advising or nominated bank, the issuing bank must honour to pay (accept and pay at maturity of the usance D/C) such documents.

An irrevocable credit, on the other hand, can be neither amended nor cancelled without the agreement of the issuing bank, confirming bank (if any) and the beneficiary once the credit is issued. The issuing bank in such a credit gives an irrevocable undertaking to pay, accept and pay under usance credit, or negotiate against submission of a full set of compliant documents; or to pay a deferred payment credit on the maturity date determinable in accordance with the stipulations of the credit. As this type of credit offers greater protection to the exporter, it is more acceptable to the exporter and is therefore more widely used.

3 Issue, Amend

Based on the instructions of the D/C application, an opening bank issues a D/C for its customer. The applicant should give clear and concise instructions as to the terms and conditions and should at all times avoid giving confusing and conflicting instructions.

If the applicant has difficulties in completing an application form, he should seek the advice of his bankers. A D/C can be opened by three different methods as follows, each with a different speed to reach the beneficiary.

(a) By airmail — The credit is typed in a letter, signed by the authorized signatory(ies) of the issuing bank and sent to beneficiary via the advising bank by airmail. The speed of this type of issue is the slowest but cheapest among the three methods.

(b) By brief cable (brief telex, brief teletransmission or pre- advice) — A preliminary advice (known as pre-advice) of the credit is sent by telex to the beneficiary. This telex message showing the key elements of a credit such as D/C amount, name and address of the applicant and of the beneficiary, shipment date, expiry date and brief description of goods, etc., is sent to the beneficiary. According to UCP–500, Article 11, a brief message can be construed as the operative credit instrument (or operative amendment) unless it states "full details to follow" or that the mail confirmation is to be the operative instrument (or operative amendment). However, it is the normal practice for the issuing bank to state "full details to follow" in the pre-advice. Therefore, in these circumstances, a pre-advice cannot, strictly speaking, be construed as the operative credit instrument.

Despite the fact that the mail confirmation is the operative credit instrument, the issuing bank having given such pre-advice shall be irrevocably committed to issue the airmail confirmation. It is clear that the issuing bank is not allowed to issue the pre-advice without the airmail confirmation. Besides, the full details of the D/C should be sent by airmail without delay and in terms consistent with the pre-advice. If, immediately after the issue of the pre-advice, the applicant finds the need to extend the expiry date in the airmail confirmation, the issuing bank cannot meet this request. Instead, the issuing bank can meet the customer's need by means of the issue of an amendment to amend the expiry date, not simply changing the expiry date in the airmail confirmation.

(c) By full cable (full telex, full teletransmission) — Here, the credit is typed and the entire D/C message is sent by telex. The telex message is deemed to be the operative credit instrument. No mail confirmation will be sent. A D/C issued by full cable will enable the beneficiary to receive it much faster than if issued by airmail.

3.1 Principal Contents of a Documentary Credit

(a) The amount of the D/C — This must be expressed in figures and words. It is important that the value of both should be consistent. Sometimes, "about a certain amount e.g., about HK$100,000" may be shown as the value of the D/C. The word "about" here means the D/C signifies a tolerance not to exceed 10% more or less than the stated amount. Banks in Hong Kong discourage the use of this type of amount although it is acceptable according to UCP–500.

(b) The name and address of D/C applicant — The full name and address of the applicant should be given and be accurate. If any information is wrong and in particular a typing mistake, it is not acceptable to most negotiating, paying or confirming banks.

(c) The name and address of the beneficiary — It is necessary that these details are accurate as typing mistakes on the beneficiary's name are not acceptable to most negotiating banks. The full beneficiary's address should be included so that the chance of advising the wrong beneficiary can be reduced.

(d) Credit available with.....by..... — The name and address of the nominated bank with whom the credit will be available are specified. Alternatively, the credit may be made available with any bank in which case the beneficiary can present documents to any bank of his choice. Documents sent to the named bank or any bank may be "by negotiation","by acceptance", "payment" or "by deferred payment".

(e) Latest shipment date — This is the last day the goods must be loaded on board and dispatched, accepted for carriage. Normally, this date is earlier than the expiry date so that there is enough time for the beneficiary to arrange shipment and prepare documents for negotiation. UCP–500 does not impose a requirement to include a latest shipment date in a D/C. However, it is the normal practice in the D/C to see the latest shipment date specified.

(f) Period for presentation — This refers to the maximum number of days allowed for presentation of documents after the date of transport documents.

(g) Expiry date — This is the last date for the beneficiary to present documents for negotiation, payment or acceptance failing which the credit becomes expired.

(h) Shipment from....to.... — This must be specified clearly. Sometime, it allows the goods to be shipped from one place to another place via a third place.

(i) Partial shipment allowed or prohibited — If partial shipments are not allowed, the goods must be shipped in one lot. One payment will be effected under the credit. This depends on whether the D/C applicant would need all the goods or if he would like to receive the goods at regular intervals according to the needs of its manufacturing department. Costs for storage of the goods may also be one of the considerations. According to UCP–500 Article 40a, partial shipments are allowed if the D/C does not specify whether partial shipments are allowed or prohibited.

(j) Shipment by instalments — If shipment by instalments and drawings are specified within a given period in the D/C, it is necessary to note that, according to UCP–500 Article 41, if any instalment is not shipped and not drawn within the period allowed for that shipment and instalment, the credit will be invalid for that and all subsequent instalments. In other words, if shipment is not effected according to the shipment schedule, the credit will cease to be available immediately.

(k) Transhipment allowed or prohibited — Traditionally, transhipment is considered to be unloading of goods from one vessel and reloading of them to another vessel during the course of ocean carriage . The bill of lading covers the voyage from Port A to Port C with transhipment effected at Port B from one vessel onto another.

In UCP–500 Article 23d, banks will accept a bill of lading in the following cases even if the credit does not allow transhipment: if it indicates that (1) the carrier reserves the right to effect transhipment; (2) transhipment will take place so long as the cargo is shipped in containers, trailers and/or

LASH barges as evidenced by the bill of lading provided that the entire ocean carriage is covered by only one and the same bill of lading. It can be seen that transhipment is interpreted in a practical way, particularly in connection to shipment effected by containers, or trailers, etc.

(l) Description of goods — Excessive details in the description of goods is discouraged. The description should be concise and specific. According to UCP–500 Article 37c, the description of the goods in the commercial invoice must **correspond** with that of the credit. Obviously, the ICC leaves room here for flexibility in the description of goods in the documents. It does not use the words "must be exactly the same as" or "must exactly equal to". However, it is prudent to make sure that the description of goods on the invoice is exactly the same as the credit. In other documents, the goods may be described in general terms not inconsistent with the credit and other documents.

(m) Documents required — Documents normally include commercial invoices, packing lists, bills of lading, air waybills, insurance documents, inspection certificate, certificate of origin etc. The names of documents called for must be specified clearly. The number of originals and copies must be stated precisely. Except in transport documents, insurance documents and commercial invoices, the D/C should stipulate the names of the issuer of the documents called for. If the credit calls for documents without specifying the names of issuer, any parties including the beneficiary can issue such documents (UCP–500 Article 21). Besides, UCP Article 20 discourages the use of an ambiguous party as the issuers of documents. Those terms such as "first class", "well known", "qualified", "independent", "official", "competent", "local" etc. shall not be used to describe the issuers of any documents. If such ambiguous issuers are specified, any parties can issue the documents so long as they are not issued by the beneficiary.

(n) Instructions to negotiating bank — This contains instructions as to whether the documents after negotiation would be sent to the issuing bank in one lot or two lots, whether the documents would be sent by airmail or courier service or speed post etc. It also contains an important clause to the negotiating bank as to how to obtain reimbursement and whether the negotiating bank is instructed to claim reimbursement from a third bank or from the issuing bank.

4 Liability of Issuing Bank in Various Forms of Documentary Credit

4.1 A Sight Payment Credit

A sight payment credit is a credit calling for immediate payment. The bank nominated in the credit to pay the seller may be the issuing bank itself, the advising bank or any bank named in the credit. The D/C will be made available with the issuing bank/advising bank/any named bank, for payment. The seller presents documents to the issuing bank or the named bank for payment which will then pay the seller and send the documents to the issuing bank for reimbursement.

4.2 A Deferred Payment Credit

A deferred payment credit is a credit calling for payment upon maturity. Drafts would not be called for under a deferred payment credit. No document is accepted by the issuing bank in the sense of an acceptance credit. The issuing bank simply guarantees that payment will be made at maturity. Again, the bank nominated in the credit to effect deferred payment may be the issuing bank itself, the advising bank or any bank named in the credit. The D/C will be made available with the issuing bank/advising bank or any named bank by deferred payment. The beneficiary presents documents to the issuing bank for payment or the named bank which will pay him upon maturity.

4.3 An Acceptance Credit

An acceptance credit is a credit calling for acceptance of a draft drawn by the beneficiary on a bank. The bank nominated in the credit to effect acceptance of the credit may be the issuing bank itself, the advising bank or any bank named in the credit. The credit will be made available with issuing bank/advising bank or any named bank by acceptance. When the draft under the credit is accepted by the nominated bank, after checking documents to its satisfaction, it becomes a banker's acceptance. The accepted draft is returned to the beneficiary who may present it to his banker to be discounted or keep it until being paid at maturity.

4.4 A Negotiation Credit

A negotiation credit is a credit in which the issuing bank may either nominate a specific bank for negotiation (restricted negotiation) or make the credit freely negotiable by any bank (free negotiation). The bank nominated in the credit to effect negotiation of the credit may be the advising bank, exporter's banker or any bank other than the issuing bank. When the nominated bank has checked the documents to its satisfaction, that bank will negotiate the draft and pay the exporter. The negotiating bank then sends the documents to the issuing bank for reimbursement. In a negotiation credit, the issuing bank undertakes to reimburse the negotiating bank against the beneficiary's submission of documents in full compliance with credit terms and conditions.

5 Bank Considerations in Issuing a Documentary Credit

When a customer submits an application for documentary credit, an opening bank would consider the following factors before issuing the D/C:

(a) The credit standing of the applicant — An opening bank needs to ensure that the applicant is a customer with high integrity and repayment ability. For a new customer, a marginal deposit may be required and this depends on a case-by-case basis. For existing customers with a credit limit, a D/C line of credit will be earmarked and deducted for the amount of the credit or added to their existing facilities.

(b) The credit standing of the beneficiary — As a D/C constitutes a definite undertaking by the issuing bank to pay the beneficiary, an issuing bank is quite concerned about the latter's integrity which will decide if the goods to be shipped are as stated by him. It should be noted that the beneficiary has no liability under a D/C. So, the buyer should conduct a status enquiry on the seller to establish identification and integrity.

(c) The nature of goods — A D/C issuing bank undertakes to pay a seller against his goods as the collateral. Therefore, the bank is quite concerned about the nature of the goods and in particular its marketability and durability. Although a pledge is usually contained in a D/C application form, this affects the applicant rather than the beneficiary. Hence, the nature of the goods is an important consideration and, in particular, quite valuable to the issuing bank when the applicant becomes insolvent or has no money to pay for the shipping documents.

(d) Control of goods and of title documents — In all cases, an opening bank is prepared to issue a credit calling for a full set of title documents. This allows the issuing bank to take control over the goods only if the bills of lading are made out in the name of the issuing bank or, "to order" and "blank endorsed". If an opening bank is requested to issue a credit calling for 2/3 set (full set less 1) transport documents, the bank will lose control over the goods in which case, further security support will be taken, e.g., it will ask for marginal deposit or earmark a Trust Receipt for the credit amount.

(e) The nature of the credit — Whether it is a local D/C or a foreign D/C and in particular the means of delivery of the goods.

(f) The type of currency — Whenever a documentary credit is issued in a currency other than that of the buyer, an exchange risk occurs. If the credit is issued in a foreign currency which is a rare currency or exposed to great fluctuation, it is advisable for the issuing bank to remind its customer to take foreign exchange cover.

(g) New business and cross-selling — The possible volume of new business and the chance of cross-selling may also be a consideration.

6 Bank Considerations in Examination of Import Documents

Upon receipt of a set of import documents, the issuing bank must ensure that the documents presented are strictly in compliance with the D/C terms and conditions before effecting payment. In the examination of documents (refer also to section 5.10 for the two schools of thought a checker can apply), the issuing bank must, according to UCP–500, determine on the basis of the documents alone and exercise its own judgement whether the documents appear to comply with D/C terms or not. UCP–500 lays down a set of standards for the examination of import documents.

7 Standards for Examination of Documents

(a) Banks must examine all documents under the credit with reasonable care to decide whether to take up such documents or to refuse them.

(b) The issuing bank shall have a reasonable time to examine the documents upon receipt of documents. The maximum number of days for examination is seven banking days following the day of receipt of the documents. In *Hing Yip Hing Fat Co Ltd v Daiwa Bank Ltd [1991]*, it was held that three days was considered to be the reasonable time taking into account the total quantity of documents, size of bank, peak business or not, etc. Hence, reasonable time depends on the circumstances of the case. "Seven banking days" do not mean that every presentation of documents is automatically given seven working days for examination.

(c) Documents not being called for under the credit will not be examined. Furthermore, a D/C containing conditions to be fulfilled but not calling for documents to evidence them will deem such conditions as not stated in most circumstances and therefore will be disregarded.

8 Techniques and Procedures in Checking Import Documents

Upon receipt of a set of import documents, make sure that the documents are addressed to the right bank. That is, the documents received are under the D/C issued by the issuing bank.

(a) The bank cover (covering letter/covering schedule) is dated.
(b) The reimbursement instruction must be clear.
(c) Attention should be drawn to the special instructions in the bank covering letter, if any.

8.1 Draft

Make sure that:

(a) the amount in figures and amount in words are the same;
(b) it is dated (it is important that it is dated if it is a tenor draft with maturity calculated from the date of acceptance or the date of draft whichever is applicable);
(c) it is drawn on the issuing bank or the drawee bank etc. unless otherwise stipulated in the D/C;
(d) the tenor is the same as in the credit;
(e) "drawn clause" is included if D/C mentions "credit available with draft ......drawn under D/C number xxxxx";
(f) there is no irregular endorsement.

8.2 Invoice

Make sure that:

    (a)   the number of originals and copies if any, is the same as per D/C stipulated;

    (b)   it is issued by beneficiary and made out in the name of D/C applicant unless a transferable credit or otherwise stipulated;

    (c)   it contains a detailed description of the goods, unit price if any, trade terms, shipping marks if any, as stipulated in the credit;

    (d)   the description should be as simple as possible and must correspond with that in the credit. Although UCP implicitly does not forbid additional information in the description of goods, make sure that such additional information is not harmful to and/or does not change the description in the credit nor the quality of the goods. Again, it is prudent to ensure that the description is the same as the credit;

    (e)   invoice amount is the same as draft amount unless otherwise stipulated in the credit, e.g., draft only drawn for 90% of invoice value. 10% of invoice value has been paid as downpayment. In that case, the invoice value is larger than the draft amount.

    (f)   an invoice need not be signed unless D/C calls for "Signed commercial invoice". However, most issuing banks in Hong Kong open D/C calling for "Signed commercial invoices" in which case, the invoices must be signed.

    (g)   if D/C calls for more than one fold (e.g., triplicate), then at least, one fold must be marked or evidenced as the original.

8.3 Packing List

Make sure that:

    (a)   it is not combined with other documents;

    (b)   it shows the number of packing cases and the contents of each package;

    (c)   the gross weight if any, is consistent with that in the bill of lading. It is necessary to be careful to ensure such consistency even though the D/C does not specifically require the gross weight to be shown in the packing list;

(d) description in general terms is acceptable provided that the description is consistent with the credit and other documents;

8.4 Bill of Lading

Make sure that:

(a) a full set of originals and copies if any, are presented. Non-negotiable copies are normally not treated to be the same as photostat copies;

(b) a full set is duly endorsed where necessary;

(c) the B/L contains no superimposed clause that declares a defective condition of the goods and/or its packaging. For example, no such clause as "1 case broken" or similar words appear;

(d) the goods are certified to be "On Board" unless otherwise specified. Preprinted on board notation or certification to this effect are acceptable;

(e) notify party, port of loading, port of discharge, consignee are the same as per D/C stipulation;

(f) marked "Freight Prepaid" or "Freight Collect" depending on trade terms;

(g) appropriately signed by:

(1) a named carrier, or
(2) a named agent for the carrier, or
(3) the master, or
(4) a named agent for the master.
(It is necessary to ensure that the word "Carrier" must be identified in every case even though the bill of lading is issued by a shipping company.)

(h) it is not a charter bill of lading;

(i) it is not a forwarder's bill of lading unless the forwarder is acting as:

(1) carrier in its own capacity

(2) an agent for a named carrier

(j) description can be in general terms not inconsistent with the D/C and other documents.

8.5 Insurance Policy/Insurance Certificate

Make sure that:

(a) a full set is presented unless otherwise stipulated in the credit. D/C may stipulate the number of originals required to be presented. If there is no such stipulation, any number of originals issued by the insurance company is considered "full set";

(b) a full set is duly endorsed where necessary;

(c) issue date is the same date as or before the "On Board" date of the bill of lading unless it appears from the insurance document that the cover is effective at the latest from the date of loading on board or the taking in charge of the goods;

(d) issued and signed by insurance companies or underwriters or their agents;

(e) the type of insurance cover is the same as the credit stipulated;

(f) the minimum amount is CIF or CIP plus 10% or 110% of payment amount or invoice value whichever is the greater unless other stipulated;

(g) cover is in the same currency as the credit unless otherwise stipulated in the credit;

(h) description can be in general terms provided that it is consistent with D/C and other documents;

(i) "cover note" is not acceptable.

8.6 Inspection Certificate

Make sure that:

(a) the correct number of originals and copies if any, is presented;

(b) it is necessary to be signed as it is a certificate;

(c) inspection requirement is shown. For example, description of goods in the D/C is "Chemicals 20% Phosphate 60% Chloride 20%". In that case, inspection certificate must have such component percentage if no other special inspection requirement is included in the credit. Additional words such as "we certify that the goods are in good order and condition" are always found in an inspection certificate;

(d) goods can be described in general terms not inconsistent with D/C and other documents. However, for a professional banker, it is more prudent to see the same description as the invoice.

9 Obligation of Issuing Bank to Pay/Accept

If documents presented comply with D/C terms and conditions, the issuing bank must effect payment . This is based on its undertaking in the "Engagement Clause" of the D/C.

If documents presented do not strictly comply with D/C terms and conditions, the documents are said to have discrepancies (or irregular documents) which constitute grounds for the issuing bank to refuse payment. In other words, if the issuing bank finds discrepancies in the documents, its undertaking to pay the beneficiary can be withdrawn. However, the issuing bank will make use of the "maximum seven banking days" to refer all the discrepancies to applicant who will decide if he still wishes to take up the documents and pay the beneficiary despite the discrepancies. If the applicant accepts all the irregularities in the documents, the issuing bank will effect payment as if the documents were completely in order.

10 Reimbursement under a Documentary Credit

A D/C must contain a reimbursement clause which provides the negotiating bank with the name of the bank through which to be repaid (to be reimbursed). There are several kinds of reimbursement instruction. The negotiating bank may be instructed to claim reimbursement from the D/C issuing bank, in which case the issuing bank acts as the reimbursing bank. Alternatively, the negotiating bank may be instructed to claim reimbursement from a third bank which normally is situated in a country other than that of the issuing bank and the negotiating bank, when the D/C is in terms of the currency of the reimbursing bank etc. Below are the common types of reimbursement instruction clauses found in documentary credits.

(a) "Upon receipt of documents which are fully in compliance with credit terms and conditions, we shall reimburse the negotiating bank according to its instruction." If this is the reimbursement clause in the D/C, the issuing bank maintains no settlement account with the negotiating bank. It will remit the proceeds to the bank as specified by the negotiating bank to the credit of the negotiating bank's account.

(b) In the D/C (restricted negotiation), the reimbursement clause may read: "Upon receipt of documents which are fully in compliance with credit terms and conditions, we shall credit your account with us." In this case, the negotiating bank has maintained a Hong Kong-dollar (same as D/C currency) account with the opening bank which will reimburse the negotiating bank by crediting negotiating bank's account with it.

(c) In the D/C (restricted negotiation), the reimbursement clause may read: "Please debit our account with you under telex advice to us if documents submitted are fully in compliance with credit terms and conditions". In this case, the Hong Kong issuing bank maintains a foreign currency account (same as D/C currency) with the negotiating bank which is authorized to debit the account of the issuing bank maintained with it.

(d) In the D/C, the issuing bank may authorize a third bank known as the reimbursing bank to honour reimbursement claims by the negotiating bank. A separate reimbursement message known as "Reimbursement Authorization" would be sent by the issuing bank to the third bank to read as follows:

"Please honour negotiating bank's claims by debiting our account with you under telex (or airmail) advice to us quoting our reference number." For certain currencies, the issuing bank may require the negotiating bank to send a telex advice to the issuing bank three or more days before the latter sends a claim to the reimbursing bank . This allows the issuing bank to place enough funds in its account with the reimbursing bank. Reimbursement of this kind is subject to Bank-to-Bank reimbursement Rules URR–525.

It is worth pointing out that if the reimbursing bank fails to effect payment to the negotiating bank, the issuing bank cannot be relieved from its obligation to provide reimbursement. The issuing bank is the instructing party which authorizes a bank to act on its behalf and therefore is ultimately responsible to pay the negotiating bank.

11 Procedures in Handling Irregular Import Documents

If the applicant chooses not to accept the discrepancies, the issuing bank will send a notice of refusal to the remitting bank (normally the negotiating bank) to reject the documents. In refusing documents, the issuing bank must observe the following rules as laid down by UCP–500:

(a) It must give notice of refusal to the remitting bank by telecommunication or other fastest means no later than the close of the seventh banking day following the day of receipt of the documents.

(b) The notice of refusal must state all the discrepancies. In its notice of refusal, the issuing bank must state whether the documents are kept in its premises pending further instruction from the remitting bank, or are being sent back to the presenter (e.g., the remitting bank).

(c) It has been seen that a bad opening bank may suddenly return the documents and in its notice of refusal state that "Documents are being held at the disposal of the remitting bank". Theoretically, the opening bank should wait for further instructions from the remitting bank. If it really wants to return documents before receipt of new instructions from the remitting bank, it is advisable to send a telex of its intention to the remitting bank before the return of the documents.

12 Outcome If Issuing Bank Does Not Follow the Aforementioned

According to UCP–500, if the issuing bank fails to act in accordance with the above, it shall be precluded from claiming that the documents are not in compliance with the terms and conditions of the D/C. In other words, if the issuing bank fails to observe the aforementioned rules, it cannot subsequently say that documents presented do not comply with D/C terms and conditions. For example, if the issuing bank fails to send a notice of refusal to the negotiating bank within the seven banking days following the day of receipt of documents, it is assumed that it accepts the documents and its undertaking to pay the beneficiary is still in force.

13 Notes for the Exporter upon Receipt of a Documentary Credit

(a) Unless the issuing bank is specifically mentioned in the sales contract, it is the buyer's discretion to choose his own banker as the D/C opening bank. And in most cases, an exporter does not know in advance which bank is going to be the credit issuing bank. Therefore, in order to be sure of being paid, an exporter should request a D/C to be issued by a reputable bank. If he receives a D/C issued by a bank of an underdeveloped country with doubtful integrity, it is better for him to request the D/C to be confirmed by a bank in his own country. In that case, the payment default of the issuing bank arising either from liquidation or its country's exchange control to prohibit funds movement only terminates one of the two sources of payment. Default by the opening bank does not affect the definite undertaking of the confirming bank to pay the beneficiary.

(b) Is the D/C irrevocable as required in the sales contract? This is important for an exporter as a revocable D/C can be cancelled at any time (up to the calling up of documents by a bank) after its issue without the exporter's agreement.

(c) Is the exporter's name complete and spelled correctly? If the name is incomplete or spelled wrongly, this affects him badly in subsequent negotiations. Negotiating banks normally stick to "Principle of Strict Compliance" in checking this area. Bankers would need to be assured that the name of the beneficiary is exactly the same as that stipulated in the D/C. It is therefore necessary for an exporter to amend the credit to the correct name before negotiation at the earliest moment.

(d) Can the exporter meet the latest shipment date and expiry date? Some time may have passed after the completion of a sales contract and the subsequent issue of a documentary credit. It may be necessary for the exporter to postpone shipment and presentation of documents, for example, there may be a delay in the supply of raw materials. Therefore, it is wise for an exporter, upon receipt of a D/C, to check carefully whether an amendment is necessary to be requested to extend the latest dates for shipment and the expiry date for submission of documents.

(e) It is then necessary to check carefully if the terms and conditions of the D/C are the same as those stipulated in the sales contract. This includes checking:

(1) amount and currency of the credit;
(2) the description of goods;
(3) Incoterms;

(4) partial shipment and transhipment allowed as in the contract;

(5) points of shipment and destination as agreed;

(6) number and types of shipping documents as stipulated in the contract;

(7) whether the credit specifically authorize some terms contrary to the rules and practices, e.g., if a chartered vessel is to be used for shipment, does the credit specifically specify "charter party bill of lading allowed";

(8) whether certain documents, e.g., consular documents, are able to be issued and obtained from the government body.

(9) who is to bear the banking charges outside the applicant's country as stated in the contract.

It must be noted that not all the contents of a D/C are the same as those in the sales contract. A credit, by its nature, is separate from the underlying sales contract. If an exporter finds it impossible to check the contents of a D/C against those of the sales contract, it is advisable for him to figure out if the shipping documents which he is going to prepare and obtain can comply with the D/C. Furthermore, he has to ask himself the question of whether he can manage to prepare them or obtain them from relevant bodies.

Also, an issuing bank may have inserted in a D/C some terms and conditions to protect itself. These terms may affect the beneficiary badly in terms of cost and /or increase the chance of failure to comply with credit terms. Therefore, a beneficiary must be aware of this potential "trap" and must request clarification with his overseas buyer and ask for an amendment to have potentially unreasonable or unfavourable terms deleted.

14 Bank Considerations in Examination and Negotiation of Export Documents

Upon receipt of a set of documents presented by the beneficiary, the staff in a bank's export negotiation department will check the documents. In examination of documents, a bills checker must, according to UCP–500 Article 13, check with reasonable care to ascertain that documents appear on their face to be in accordance with the terms and conditions of the D/C. In practice, a checker should:

(a) ensure that the number of documents presented is as listed in the application form and in particular, as per the requirement under the D/C;

(b) check every document against D/C terms and conditions (Documents vs D/C) to ensure that they are compliant;

(c) check other conditions and, in particular, the information not specified in the D/C in each document (but which exist in the documents) which may be inconsistent between documents. For example, it is necessary to ensure in the packing list that such information as gross weight and measurement be consistent with those on the bills of lading although D/C does not specifically require such information to be shown in the packing list and bill of lading (Documents vs Documents).

In document checking, there are two schools of thought which a checker can apply. One school is "Doctrine of Strict Compliance" in the sense that the documents should be checked strictly in accordance with the credit terms and conditions. The other school of thought is "Doctrine of Substantial Compliance" in the sense that the documents to be examined do not necessarily have to be exactly the same as stipulated in the D/C provided that they are substantially compliant with the D/C terms and conditions. In other words, this school of thought allows flexibility in acceptance of documents provided that the minor variations are immaterial. This depends on what the issuing bank will tolerate.

If the bank is satisfied with all the information in the documents, it may be prepared to effect negotiation. Negotiation means examination of documents as well as provision of a financing facility from a bank to its customer without the customer having to wait for the actual collection of payment from the issuing bank. This can enhance the customer's liquidity position. Based on the relationship between the negotiating bank and its customer, the bank may pay the exporter the face value of the bill. The credit standing of the beneficiary and of the issuing bank, and the past experiences of sending similar bills for reimbursement are the important considerations in negotiation. In negotiation, the financing bank in fact, purchases the documents and becomes the holder of the bill and is entitled to payment from the drawee of the bill in its own right. It may also have a recourse agreement depending on its relationship with the beneficiary.

15 Discrepancies and Indemnities

If the documents presented by the beneficiary do not comply with any of the D/C terms and conditions, no matter how minor the inconsistency, the documents are said to have discrepancy(ies). If that is the case, the issuing bank may refuse to reimburse the negotiating bank as the issuing bank's undertaking to pay is only on condition that the documents presented are in order (without discrepancies).

Upon receipt of a set of irregular documents, the exporter's banker may deal with them in the following four ways:

(a) It agrees to pay the beneficiary despite the discrepancies provided that:

(1) the exporter has a good relationship with his bank;

(2) the exporter has signed a Letter of Indemnity to the bank in which ;

(3) the exporter undertakes to indemnify his banker against non-payment from the issuing bank.

(b) If the exporter's banker is unwilling to negotiate a set of documents containing discrepancies, it may send the export documents to the issuing bank for presentation to the applicant for acceptance of discrepancies and payment. The exporter's bank, in this process, acts as an agent as if in a documentary collection to collect the proceeds for its customer. Upon receipt of the import documents, the issuing bank will spot the discrepancies which are then referred to the applicant for acceptance. If the discrepancies are accepted by the applicant, payment under the credit will be made in due course.

(c)   The third way is by means of cable negotiation. The negotiating bank sends a telex to the issuing bank for permission to pay despite the discrepancies. It lists all the irregularities to the issuing bank which then refers them to applicant for acceptance and agreement to pay the bill despite the said discrepancies. The cost of the cable will be charged to the beneficiary's account.

(d)   Documents could be corrected/amended by the beneficiary.

It is worth pointing out that if the D/C has not been fully utilized (e.g., only partial shipment is effected), it is advisable for the exporter to request a D/C amendment from the issuing bank to avoid committing the same documentation errors in future.

16   Documentary Credit Dispute Expertise System (DOCDEX)

There is a growing number of disputes between parties to documentary credits, and these disputes cannot be resolved by referring to UCP–500 AND its Opinion Papers. To respond to a call from the international banking community for a rapid, cost-effective, expert-based dispute resolution mechanism for documentary credit practice, the DOCDEX was introduced in October 1997 by the International Chamber of Commerce. DOCDEX is made available through its International Centre for Expertise (the Centre) under the auspices of the ICC Commission on Banking Technique and Practice (the Banking Commission). When a dispute is submitted to the Centre, it will appoint three experts from a pool of ICC-appointed experts. The three appointed experts shall make a decision which after consultation with the Technical Adviser of the Banking Commission, shall be rendered by the Centre as a DOCDEX Decision. The costs of the DOCDEX service shall be the standard fee (USD 5,000) which has to be paid when the dispute is submitted to ICC. The standard fee includes administrative expenses and expert fees and is not recoverable no matter what the outcome of the resolution is. An additional fee may be payable which shall be fixed by the Centre at its discretion and may be up to 100% of the standard fee.

The advantage of making use of this system is that the three independent experts selected at random from the pool of experts by the ICC provides an impartial decision. Also, instead of using relatively technical terminology as in arbitration, DOCDEX is based on the Uniform Customs and Practice for Documentary Credits UCP–500 and Uniform Rules for Bank-to-Bank Reimbursement under Documentary Credits (URR–525) which are well known to most bankers. It may be cheaper than arbitration and also less time-consuming.

17   Certified Documentary Credit Specialist (CDCS)

CDCS is a professional designation for individuals who successfully complete the requirements for a Certified Documentary Credit Specialist. This has been developed in partnership between the Chartered Institute of Bankers (CIB) and the International Financial Services Association (IFSA). The certification is endorsed by the International Chamber of Commerce (ICC).

After being qualified to be a CDCS, a banker can demonstrate his knowledge and understanding of the complex issues in documentary credits. He may be more authoritative and professional in his field. The first examination is scheduled for 1999 and the method of assessing the candidates is by means of multiple choice. The syllabus of the examination is as follows:

Core knowledge:

(a) Understanding types of documentary credits
(b) Understanding bank operation risks

   (c)   Understanding   applicable   regulations,   rules   and
        responsibilities

Processing responsibilities:

(a) Issuing and amending
(b) Advising and confirming
(c) Examining documents
(d) Effecting payments

In summary, the examination is about purposes, types and uses of documentary credits, characteristics of documentary credits, applicable rules and local law.

The examination is held at various locations around the world. [1]

As banks are moving in the direction of offering professional services, the CDCS examination provides a professional certification examination which certifies that staff with CDCS are competent in D/C operations and knowledgeable professionals. It is hoped that with the help of the examination, the techniques in dealing with D/C transactions can further be upgraded towards a uniform standard.

Note

1.   Quote from U.S. Council on International Banking, Inc., One World Trade Center, Suite 2269, New York NY 10048, U.S.A. (now the International Financial Services Association).

Revision Questions

1. State the procedures for handling unclean import documents by a banker.

2. If documents presented by your customers do not comply with credit terms, explain the different ways you can help your customer.

3. What are the considerations you would have in mind before the issue of a documentary credit?

4. Upon receipt of a documentary credit, what are the main points an exporter should look at carefully?

5. What do you understand by DOCDEX? How do you compare DOCDEX and ICLOCA Rules?

6. What do you understand by CDCS?

7. Titanic Decorations Ltd. are your customers who have been importing furniture from Europe. Recently, they have had difficulties in obtaining supplies from their current suppliers. To cope with company's growth, they started working with a reputable Indonesian company which has offered, subject to receiving finance for each transaction, to buy furniture from various suppliers in Jakarta and to ship the furniture to Hong Kong for Titanic Decorations Ltd. Today, Mr. Robert Cheung, financial controller of Titanic Decoration Ltd. approaches you for advice.

   Required:

   Explain briefly any method by which your customer, Titanic Decorations Ltd., might arrange for the finance of such transaction by using documentary credits. You are expected to give details on the nature of finance, parties involved and the practical procedures of providing this finance.

   Banking Practice in Hong Kong, HKIB Associateship Examinations, May 1998.

8. Your customer, Johnson & Brothers, have maintained a good relationship with your branch over the last five years, You have

granted them facilities to open D/C and settle transactions under trust receipt. They used to purchase steel and spare parts from Europe. Today, Mr. Michael Cheung, financial controller of the company, calls and advises you that they have received a quotation from Germany for the supply of special steel. The supplier asks them to arrange an irrevocable documentary credit which is transferable and confirmed. They have no experience in handling this special type of D/C.

Required:

(a) State briefly what the seller requires. Quote relevant articles of UCP–500 as necessary.

(b) State what factors Johnson & Brothers should consider before signing the contract.

(c) If partial shipment is prohibited, can the supplier transfer the D/C to more than one second beneficiary? Quote relevant UCP–500 article in your answer.

Banking Practice in Hong Kong, HKIB Associateship Examination, October 1998.

9. Your customer, Great Electronics Ltd., has been importing electronic components from a supplier, High Impact Conductors Inc. in Europe. This supplier has required Great Electronics Ltd. to arrange for the D/Cs to be issued three months before shipment and the payment term is 90 days from date of shipment.

Mr. Terence Fong, the operations manager of Great Electronics Ltd., calls you today and tells you that their supplier in Europe wishes to receive future L/Cs without bills of exchange and wants to replace sea waybill instead of marine bill of lading.

Required:

(a) Why might High Impact Conductors Inc. have required D/Cs to be issued three months before shipment?

(b) What are the characteristics of the future D/Cs to be applied by Great Electronics Ltd.?

(c)   Compare, in tabulated form, the functions of a marine bill of lading and a sea waybill.

Banking Practice in Hong Kong, HKIB Associateship Examination, May 1999.

Further Reading

1.   Charles del Busto, *ICC Guide to Documentary Credit Operations*, International Chamber of Commerce.

2.   H. C. Gutteridge Maurice Megrah, *The Law of Bankers' Commercial Credit*, Europa Publications Limited, London.

3.   Charles del Busto, *The New Standard Documentary Credit Forms for the UCP–500*, International Chamber of Commerce.

4.   Abdul Latiff Abdul Rahim, *Guide to Documentary Credit Rules: UCP–500*, Institute of Bankers, Malaysia.

5.   Abdul Latiff Abdul Rahim, *Documentary Credit*, Nalco Associates.

6.   *DOCDEX Rules*, International Chamber of Commerce.

7.   Lakshman Wickremeratne and Michael Rowe, *Trade Finance: The Complete Guide to Documentary Credits*, CIB 1998.

6

Banking Facilities and Services for Exporters and Importers

❑ Export Facilities and Services:
- ❑ Overdraft facilities (O/D)
- ❑ Negotiation of export bills under documentary credit (D/C)
- ❑ Negotiation under documentary collection
- ❑ Bills advance
- ❑ Documents presented for negotiation with and without recourse
- ❑ Bills discounted under D/C available by acceptance
- ❑ Usance draft payable at sight basis under D/C
- ❑ Acceptance credit facility under documentary collection
- ❑ Performance bond, letter of indemnity, standby credit, red clause credit, packing loan
- ❑ Factoring

❑ Import Facilities and Services:
- ❑ Loan against imports (LAI)
- ❑ Trust receipt facilities (T/R)
- ❑ Shipping guarantee
- ❑ Overdraft D/C facility

Export Facilities and Services

1 Overdraft Facilities (O/D)

Overdrafts are granted to customers to finance their daily business requirements, and particularly assist their cash flow position.

An overdraft may be secured or unsecured and there are usually upper limits on the amounts provided over a period of time. The facilities are reviewed annually.

The interest rate charged is usually higher than other forms of finance and is calculated based on prime rate plus a margin. It is quite common for the commercial bank to charge O/D interest based on prime rate plus 1.5%–4% and this depends on the relationship between the bank and the customer. Unlike in the fixed loan, O/D interest is charged only on the actual amount overdrawn on a daily basis. Therefore, an overdraft is most suitable for customers with temporary liquidity needs and is more flexible to customers.

2 Negotiation of Export Bills under Documentary Credit

When the exporter who has effected shipment presents the relevant documents to his bank, that bank will send the documents to the overseas bank for onward delivery of documents and, upon receipt of payment from the overseas bank, will credit the exporter's account held with it. This period normally would be seven days or more and is called the transit period. The interest so incurred during this period is known as transit interest.

If the exporter cannot afford to wait for this period or if he wants to further improve his liquidity position, he can apply for a negotiation facility from his banker. Negotiation means documents being checked and value given by his banker. In other words, it is a kind of post-shipment finance granted by the negotiating bank to him when he has presented a set of documents strictly in compliance with D/C terms and conditions. That his banker may be willing to offer him this type of finance is based on the expectation that payment will be effected by the overseas bank in due course. This source of payment is almost certain provided that:

(a) the exporter is able to submit a set of documents which is strictly in compliance with credit terms and conditions (in D/C), or;

(b) the overseas buyer accepts the documents despite the discrepancies and pays via his banker (in D/C).

Sight bills or term bills might be negotiated by the exporter's banker. The bill, with shipping documents, will be handed to the bank, which will:

(a) pay the exporter the amount of the bills. This, in effect, is equivalent to buying them from the exporter;

(b) send the bills and documents in their own right for reimbursement.

In negotiating bills of exchange drawn under documentary credits, the negotiating bank purchases the bills and sends the documents in its own right for reimbursement. In a documentary credit, the bills should be drawn on the issuing bank. Negotiation under D/C may be granted on a with recourse or non-recourse basis (without recourse basis). It is a with-recourse finance unless the negotiating bank has added its confirmation to the credit. Besides, the right of recourse can only be exercised by the negotiating bank should the issuing bank fail to pay (accept bills and honour to pay upon maturity) for reasons other than discrepancies being found in the documents. In other words, the negotiating bank has no right of recourse to the exporter in the following situations:

(a) it has confirmed the credit;

(b) it has failed to spot discrepancies and the issuing bank has refused to reimburse the negotiating bank.[1]

3 Negotiation under Documentary Collection

Bank may offer a negotiation facility in documentary collection. In negotiating documentary collection, the negotiating bank examines the documents and credits its customer's account if it is satisfied that the overseas buyer will pay via the collecting bank. Meanwhile, it is given the right to vary the customer's instructions in the collection instruction if it so wishes. For example, a negotiating bank may prefer to add "protest in case of dishonour"in its collection instruction when its customer prefers not to do so. A negotiating bank may insist on adding the clause "store and insure the goods in case of dishonour" while its customer does not specify such an instruction in the collection instruction. In a simple collection, a bank would not take the initiative to add instructions other than those given by the customer. In negotiating a collection, the bank has purchased the bills and other documents and collects the proceeds in its own right.[2] It is understandable that the bank would like to add on terms which can protect its own interests. Such finance is on a with-recourse basis.

4 Bills Advance

Bills advance is similar to negotiation in that the bank offering the advance grants post-shipment finance to the customer. It works in the similar way as in negotiation of export bills. However, the bank usually advances only a percentage of the bill amount. It also differs from negotiation in that the bank can have a right of recourse to its customer at any time after the finance. Therefore, a bank may choose to advance the bills other than to negotiate the bills when:

(a) it may have doubts about the payment obligation of the issuing bank and/or that of the buyer.

(b) a nominated bank other than the exporter's banker is authorized to negotiate the documents.

The following case is a common example of bills advance in Hong Kong:

If an exporter receives a D/C which is available with a restricted bank for negotiation, he should present documents to this nominated bank for negotiation and obtain finance from it. However, if this restricted bank is not his banker, it is unlikely that the bank will accept his application for negotiation. Neither is the bank willing to provide him with any type of finance. In order to obtain finance, this exporter can apply for bills advance from his own bank which knows him well and is ready to check the documents and provide his customer with finance. His bank subsequently presents the documents to the restricted bank for negotiation on a with-recourse basis. Hence, bills advance is a kind of finance to the exporter from his banker before he receives payment from the nominated bank.

The bank may agree to offer this type of finance if it is satisfied that the exporter is reliable. Under any circumstances, the bank offering such advance can have a right of recourse to its customer upon default of payment from the issuing bank via the restricted negotiating bank.[3]

5 Documents Presented for Negotiation Without Recourse

When the beneficiary receives a confirmed documentary credit which is available with the confirming bank by negotiation, the exporter's bank cannot negotiate this document. Instead, it has to present it to the confirming bank for "negotiation without recourse". This means that:

(a) Documents have not been checked by the presenting bank (exporter's banker).

(b) It is the responsibility of the nominated negotiating bank (i.e., the confirming bank) to check the documents.

(c) Upon receipt of funds from the confirming bank, the exporter's bank will credit its customer's account. The nominated negotiating bank has no right of recourse to the presenting bank once it has paid the bill.

6 Documents Presented for Negotiation With Recourse

When the beneficiary receives a documentary credit which indicates a restriction to the nominated bank for negotiation or that the nominated bank holds a reimbursement instruction, the exporter's banker cannot negotiate this document. Instead, it has to present it to the nominated bank for "negotiation with recourse". This means that:

(a) Documents have been checked by the presenting bank (exporter's banker).
(b) The nominated bank needs not re-check the document.
(c) Upon receipt of funds from the nominated bank, the exporter's bank will credit its customer's account.
(d) The nominated bank has a right of recourse to the presenting bank if the issuing bank subsequently fails to make payment.

In the above presentations, either with recourse or without recourse, documents may still be negotiated by the nominated bank against a "Letter of Indemnity" which is signed by the presenting bank (exporter's banker) in favour of the nominated bank (see Section 11 Letter of Indemnity).

7 Bills Discounted under Documentary Credit Available by Acceptance

An acceptance credit may require the bills to be drawn either on the nominated bank in the beneficiary's country or on the issuing bank. Having effected shipment using this type of documentary credit, the beneficiary will send the draft and other shipping documents to the bank where the credit is available for acceptance. After having checked the documents (if the documents comply with credit terms and conditions), the bank will signify its acceptance on the draft and return it to the beneficiary. As the bill is accepted by the nominated bank, the bill becomes an eligible bill. The discount rate will be at a fine rate. The beneficiary may present the bill to his bank/the discount house to be discounted or alternatively keep the bill until the maturity date for payment. When the beneficiary chooses to request his bank/discount house to have the bill discounted, he can get immediate and cheap funds from his bank/discount house which will be reimbursed from the nominated bank upon maturity.

This kind of facility is popular in the United Kingdom and some Asian countries. However, it is rarely seen in Hong Kong. It is time for our bankers to further explore this new business opportunity. It remains to be seen whether this type of facility can be developed in our market.

8 Usance Draft Payable at Sight Basis under Documentary Credit

A beneficiary may receive a documentary credit which is available with a nominated bank/any bank in Hong Kong by acceptance, payable at a future date (e.g., 180 days sight). Meanwhile, the nominated bank in Hong Kong is instructed to treat the draft at sight basis and that acceptance commission and discharge interest are for account of the D/C applicant. Hence, the beneficiary is paid at sight despite the fact that this is a term bill. The D/C applicant need not pay the bill until it falls due at maturity. The nominated bank is instructed to claim the acceptance commission and discount interest which it should earn from the issuing bank, besides the bill amount.

This kind of facility has the following characteristics:

(a) The interest rate in the exporter's country is lower than that of the buyer's country.
(b) The buyer enjoys the benefit of a lower interest rate in the seller's country and only has to make payment upon maturity.
(c) The seller gets immediate payment from the negotiating bank.
(d) This is effected under documentary credit.

9 Acceptance Credit Facility under Documentary Collection

This is a form of discounting similar in concept to a documentary acceptance credit.

When the exporter engages in a series of transactions with the overseas importer, he may arrange with his banker an acceptance credit line, with the help of documents under collection as security for the facility. Then, the exporter is authorized to draw a term bill on his bank (acceptance house) which is processing collection bills for him. It is important to note that this bill is separate from the underlying trade bill which is drawn by the seller on the overseas buyer. Therefore, the exporter has drawn two separate bills, one drawn under the trade bill for payment from the overseas importer and one drawn under the term bill for acceptance from his bank (or acceptance house). When the bill has been accepted, it becomes an "eligible bill". The exporter will have it discounted by the discount house at a fine rate and his account will be credited with the face value of the bill less discount charges and acceptance commission.

When the bill matures, the discount house will present it to his bank (acceptance house) for payment. By this time, his banker should have obtained reimbursement from the exporter's underlying trade bill. Hence, based on the underlying trade bills as the security and source of payment, his banker is ready to accept the bills for the exporter against an acceptance commission. An acceptance credit facility is granted on a with-recourse basis.

It is necessary to point out that the bill drawn by the exporter on his bank (acceptance house) for acceptance must have an expiry date later than that of the underlying trade bill. The time difference between the two bills represents the time required for the proceeds from the underlying trade bill to be remitted to settle the accepting bill.

This kind of facility is popular in the United Kingdom and in some Asian countries like Malaysia. For example, the exporter's credit standing must be undoubted and the minimum transaction level is GBP 100,000 in the U.K. market.

10 Performance Bond

This is a written instrument, issued by a bank or a surety company, (e.g., insurance company) stating that the exporter will comply with the terms of the contract with the buyer, otherwise the buyer will receive compensation for any losses suffered as a result of the exporter's failure to perform as agreed.

This is common where a contractor has made a bid for a government project. When the bid bond has expired, a performance bond is requested to be issued in favour of the relevant overseas buyer or government department to guarantee against the contractor's non-performance or poor performance of the contracted work.

If the contractor fails to fulfil the terms of the contract, the bank will (because usually the bond is on demand) take the responsibility to pay the buyer (government department). Usually, security is required for the issue of the bond and in return, the bank will charge a fee for the potential risk taken and the service provided. This impacts on the exporter's borrowing facilities (refer to Chapter 13 for further details).

11 Letter of Indemnity

In a negotiation credit, if the exporter cannot fulfil all terms and conditions, he can still request his bank to negotiate the documents against signing a Letter of Indemnity.

The Letter of Indemnity is signed and given by the exporter in the bank standard form. Upon receipt of a letter of Indemnity, the bank agrees to negotiate the exporter's documents despite the discrepancies. Meanwhile, the exporter agrees to indemnify the bank against any losses arising from the negotiation.

A Letter of Indemnity may be signed by the exporter's bank to the nominated bank under a set of documents sent for negotiation with recourse or without recourse.

In a restricted negotiation credit, if another bank other than the advising bank (assuming that we are the exporter's bank) is the nominated bank for negotiation, we have to present the shipping documents to this bank on behalf of our customer (also assuming that the customer maintains no account with the nominated bank).

If the shipping documents which have been prepared by our customer are not in order, the nominated bank may be unwilling to negotiate the documents unless it is given some kinds of protection. We can help our customer by submitting a Letter of Indemnity to the nominated bank with regard to negotiating the discrepant documents.

A Letter of Indemnity, signed by our customer, countersigned by our bank, will be presented with the shipping documents to the nominated bank. With this indemnity, the nominated negotiating bank will be happy to negotiate the documents because it has a right of recourse to us if the discrepancies turn out to be unacceptable to the D/C applicant. Any commissions or charges so incurred will be paid by our customer. Meanwhile, we have a right of recourse to our customers.

12 Standby Letter of Credit

A pure loan type of standby credit is a guarantee given to the advising bank against its finance to the exporter, on the instruction of, and at the risk of the issuing bank (see standby credit in Chapter 12 for details).

13 Red Clause Credit

It is a pre-shipment finance granted to the exporter by, and at the risk of the issuing bank (see red clause credit in Chapter 12 for details).

14 Packing Loan

The purpose of packing loan is to help the exporter to buy raw materials for production or to buy the necessary goods required by the D/C. This is similar to a red clause credit in that it is a pre-shipment finance granted to the exporter.

However, unlike the red clause credit where the issuing bank has to bear the risk, a packing loan is granted against the deposit of the documentary credit as the collateral. Hence, it is the exporter's banker which has to bear the potential risk.

Under a packing loan agreement, the customer is required to present documents to the same bank (the bank having granted the facility) before the latest shipment date and expiry date. Should the customer fail to present documents as agreed, the bank can ask for refund of the packing loan from him.

15 Factoring

Factoring is a special type of trade service usually targeted at exporters, incorporating debt collection, finance, cash flow management and credit insurance, aimed largely at open account sales. It is usually provided by the subsidiary or associate company of the bank, known as the factor or the factoring company. The factor usually is a member of the Factoring Association.

15.1 Reasons and Conditions for Factoring

The market for the firm's product is highly competitive, making it essential for the exporter to offer favourable credit terms to the importer. The credit terms usually range from immediate sight payment to 180 days (typically 90 days) open account. Besides, the client base is broad and located throughout the world, with the characteristics of repetitive sales. The exporter may need financial support and he may find it too costly to set up a credit collection department. As an alternative to ease one or more of the above, the exporter can look for a factor for assistance.

15.2 Scope of Factoring Services

A. Debts Collection

When the seller has shipped the goods, he will submit relevant invoices to the factor which will find an overseas correspondent to onward transfer the documents to the overseas buyer for payment. The overseas correspondent, which is usually a member of the Factoring Association, is more familiar with the buyer's customs, language and possible reason to defer payment. In this way, the factor collects the account receivable for the seller. However, it looks as if it were the exporter's debt collection department sending invoices, making collections from debtors, keeping records and sending reminders as necessary.

B. Finance

Finance is a very important service within the definition of factoring. Upon receipt of an invoice, the factor may pay the exporter a percentage (up to 80%) of the invoice value. The factor, in fact, purchases the bill of exchange which is drawn on the importer. Under the agreement, the factor retains a right of recourse to the exporter unless credit insurance is also incorporated in the agreement.

C. Credit Insurance

If the factor also provides credit insurance in a factoring service, in addition to providing finance, it has to check the buyer's credit standing very carefully. If the factoring service incorporates credit insurance, the finance is granted on a non-recourse basis. In other words, the factor also provides against bad debts. It should be noted that the scope of cover is usually against the buyer's insolvency arising from protracted default (unwilling or unable to pay). Political risk may not be covered. Therefore, this type of credit insurance provided under factoring is most suitable for exporters who are selling goods to markets in which political risks do not exist or are minimal.

Banks may offer one or a combination of the above services, depending on the customers' need. Some factors may completely refuse to provide insurance cover in a certain region because of the high default risk.

15.3 Advantages of Factoring Services to the Exporter

Factoring services allow exporters to become more competitive in the existing markets. An exporter can grant longer credit terms to the overseas importer on the understanding that the factoring company can provide him with finance by purchasing his account receivables.

Undoubtedly, offering a longer credit period to the buyer is an effective way to compete successfully in the existing market.

Factoring services can also enhance the exporter's cash flow. A factor may provide the exporter with up to 80% of the invoice value. This enables the exporter to recycle his funds back to the business for other useful purposes.

Factoring services may lead to a gain in controlling administrative costs and improvement in debt management. With the help of a professional factor who offers expert advice (although at relatively high charges), the exporter may have an overall gain in administrative costs and a much more effective way of collecting payment. He does not need to set up his own debt collection department but this is at the expense of a discount charge and service fee.

With the help of a factor, the exporter does not need to spend time and take the trouble to collect the debts. He can concentrate more on other management functions such as marketing, manufacturing, and quality control etc.

A factoring service may enable the exporter to explore new markets more easily and safely. Factoring companies provide much information about the buyers' credit standing, which enables the exporter to adopt a bolder marketing strategy and render him more willing to enter into new markets.

15.4 Advantages of Factoring Services to the Factor

The factor can increase its income in the form of discount charges and service fees. The discount charge is based on the amount actually drawn down by the exporter against each invoice and its tenor until full payment is received from the overseas buyer. With respect to service fees, factors in Hong Kong usually charge 0.25%–3.5% of the invoiced value and the exact percentage depends on the range of services provided, and the volume of the client's business. The range of services usually includes:

(a) answering customers' enquiries;
(b) handling customers' wholesale ledger;

(c) collecting debts by means of sending out statements and regular reminders/chasers;

(d) credit insurance against default payment.

The factoring business can be quite profitable.

15.5 Factoring and Invoice Discounting

Factoring is quite similar to invoice discounting. It is similar to invoice discounting in that it provides a financial benefit to the customer. It differs from invoice discounting in that the latter enables the exporter to maintain complete control over their relationship with their overseas importers. In other words, the overseas buyers may be unaware that the documents are purchased in invoice discounting whereas, in providing a factoring service, the factor deals with the overseas buyer. Besides, invoice discounting is limited to smaller amounts compared to factoring.

15.6 Concluding Remarks

Initially growing quickly, factoring services seem to be declining recently. Recent financial turmoil which reduces the trading activities worldwide may be one of the reasons for the decline. Besides, open account sales are not as popular as other terms of payment in Hong Kong (although 70% of world trade is by means of "open account"). Factoring services are mainly provided by foreign financial institutions and a few subsidiaries of local banks. An example of the local factor is East Asia Heller Limited, jointly owned by Bank of East Asia and Heller International Group. Transactions are not as numerous as with documentary credits and documentary collections.

Import Facilities and Services

16 Loan against Imports (LAI)

LAI is an advance to the importer based on the imported goods as the security.

When the goods under a D/C arrive but where the customer does not wish to effect immediate payment, he can request the bank to effect payment for him and arrange to have the goods stored in a godown under the name of the bank. In other words, the bank can always maintain physical control of the goods although it has effected payment to the beneficiary.

In case the customer wants to take delivery of the goods, he can arrange with his bank and the godown to take delivery of them against payment to the bank or against trust receipt.

The customer can take partial delivery of the goods against proportional payment (or trust receipt) in which case, a delivery order will be issued. This kind of service is most useful for those customers who do not need all the goods at one time. His credit lines are earmarked for the amount of the goods he has taken delivery of. His liquidity position is, therefore, enhanced. However, loans of this kind are restricted to good customers.

In practice, the bank must make sure that there is adequate fire insurance and marine insurance coverage for the goods. Besides, LAI is limited to goods which are not easily perishable and whose marketability is high.

17 Trust Receipt (T/R)

This is a document executed by a customer who agrees to hold the goods in trust for and on behalf of the bank. It is a sub-limit of the customer's import line, granted together with the line of documentary credit. The customer who takes delivery of goods against a trust receipt agrees to hold the goods in trust for the bank and acknowledges the bank's vested interest in the goods. He further undertakes to repay the bank from the sales proceeds.

17.1 Advantages of Trust Receipt Facility

From the customer's point of view, it allows the importer to take delivery of the goods for sale or further processing (as in the case of buying raw materials) and not pay for them until the expiry of the T/R as agreed. His liquidity position is therefore enhanced.

From the bank's point of view, the finance is self-liquidating in the sense that its customers repay the bank from the sales proceeds.

17.2 Disadvantages of Trust Receipt Facility

From the customer's point of view, not every customer is entitled to such facility. It is granted to customers of high integrity and against adequate collateral.

It is granted with time constraints, normally ranging from 60 days to 180 days (but with exception) depending on the types of trade and customers. Interest, especially overdue interest, is high.

From the bank's point of view, it loses physical control of the goods.

The goods and the proceeds may be subject to prior charge and, sometimes, goods may be intermingled and not be identifiable. Besides, it may be the case that the proceeds of the sale are not traceable. (*Romalpa Aluminium Ltd v Aluminium Industrie Vaassen*)

The customer's creditworthiness may also worsen and goods may be perishable or become out of fashion which may render the goods valueless.

18 Shipping Guarantee

A shipping guarantee is an undertaking given by the bank on behalf of its customer to the shipping company to return the original shipping documents.

In return, the shipping company allows the customer of the bank to take delivery of goods against a shipping guarantee without producing the original bill of lading.

The reason why this facility is needed by the customer is that sometimes, goods arrive at Hong Kong long before the arrival of documents. This may happen if an importer opens a documentary credit with goods shipped from China or Asian countries to Hong Kong. Normally, it takes two or more days for the goods from China to arrive in Hong Kong while the shipping documents may not arrive until a week later.

In order to allow the importer to take delivery of the goods at the first moment upon their arrival and also to avoid demurrage charges (shipping companies usually grant a few days or more free storage known as the grace period, after which a storage penalty known as the demurrage charge is imposed on the consignee to encourage him to take delivery), the bank is ready to provide its customers with this service.

In practice, a shipping guarantee is given on the pre-printed form of that shipping company, signed by the customer and countersigned by the bank.

Since the bank loses physical control of the goods upon signing a shipping guarantee, it requires protection such as full margin or a trust receipt line being earmarked.

As to the importer, he must be clearly aware of his position. Once he has taken delivery of the goods, he must accept the documents which he will receive later. Any discrepancies which are found in the shipping documents afterwards cannot be grounds for the rejection of payment.

In addition, poor quality of the goods cannot be used as a reason to refuse payment, so the intended protection inserted in the terms and conditions of the D/C is lost.

Below is a summary of the advantages and disadvantages of a shipping guarantee to the importer:

18.1 Advantages

(a) The importers can possess the goods immediately upon their arrival.

(b) He can avoid paying additional charges imposed by the transportation company such as paying demurrage charges.

18.2 Disadvantages

(a) In case he has taken delivery of goods against shipping guarantee, he has to pay for the bills. He is obliged to pay regardless of any discrepancies in the documents. Therefore, the intended protection of the terms and conditions in the D/C is lost.

(b) Marginal deposit, Trust Receipt or other credit lines are normally taken as security to support the delivery. This will utilize existing credit lines.

19 Overdraft

Overdraft for importer works in the same way as for exporter (see Section 1 for details).

20 Documentary Credit

This is an undertaking given by the issuing bank on behalf of the importer to pay the exporter against the latter's submission of a set of compliant documents (see Chapter 5 for details).

Notes

1. This kind of facility is offered by banks in Hong Kong under: (a) documentary credit issued at sight or usance; (b) documentary collection with a sight bill or term bill.

2. The bill of exchange should be drawn on the buyer in a collection.

3. In the U.K., a bill advance is only used with documentary collections and is credit insured to make the transactions without recourse.

Further Reading

Watson/Paul Cowdell/Derek Hyde, *Finance of International Trade, 6th Edition*, The Chartered Institute of Bankers, Chapter 17.

7

Export Credit Insurance

1 Meaning of Export Credit Insurance

Export credit insurance provides exporters with insurance against buyers' credit risk and country risk. Specifically, it provides an additional security to banks on behalf of the exporters so that the bank is more willing to lend money to the exporter. In Hong Kong, the Hong Kong Export Credit Insurance Corporation (ECIC) is responsible for providing export credit insurance. Insurance policies issued by ECIC are well accepted by the banking community as useful collateral against the export bills they discount. The scope of cover in credit insurance is usually against (a) buyer risks (commercial risks) and (b) country risks (market risks or political risks).

2 The Hong Kong Export Credit Insurance Corporation

The Hong Kong Export Credit Insurance Corporation was created by statute in 1966. The purpose of its formation is to provide insurance protection for Hong Kong exporters against non-payment risks arising from commercial and political events. Its capital is wholly-owned by the Hong Kong Government.

Apart from the capital of HK$20 million issued by the Government, the Corporation is required, under its enabling statute, to secure sufficient revenue to meet its expenditure from one year to another. The contingent liability, which the Corporation may assume under its contract of insurance, is determined from time to time by the Legislature. The current maximum contingent liability is HK$10 billion. However, it has not been necessary for the ECIC, throughout its 33 years of operation, to invoke the Government guarantee.

In its day-to-day operations, the ECIC functions as an autonomous entity and is empowered to take on risks based solely on commercial considerations, without any directive from the Government. The classes of insurance contracts and the nature of the risks that may be covered by the corporation, however, are subject to the approval of the Financial Secretary. For major formulation and changes in policy, the ECIC may seek the advice of a 12-member advisory board consisting of representatives from the finance, insurance, trade and industrial sectors and Government officials.

2.1 Roles of the ECIC and the Range of Services Provided

The role of the Corporation is to encourage and support export trade through the provision of professional and customer-oriented services.

The Corporation provides a wide range of insurance facilities to Hong Kong exporters of goods and services trading on credit terms with overseas buyers on credit periods of up to 180 days. The facilities are to cover non-payment risks for goods exported and services rendered arising from the buyer's inability or refusal to pay, or political and economic events including shortage of foreign exchange, import bans, war and civil disturbances, or natural disasters.

The indemnity provided in the Corporation's facilities is normally up to 90% of the losses incurred. Apart from insurance coverage, the Corporation also provides a credit advisory service on the extent of credit it considers prudent to offer to buyers. The Corporation maintains a database of over 50,000 buyers all over the world and regularly monitors their creditworthiness and integrity. The credit information is derived from an international network, including status information agencies, banks and other credit insurers and is constantly updated and expanded through a computerized system.

With its world-wide network of lawyers and debt-collectors, the Corporation can also assist in solving payment problems and advising the course of action which a policyholder may undertake to prevent or minimize loss. If necessary, the Corporation may share up to 90% of the legal costs or charges incurred for the purposes of pursuing overdue payment.

3 Advantages of Having ECIC Cover

By having ECIC cover, an exporter enjoys the following advantages:

(a) Protection of up to 90% indemnity — By paying a low and reasonable premium under an ECIC policy, an exporter no longer has to worry about the risks of non-payment by his overseas buyers. He takes 10% of the risk.

(b) Credit management — Many exporters do not have the time, experience and expertise to assess the creditworthiness of their buyers. The ECIC solves this worrying problem by checking the credit standing of overseas buyers and constantly updates status information on them.

(c) Expansion of export business — With the ECIC's protection and guidance, an exporter should normally be able to expand his business better and faster and be able to develop new markets. He no longer has to reject buyers who ask for credit.

(d) Easy finance for an export from his banker — Although the ECIC itself does not provide finance, exporters will find that an ECIC policy is a very useful form of collateral security in negotiating export finance facilities with their bankers when the bankers know their clients' receivables are credit insured at 90%.

(e) Assessment of country risks — ECIC keeps a close eye on the economic and political developments in all overseas markets for Hong Kong goods. It also has due regard to the products involved and other aspects of marketing.

How can an ECIC Policy help an exporter obtain export finance from his banker? It is by means of a Letter of Authority (LA) — The protection accorded to a policy holder may be extended to the policyholder's bank by way of a Letter of Authority, which enables claims to be paid directly to the bank. Insurance policies issued by the Corporation are accepted by the banking community as useful collateral against the export bills they discount. The common types of Letter of Authority are:

(a) Whole Policy LA
(b) Specific Countries LA
(c) Specific Buyers LA

4 Common Types of Insurance Policy Offered by ECIC

4.1 Comprehensive Cover Policy (CCP)

The Comprehensive Cover Policy (CCP) is a policy designed for the Hong Kong exporters and manufacturers. The policy provides cover not only for all seller's export business on credit terms with goods shipped from Hong Kong, but also those transported directly from suppliers' countries to their destination without passing through Hong Kong. The policy was introduced in May 1997 and has been widely used in the market. It is expected that Comprehensive Cover Policy will replace Comprehensive Shipments Policy and External Trade Shipment Policy.

ECIC provides cover for such transactions under the Comprehensive Cover Policy (CCP) as long as the exporter is the principal in the contract of sale. All protection commences from the date of shipment.

Risks covered by CCP can be classified as follows:

(a) Buyer risks — These include buyer's insolvency and bankruptcy; default in payment; and failure or refusal to take delivery of goods.

(b) Country risks — These include blockage or delay in foreign exchange remittance; cancellation of import licences; import bans; payment moratorium; and war, civil disturbances and natural disasters.

For indemnity, the maximum percentage for all event of loss is 90% due to the following reasons:

(a) For insolvency or bankruptcy of the buyer, claims are settled as soon as all relevant documents are submitted.

(b) Where the buyer fails to pay for goods he has taken delivery of, claims are settled four months from the due date of payment.

(c) Where the buyer fails or refuses to take delivery of the goods, claims are settled immediately after the resale of goods.

(d) For any other event involving loss, claims are settled four months after the occurrence of the event.

4.2 Comprehensive Shipments Policy (CSP)

CSP has once been the most commonly used insurance policy. The policy covers exports of all kinds of consumer goods, semi-finished goods and raw materials from Hong Kong and re-exports through Hong Kong, on credit terms not longer than 180 days. The exporter may be trading under Documents against Payment or Open Account. The policy gives the exporter protection from the day goods are shipped.

The risks covered by Comprehensive Shipments Policy and its conditions of indemnity are the same as those of the Comprehensive Cover Policy (CCP). It is worth pointing out, however, that CSP will be gradually replaced by CCP.

4.3 External Trade Shipments Policy (ETSP)

ECIC recognizes the increasing trend for Hong Kong exporters and manufacturers to source goods from other countries due to pricing or other reasons. This means that while the banking and shipping documents and the decision to extend credit to overseas buyers are done in Hong Kong, the goods will be shipped direct from supplier's countries to their destination without passing through Hong Kong.

ECIC provides cover for such external trade transactions under its External Trade Shipments Policy (ETSP) as long as the exporter is the principal in the contract of sale. Protection commences from the date of the shipment.

Risks covered by ETSP can be classified as follows:

(a) Buyer risks — These include buyer's insolvency and bankruptcy, default in payment and failure or refusal to take delivery of goods.
(b) Country risks — These include blockage or delay in foreign exchange remittance; war, civil disturbances and natural disasters.

For indemnity, its conditions are the same as those of Comprehensive Cover Policy (CCP). Also, ETSP will be gradually replaced by CCP.

5 Cover on Export of Services

This type of service is tradable internationally. It helps to promote and support the export of services. Besides, it provides comprehensive protection to the Hong Kong service sector when rendering services to overseas clients on credit terms. The service offers a tailor-made policy, available to cater for the unique requirements of the trade. The cover starts on the date of rendering services.

The major benefits of the services are that the Percentage of Indemnity can be as high as 90%, credit management services, collateral for financing, risk management services, and sharing up to 90% of the expenses for pursuing debts.

5.1 Scope of Cover

Services covered may include freight forwarding and transport, computer software development, advertising and market research, engineering, construction and architectural services, media and publishing services, management consultancy.

5.2 Risks Covered

The risks covered are commercial risks and country risks. Commercial risks include insolvency and bankruptcy, default in payment. Country risks include blockage or delay in foreign exchange remittance, payment moratorium, war, civil disturbances and natural disasters.

6 Small and Medium Enterprises Policy (SMEP)

SMEs in general lack manpower and tend to overlook the risks inherent especially in new business. SMEP offer comprehensive protection over accounts receivable.

6.1 Major Benefits

The major benefits are easy to administer. Besides, the percentage of indemnity can be as high as 90%. It provides collateral for the exporter's banker in discounting export bills. It also provides credit management services. SMEP can share up to 90% of the expenses for pursuing debts.

6.2 Scope of Cover

Exports and re-exports from Hong Kong or from: China, The Philippines, Indonesia, Singapore, South Korea, Sri Lanka, Macau, Taiwan, Malaysia, Thailand on payment terms of Documents against Payment, Documents against Acceptance and Open Account.

6.3 Risks Covered

The risks covered are buyer risks and country risks. Buyer risks include insolvency and bankruptcy, default in payment, and failure or refusal to take delivery of goods. Country risks include blockage or delay in foreign exchange remittance, cancellation of import licences, import bans, payment moratorium, war, civil disturbances and natural disasters.

7 Cover on Sales to Local Exporters

Hong Kong manufacturers may supply goods to local exporters who in turn sell the goods to overseas buyers. Where credit sales are involved, the local manufacturer is exposed to the risks of non-payment in the event the local exporter defaults or becomes insolvent. It covers the credit risks arising from sales by Hong Kong manufacturers to exporters in Hong Kong

7.1 Eligibility for Cover

The policyholder must be a manufacturer and the exporter must be a locally registered business entity. Goods must be intended for export.

Contracts, shipping documents, and export declarations are evidences to support the intention.

7.2 Risks Covered and Indemnity

Risks covered include insolvency and bankruptcy of the local exporter and, payment default by the local exporter. The maximum compensation is 90% of loss.

8 Cover on Sales to Overseas Buying Offices in Hong Kong

There is a tendency for overseas buying offices in Hong Kong to act as the principals in their own right in transactions with local manufacturers or suppliers.

Where credit sales are involved, the local manufacturer is exposed to the risk of non-payment and has no legal right to pursue payment from the parent company of the buying office. The cover insures against credit risks arising from sales by Hong Kong manufacturers and suppliers to buying offices set up in Hong Kong.

8.1 Eligibility for Cover

The goods involved must be intended for export to the parent company of the buying office or the parent's designated consignees. Contracts, shipping documents, and export declarations are evidence to support the intention.

8.2 Risks Covered and Indemnity

Risks covered include insolvency and bankruptcy of the buying office, and payment default by the buying office. The maximum compensation is 90% of loss.

9 Tailor-made Policies

9.1 Comprehensive Contracts Policy

This covers non-payment risk for exports or re-exports of goods from Hong Kong. It also covers both pre-shipment and post-shipment risks starting from the date of the contract of sale. It is most suitable for: Exports of general consumer merchandise, e.g., garments, toys, electrical appliances, electronics, clocks and watches, shoes, etc.

9.2 Comprehensive Confirming House Shipments Policy

This covers the confirming house for the non-payment risk for exports or re-exports of goods from Hong Kong. It is most suitable for: Exports financed on a non-recourse basis by the confirming house which in turn grants credit terms to the overseas buyer.

9.3 Extended Terms Policy

This covers non-payment risk for exports and re-exports of consumer durables and semi-capital goods effective from the date of shipment. The policy covers a credit period between 181 days and two years.

9.4 Specific Shipments Policy

This covers non payment risk for exports of capital goods and production equipment effective from the date of shipment. It covers a specific contract of sale.

9.5 Specific Contracts Policy

This covers non-payment risk for exports of capital goods and production equipment effective from the date of the contract of sale. It covers a specific contract of sale.

10 Premium Rates

The ECIC's premium system consists of a premium matrix of basic rates and a scale of loadings. The basic rates are the minimum rates to be charged under the standard policy to be issued to an exporter who offers a substantial volume of insurable business with a good spread of risks. A loading (plus or minus) is an increment expressed in percentage points over the basic rates in the matrix. The major factors in determining the pricing and loadings include:

(a) likely insurable turnover;
(b) nature of goods;
(c) spread in terms of markets and buyers;
(d) overall quality of insurable buyers;
(e) credit control and management expertise of the exporter; and
(f) the ECIC's claims experience in the trade market.

The average premium rate for 1996–97 was about 0.54% of the gross invoice value of goods exported.

11 Claims and Recoveries

The ECIC's claims and recoveries activities stem from its obligations under the various contracts of insurance. Under the terms of the policy, the insured, that is the Hong Kong exporter, is required to report overdue payments from overseas buyers 60 days after the due date. Upon receipt of such report or other adverse information about the buyer, the ECIC will work closely with the insured to resolve the payment difficulties and to minimize losses. In this regard, the ECIC has established contacts with an international network of over 50 law firms and debt-collection agencies.

If the payment problems cannot be resolved, the ECIC will settle the claims on expiry of a waiting period in accordance with the terms of cover. In examination of claims, the ECIC always adopts a pragmatic approach rather than relying on the fine print of the policy. Quite a number of claims have been settled on an ex-gratia basis.

After payment of claims, the ECIC will continue to work with the insured to pursue recoveries. About 10% to 15% of the claims paid are normally recovered.

12 Risk Sharing

The ECIC has a Quota Share reinsurance agreement with a group of international reinsurers. Under this agreement, the ECIC retains 55% of the commercial risks. In addition, the ECIC has also arranged a separate Excess of Loss reinsurance treaty with another group of insurers to cover a part of the commercial losses retained under the quota share treaty.[1]

Note

1. *Annual Report 1996–97*, product leaflets and updated information provided by Hong Kong Export Credit Insurance Corporation.

Revision Question

1. Chins Trading Company is one of your valuable customers
    and has been maintaining a good account relationship for the
    last five years. They used to do business with overseas
    partners under L/C terms.

    Today, Mr. Kenneth Chin, the managing director of Chins
    Trading Company, comes to see you and tells you that their
    company has decided to expand their export business to
    South East Asia. They intend to allow some of their valuable
    customers to use open account or D/A terms. Because of this,
    they would like to apply for some trade financing. Mr. Chin
    states that they have contacted Hong Kong Export Credit
    Insurance Corporation and knows that one ECIC policy, which
    has been launched since May 1997, will provide cover not
    only for export business on credit terms with goods shipped
    from Hong Kong, but also for those transported directly from a
    supplier's country to their destination without passing through
    Hong Kong.

    Required:

    (a) What is the function of Hong Kong Export Credit
         Insurance Corporation?

    (b) Discuss the type of ECIC policy Mr. Chin has mentioned
         to you.

         Banking Practice in Hong Kong, HKIB Associateship
         Examination, May 1999.

8

Important Trade Promotion Institutions in Hong Kong

- ❏ The Trade Department
- ❏ Hong Kong Trade Development Council
- ❏ Federation of Hong Kong Industries
- ❏ The Chinese General Chamber of Commerce
- ❏ The Chinese Manufacturers' Association of Hong Kong
- ❏ The Hong Kong General Chamber of Commerce
- ❏ The Indian Chamber of Commerce

1 The Trade Department

The Trade Department is responsible for Hong Kong's commercial relations with foreign governments. It implements trade policy and agreements, procedures for import and export licensing and origin certification. Since moving from rented premises in Ocean Centre to permanent accommodation at the Trade Department Tower in Mongkok in 1990, the Trade Department has been able to improve its services in conducting all commercial relations of the Hong Kong Special Administrative Region (HKSAR) internationally. In addition to bilateral and multilateral relationships, issues such as certificates of origin, export and import licensing including textiles, and strategic and reserved commodities are also included. The ten overseas offices established by the Government of the HKSAR conduct the territory's commercial relations on behalf of the Trade Department and are located in Brussels, Geneva, London, Washington DC, New York, San Francisco, Toronto, Tokyo, Sydney and Singapore.

Under the World Trade Organization Agreement on Textiles and Clothing (ATC), Hong Kong's exports of certain textiles and clothing products to three overseas markets (i.e., the USA, the European Union [EU] and Canada) are subject to quota restraint. The Trade Department operates a textiles export control system with the following broad objectives:

(a) To ensure that Hong Kong discharges fully its obligations arising from ATC;

(b) To optimize the use of limited quotas available under the Agreement;

(c) To provide accurate and up-to-date information on the pattern and destination of Hong Kong's exports and re-exports of textiles.

Hong Kong maintains an import licensing system for textile imports from all sources in order to assist with the surveillance necessary to complement the enforcement of the textiles export control system. Importers, unless exempted, must lodge with the Trade Department an import license application prior to the actual arrival of the consignment.

The import and export of strategic commodities, as set out in the Schedules to the Import and Export (Strategic Commodities) Regulations made under the Import and Export Ordinance, Chapter 60 of the Laws of Hong Kong, are subject to licensing controlled by the Director-General of Trade. The purposes of licensing are to monitor and control the flow of strategic commodities to prevent Hong Kong from being used as a conduit for the proliferation of weapons of mass destruction and to secure continued access to high technology products.

The main services provided by the Trade Department are:

A. Licensing Services

Under the Import and Export Ordinance (Cap. 60), the Reserved Commodities Ordinance (Cap. 296), the Ozone Layer Protection Ordinance (Cap. 403) and their subsidiary legislation, imports and exports of certain articles are subject to licensing control by the Director-General of Trade. For example, textiles, pharmaceutical products and medicines, reserved commodities, strategic commodities and ozone-depleting substances are subject to import license and export license control. Radioactive substances are also subject to import license control. Therefore, a major function of the Department is to serve the trade by providing various licensing or certification facilities.

The licensing requirements in respect of pharmaceutical products and medicines are for health and safety reasons. Those in respect of reserved commodities, which include rice, frozen meat and frozen poultry, are to ensure the availability of certain essential foodstuffs for emergency situations. For ozone-depleting substances, the purpose of licensing control is to ensure that the local consumption of controlled substances does not exceed levels agreed under the 1987 Montreal Protocol on Substances that Deplete the Ozone Layer, as amended from time to time.

B. Issue of Certificates of Origin

The Trade Department administers a certification of origin system to establish the origin of the goods which Hong Kong exports and to meet the requirements of the importing authorities. The issue of Certificates of Origin by the Department and the five Government Approved Certification Organizations is governed respectively by the Export (Certificates of Origin) Regulations of the Import and Export Ordinances and the Protection of Non-Government Certificate of Origin Ordinance.

C. Commercial Relations

The Department is responsible for conducting Hong Kong's overseas commercial relations by seeking to safeguard Hong Kong's rights and to discharge its obligations in the pursuit of free trade, to secure and preserve maximum access for Hong Kong's exports to international markets, and to monitor and respond to trade measures of other trading partners through multilateral and bilateral negotiations and other channels.

D. Dissemination of Trade Information

(a) Trade Information Circulars — Traders can subscribe to the following trade information circulars through a mail subscription service run by the Department or a facsimile transmission service operated by an appointed agent:

(1) Notice to Exporters — There are a total of six series. Notices issued under the three "O" series provide information on the implementation of the various textiles control arrangements. Those under the three "A" Series publish information on textile quota utilization by Hong Kong to all restrained markets.

(2) Certification Branch Circulars — These circulars provide information on matters relating to certificates of origin and certificates of preferences, factory registration, local sub-contracting arrangements, and outward processing arrangement and production notification for cut and sewn garments.

(3) Commercial Information Circulars — These are issued to give information on trade policies, regulations and tariffs

concerning both textiles and non-textiles matters in Hong Kong's overseas markets.

(b) Pamphlets/Publications — The Trade Department publishes a number of pamphlets and publications for free distribution to the trade on the following subjects: Certification, Textiles Export, Textiles Import, Textiles Trader Registration Scheme (TTRS), and Non-textiles Imports/Exports. In particular, the Trade Department provides guidance on how to apply for relevant certificates and/or complete the relevant applications etc.

(c) Information on Tariff and Other Import Regulations — Traders who need information on tariff and other import regulations may consult the commercial relations branches of the Asia and Americas Division, and Europe Division. Tariff schedules are available for inspection at the Trade Department. [1]

2 Hong Kong Trade Development Council (TDC)

The Hong Kong Trade Development Council (TDC) is the Special Administrative Region's statutory body for expanding Hong Kong's trade with the world. Created in 1966, the TDC has a network of 51 offices to help Hong Kong companies market their products and services globally. It also promotes the SAR as a superb place to do business. Most of the clients are small and medium-sized enterprises (SMEs) using the TDC's services to compete more effectively in world markets.

According to the TDC, they have the following mission and objectives:

(a) To develop and diversify markets for Hong Kong companies, with special reference to the needs of small and medium-sized enterprises (SMEs).

(b) To enhance the image and competitiveness of Hong Kong's products and services in world markets.

(c) To strengthen Hong Kong's role as Asia's premier business and services hub.

(d) To enhance Hong Kong's image as an open market and a good business partner, standing for free trade and the rule of law in global commerce.

To meet the above objectives, the TDC has engaged in a number of activities that include:

A. Organize Trade Fairs, Seminars, Business Groups

Organizes, co-sponsors or participates in different fairs annually. For example, Hong Kong Toys & games Fair, Hong Kong Fashion Week, Hong Kong International Jewellery Shows, etc. The Council also organizes seminars, conferences, workshops and business training courses annually, many with international speakers. To foster closer links with trade partners from around the world, the HKTDC also hosts some 500 international business groups each year.

B. Trade Services Department

Through its overseas branches, the council implements a worldwide programme of trade promotion activities and provides Hong Kong exporters and overseas buyers with business information. All overseas offices are on-line with the computer databank in Hong Kong, providing instantaneous trade enquiry services. Detailed information on local manufacturers, importers and exporters, overseas buyers, Chinese enterprises and import/export companies are stored in the computer, and the information is constantly updated.

C. Design Gallery

Hong Kong manufacturers are making great strides in upgrading product design and image. The HKTDC's Design Gallery showcases outstanding Hong Kong design. The Gallery shop stocks a wide range of high-quality, original and innovatively designed products for sale. It also organizes design competitions and provides a databank of information on design.

D. Research Information

The TDC provides a wide range of services, such as the publication of trade and statistical information on Hong Kong, its industries, export markets and trade scope. Publications include *International Market News*, *New Market Search* and *EC Monitor*, which identify market trends and opportunities for Hong Kong traders, a range of product research studies, special market reports and trade prospect forecasts.

E. Business InfoCentre

The Business InfoCentre located in Hong Kong and Convention and Exhibition Centre contains books including trade directories, journals and statistics titles, as well as documents covering all major markets. It contains a China Trade Information Centre and a Design Library and a Fashion Library.

F. Publications

The HKTDC produces product magazines, fashion magazines and a newspaper in both English and Chinese on general controlled circulation. More than 1.5 million individual copies of the magazines are circulated annually to more than 100 countries. Publications include *Hong Kong Enterprise*, *Hong Kong Electronics*, and *Hong Kong Trader*.

G. TDC–Link

This is an on-line trade information system which gives Hong Kong business executives access to data from their own PC work stations.

H. Hong Kong Trade Development Council–SME Service Centre

Located inside the TDC Business InfoCentre, the SME Service Centre is a one-stop unit providing practical services to small and medium-sized enterprises (SMEs) in Hong Kong on trade related matters. Through day-to-day advisory service and structured weekly programmes, the SME Service Centre aims to assist SMEs in various aspects of their businesses and in turn help them to enhance their global competitiveness.

Services provided by the SME Service Centre include:

(a) Trade consulting and advisory services — A team of TDC staff are stationed in the SME Service Centre to provide one-on-one consulting and advisory services to SMEs on trade related questions. In addition, external partners such as bankers, lawyers, accountants, China trade experts, business consultants, and other professionals will be lined up periodically to provide specific advice on topics like market opportunities on specific products, trade finance, legal aspects of international trade, export credit, export management, e-commerce, etc. to SMEs.

(b) Mini-exhibition and information display — Mini-exhibitions on topics pertinent to SME's interests will be on display on a regular basis. Topics may include overseas market news and recent market situations, new product information, current trade practices, TDC promotion activities, etc.

(c) Forums, workshops and networking events — The SME Service Centre will line up professionals and knowledgeable persons to present topics that are of interest to SMEs, in order to increase their awareness of the global trade environment and market opportunities. Networking events will also be held to facilitate communications between SMEs.

(d) Information technology (IT) and E-commerce demonstrations — A special demonstration section is set up at the SME Service Centre to let SMEs see the real life operation of trade and business related IT applications. Examples include commercial applications on Internet, quick access to relevant trade and market information, trade statistics, hands-on electronic data interchange (EDI) applications, contacting potential buyers and suppliers, etc.

(e) Dissemination of useful trade information — A virtual "SME Centre" (at http://www.tdc.org.hk/sme/) on the TDC website has been set up to disseminate useful information for easy retrieval by SMEs. It contains a special SME frequently-asked-question section that gathers all the popular and practical trade questions with answers for SMEs.[2]

3 Chambers of Commerce

3.1 Federation of Hong Kong Industries

Since its inception in 1960, the Federation's prime goals have been to serve the many needs of Hong Kong's industrial and business communities. It continues to play a major role in shaping the territory's prosperity.

Objectives of the Federation are to promote and foster the interests of Hong Kong's industrial and business sectors. It promotes trade, investment, technological advancement, manpower development and business opportunities in Hong Kong and represents industry's views and influences Government on policies and legislation which affect industry and business.

The Federation achieves this by representing its members on the Legislative Council and various high-level Government advisory boards and committees. It acts as a bridge between members and overseas business communities and organizes activities to promote trade, investment, technology transfer and manpower training. The Federation also plays an important role in updating members on business opportunities in Hong Kong and all over the world.

The Federation offers a wide range of services aimed to facilitate business operations and provide opportunities for businessmen to make new contacts and strengthen existing ones.

A. Issue of Certificates of Origin and Re-exports

An accurate, efficient processing service for certificates is provided by the Federation's Mongkok, Tsimshatsui and Central offices to both members and non-members. These offices also issue Form A.

B. ISO 9000 and Technical Consultancy Service

This comprehensive service, offered by the Federation's Hong Kong Q-Mark Council, provides information about ISO 9000 and other standards to small and medium-sized firms. It is available at a highly competitive price.

C. Directory of Members

This reference book has a full list of every member of the Federation, together with contact information. It is a valuable business tool for all businesses and traders.

D. Study Missions

These are well-planned visits to China and other countries to assess investment and technology transfer opportunities as well as the local business environment. High level contacts with government and industry officials not usually accessible to individual visitors can often be arranged.

E. Seminars and Conferences

Notable guest speakers regularly address topical issues ranging from labour relations and legislation to management and offshore investment opportunities.

F. Hong Kong Industrialist

This is the monthly magazine that many business people depend upon for updates on industry and business trends, valuable investment information, new policies and regulations, advances in technology, as well as news of the Federation's activities. It is mailed free of charge to all members.

G. Training Courses

Experienced trainers share their vast knowledge of issues related to business and industry. The Training Division addresses a wide range of education needs and also provides a comprehensive range of specially tailored in-house courses for companies of all sizes.

H. New Product Registered Design Service

The Federation offers services on protection and application of new product design registration in Hong Kong, China and major foreign countries at competitive rates. Free advice on infringement of intellectual property and registration of new product designs is also available.

I. Hong Kong Design Depository Service

This protects the copyright of products, computer programmes and two-dimensional design. Preferential rates are given for members.

J. Trade Mark Service

This protects the logo and brand name of the company and products against infringement and passing off.

K. Annual Awards

The Federation organizes two major awards every year to give public recognition to the outstanding achievements and innovative efforts of industrial entrepreneurs. These are:

(a) Young Industrialist Awards of Hong Kong;
(b) Hong Kong Award of Industry–Consumer Product Design.

L. Industrial and Economic Research Reports

The Federation's Industry and Research Division publishes wide-ranging studies and reports on major issues facing business and industry today. These documents are available to members and the general public free or charged at cost.

M. Trade Opportunity Listings

The Federation prepares regular listings of import/export enquiries, technology transfer and joint venture information.

N. Visa Referral Service

This is a fast and very convenient service for Federation member companies' senior staff preparing to travel to the U.S. Members are not charged for this service.

O. Laboratory Testing with HK Standard and Testing Centre

Members who need reports for pre-shipment inspection or certificates to verify the safety, quality or performance standards of their goods can enjoy a 15% discount from the HK Standard & Testing Centre.[3]

3.2 The Chinese General Chamber of Commerce

The objectives of the Chamber are:

(a) To promote trade and industry and enhance the prosperity of Hong Kong;

(b) To protect the right and interests of the business and industrial community in Hong Kong;

(c) To participate in public affairs and reflect the views of the business and industrial community;

(d) To develop international and regional communication with a view to promoting economic co-operation.

Main services provided:

A. Electronic Trade Services

The Chamber provides Electronic Trading Access Services which include restrained textile licenses and export trade declarations to the public through the Service Centre in the Chamber's office.

B. Issuance of Certificate of Origin

The chamber is authorized by the HKSAR to issue all kinds of certificates of origin recognized worldwide. Members of the Chamber enjoy preferential rates for these services.

C. Distribution of Invitations to the Chinese Export Commodities Fair

The Chinese Export Commodities Fair authorities have entrusted the Chamber to issue invitations to local firms on their behalf ever since the first fair in the Spring of 1957. Firms interested in attending the Fair are welcome to make enquiries at telephone number (852)2845-7950.

D. The Chamber's Library

The library provides trade enquiry services for members and the general public. It has a comprehensive range of reference materials, including a collection of local, foreign and the Mainland economic almanacs, trade directories and periodicals as well as statistics. In addition, the Chamber's computer allows retrieval therefrom of business information, details of the Chamber's members, trade information and library catalogue.

E. Trade Enquiries

Each year, the Chamber handles a large number of local and foreign trade enquiries. Depending on the nature of the enquiries, the Chamber would provide the requested information either by phone or by post or by e-mail. It also publishes the enquiries in the Chamber's monthly newsletter, "Business Info", so that interested members can establish business contacts by writing directly to the enquirers. The Chamber, in addition, keeps in its office a collection of local and foreign trade directories, economic literature, trade notices and circulars, etc., which are available for reference upon request. A computerized data bank is maintained by the Chamber and both members and non-members alike are welcome to utilize this service.

F. Publications

The Chamber produces two regular in-house publications, "Business Info" and "The Chamber's Bulletin". "Business Info" is a monthly newsletter providing information on business opportunities, trade fairs and exhibitions, seminars and conferences as well as updates on local trade regulation. "The Chamber's Bulletin" is a monthly magazine containing feature articles on topical economic issues contributed by prominent local businessmen, government officials and academics as well as news of the Chamber's activities.

G. The Chamber's Homepage (http://www.cgcc.org.hk)

The Chamber's homepage contains a wide range of business information which includes: Chinese economic news, trade and investment information, exhibitions, seminars and conventions news, list of Chinese Trade and Industrial Organizations, Trade Provincial and Municipal Representatives, business information of the Chamber's members, and library collection.

H. Mailing Service

The Chamber can provide a mailing service to trade and industrial organizations and companies who wish to distribute to members of the Chamber their promotion leaflets containing information of exhibitions, seminars, products and services. Such promotion material will either be inserted in the "Business Info" or in "The Chamber's Bulletin", with circulation exceeding 1,000 and 5,000 respectively. [4]

3.3 The Chinese Manufacturers' Association of Hong Kong

Established in 1934, The Chinese Manufacturers' Association of Hong Kong (CMA) is a non-profit making chamber of commerce. It is one of the oldest and most representative industrial associations in Hong Kong, with over 3,700 member companies from various sectors of industry and trade. It is well known for its public interest and community service.

CMA's primary objectives are to promote Hong Kong's industrial and trade development, to represent the industry in the formulation and implementation of public policies, to participate in community development and to foster international understanding and co-operation.

As a functional constituency, the CMA plays an active role in safe-guarding the interests of the industry and in cultivating mutual understanding and co-operation between the industry and the government. Members of the Association have the right to vote for their representative to serve at the Legislative Council (Legco). In addition, the CMA pays close attention to issues relating to land, labour, environment, infrastructure, technological development, public administration, trade policies, etc., and makes recommendations to the government and relevant authorities.

The Association provides a wide range of services and participates in different kinds of activities. It liaises with international bodies as well as overseas trade and industrial associations for the exchange of information and ideas. Besides, it is a member of the International Chamber of Commerce and maintains close contact with consulates and trade commissions of overseas governments. It also handles local and overseas trade enquiries, provides different kinds of trade information, organizes seminars and training courses, etc. In addition, it is one of the organizations authorized by the government to issue all kinds of Certificates of Origin.

The CMA Testing and Certification Laboratories (CMA Testing) was established in 1979 as an independent and non-profit making testing institute, operated under the CMA Industrial Development Trust. It provides different services including materials and products testing, production and pre-shipment inspection, ISO 9000 consultation, technical consultation, factory evaluation, laboratory design etc., and is one of the HOKLAS (Hong Kong Laboratory Accreditation Scheme) accredited laboratories in Hong Kong.[5]

3.4 The Hong Kong General Chamber of Commerce

The Hong Kong General Chamber of Commerce (HKGCC) is the oldest (founded in 1861) and largest (around 4,000 corporate members) business organization in Hong Kong. HKGCC is international in character, with membership comprising of multinational companies, Chinese mainland companies, and Hong Kong companies. It is a self-funded, non-profit organization, and a truly independent body representing the entire scope of trade, service and industry in the Hong Kong special Administrative Region.

It acts as its members' voice in advising the SAR Government in matters affecting businesses and the economy, providing members with business information and opportunities, and facilitating networking through a variety of Chamber activities. It promotes Hong Kong as an international business centre in the heart of Asia, and pledges its confidence in Hong Kong now and into the future.

Hong Kong is now part of China, but it remains an international city. The Chamber acts as an international bridge, connecting Hong Kong business with the Chinese mainland and the rest of the world. Today, corporate membership stands at around 4,000 and the spirit of the Chamber's original objective remains as demonstrated in its mission statement: "To promote, represent and safeguard the interests of the Hong Kong business community." In short, it helps its members do business.

Main services provided:

A.   Hong Kong SAR Legislative Council

The Chamber has been a functional constituency representing Hong Kong's business community in the Legislative Council since 1988. This gives members the privilege of electing the Chamber's own representative to the 60-member Legislative Council every four years.

B.   Business Policy Unit

The Chamber extensively recommends and comments to the Hong Kong SAR Government on issues affecting business and economic development of the SAR, such as inflation, taxation, trade problems between Hong Kong and the Mainland, environment, labour matters and draft legislation. These are based on input from members through over 20 active committees, as well as research by the Chamber's staff.

Apart from topical issues, representation to the Government is crucial prior to two junctures of the year: The Chief Executive's annual policy address to the Legislative Council in Autumn and the Financial Secretary's budget speech in Spring.

C.   Chamber Committees

There are over 20 committees, identified by geographical areas, business sectors and management/social issues. Chaired by a Chamber member whose expertise in the field prevails, each committee is served by a secretariat from the Chamber staff. They convene regular meetings to discuss issues relevant to their terms of reference and make recommendations to the General Committee. They also deal with representatives of foreign governments on commercial issues impacting on their business.

D.   Hong Kong Advisory Bodies

Chamber representation in Hong Kong advisory bodies is significant. Of the over 70 bodies and committees in which 64 Chamber members participate, half are official government advisory bodies such as

Labour Advisory Board, Trade Advisory Board, and Joint Liaison Committee on Taxation, etc.

E. Website

The Chamber has a website (www.hkgcc.org.hk) for access by the public. An interactive membership directory is available on the website to facilitate international traders who wish to get in contact with members of the Chamber. Members can also retrieve economic and business information; can be notified of upcoming Chamber or non-Chamber events; can be linked to trade and business website around the world; and can be matched with other members on specific business interests. The website is designed to help members obtain information to do business. The Chamber website facilitates link with business people around the world.

F. Business Information

With around 4,000 members, contacts and staff expertise, the Chamber is well-positioned to help members with specific business questions and business lead requests by using the information highway.

G. Trade Inquiries

Inquiries from overseas companies for supply of products and services are updated daily and published in the website for members' viewing.

H. Business Delegation

The Chamber organizes and arranges overseas visits for Chamber members to explore investment opportunities in developed and developing countries. In response to increasing interest from its members, it has in recent times conducted successful trade missions to Denmark, Dubai, Japan and South America. The Chamber also visits China several times a year.

Chamber members are also offered numerous opportunities to meet many visiting businessmen and officials interested in trade with Hong Kong, and through Hong Kong with China. Recent delegations include those from China, Japan, India, United States, United Kingdom, Brazil, Romania and Russia.

It also organizes a lot of trade/investment talks featuring opportunities in different parts of China such as Guangzhou, Xiamen and Dalian.

I. Product Promotion

The Chamber helps members to promote their products through different channels. These are:

(a) Bulletin — The Chamber's monthly magazine has a circulation of almost 8,000, which offers reasonable rates for display advertisement.

(b) Direct Mail — It operates a periodic direct mail service which is an effective means for message's to reach all Chamber members. Members enjoy a reduced rate for this service.

(c) Small Ad — This is a single sheet carrying small and paid advertisements and is sent to all Chamber members by post through the periodic mailing.

J. Programmes

Chamber members can attend the following programmes for information and networking:

(a) Hong Kong Business Summit — This is an annual prestigious conference for leading businessmen to review Hong Kong's economic performance for the year and to forecast that for the following year.

(b) Subscription Luncheons — Distinguished local and visiting speakers are invited to address Chamber luncheons. Recent keynote addresses were made by senior Chinese government officials, business leaders from China and overseas, the Chief Executive of the Hong Kong SAR and senior government officials like the Chief Secretary for Administration and the Financial Secretary.

(c) Seminars — Seminars are organized to provide information and to encourage exchange of views on specific topics.

(d) Roundtable Luncheons — These are gatherings of around 30 participants with an invited speaker to discuss a specific issue over lunch-time refreshments.

K. Training

Many training courses are organized for the benefit of our members to assist them in improving their staff's efficiency and productivity. These trainings are subject-oriented which include management training, sales and marketing, language training and other specific skills.

L. Certification

The Hong Kong General Chamber of Commerce is authorized by the SAR Government to issue a full range of Certificates of Origin. These are:

(a) Certificate of Hong Kong Origin
(b) Certificate of Origin — Processing
(c) Certificate of Origin — Re-export
(d) Certificate of Origin — Non-transit
(e) Endorsement of commercial documents and invoices
(f) GSP Forms A

In addition, it is the sole issuing authority of *International ATA Carnets* in Hong Kong.

Members enjoy special rates and services are available from eight conveniently located Certification Offices in Hong Kong and Kowloon.

In corporation with Tradelink, the Chamber also provides EDI Service including:

(a) Restrained Textile Licence (RTEL)
(b) Import and Export Trade Declaration (TDEC)
(c) Certificates of Hong Kong Origin (CHKO)
(d) Production Notifications (PN)

M. Economic Research Service

The Chamber has an Economic Advice and Information Unit to provide statistics and other information to members on a wide range of Hong Kong, China and international economic issues.

Organized within the Economic and Legal Affairs Division headed by the Chief Economist, the Unit also undertakes more detailed research projects on behalf of Chamber members.

N. Member Services

The Chamber offers a wide variety of services to cater to its members' social and business needs.

(a) USA Visa delivery/collection — Members can save time by sending in their non-immigrant visa applications to the US Consulate through the Chamber's visa delivery/collection service.

(b) Facility Tours — The Chamber arranges tours for members to visit major local projects and installations.

(c) Meeting Venues — Members can rent the Chamber's theatre, conference room and committee room for meeting purposes.

(d) Translation Service — Its professional translation team offers a reliable service for a fee lower than market rate.

(e) Discount Club — Some members generously offer discount for their products or services to fellow Chamber members. They range from petroleum firms, restaurants, to travel agents.

(f) Shatin and Happy Valley Race Box — Members can make reservations to attend horse racing events at the Chamber's race box in Shatin and Happy Valley.

(g) Social Clubs — Social activities such as golfing and dinning are available. Members can meet other Chamber members in the monthly meetings of the 3288 Dinner Club and the Chamber Golf Club.

(h) Event Organizing — Its subsidiary, Chamber Services Ltd., can provide large and small scale event organizing assistance.[6]

3.5 The Indian Chamber of Commerce

The Indian Chamber of Commerce in Hong Kong was founded on 12 December 1952 by Indian businessmen as a Company limited by guarantee for the purposes of promoting Hong Kong's trade and commerce.

The Chamber consists of merchants, manufacturers, bankers, members of professions, shipowners, shipbuilders and others (including corporations, unincorporated associations and societies). Membership shall be open to persons of all races and nationalities.

Objectives of the Chamber are:

(a) To promote and protect home and foreign trade, commerce, shipping and industrial products of Hong Kong and to represent and express on commercial questions the opinions of the Indian mercantile community in Hong Kong.

(b) To promote, support or oppose legislative or other measures affecting such trade, commerce, shipping and manufacture.

(c) To undertake by arbitration the settlement of disputes arising in the course of trade, commerce, shipping and manufacture.

(d) To issue certificate of origins of any goods and to undertake and conduct surveys of any goods or merchandise and to issue all necessary certificates in connection therewith.

(e) To collect and disseminate statistical and other information relating to trade, commerce, shipping and manufacture.

(f) To advance and promote commercial and technical education and to award scholarships and hold examinations or otherwise assist young persons desiring to train for commercial careers.

Main services provided:

A. Trade Promotion

Trade promotion constitutes the most important activity of the Chamber. Through its various committees, endeavours are constantly made to study the prospects and progress of trade with various countries and to remove or minimize as much as possible any difficulties faced by the members in visiting those countries or trading with them.

The Chamber has shared a pioneering role with other trade associations in organizing trade fairs in Hong Kong. It continues to be actively associated with the organization of some of the highly successful trade fairs in Hong Kong.

The Chamber issues letters of introduction to its members proceeding on business tours abroad. Credential books are also issued by the Chamber to facilitate identification of the members.

B. Trade Delegations

The Chamber, in collaboration with the Hong Kong Trade Development Council or under its own banner, organizes from time to time trade missions to various countries.

Incoming foreign trade missions to Hong Kong are also received by the Chamber and discussions by the Chamber members with them are arranged to foster better trade relations.

C. Certificates of Origin

The Chamber is authorized by the Hong Kong Government to issue certificates of origin which are recognized by customs authorities all over the world as equivalent to standard certificates of origin issued by the Trade Department.

D. Dissemination of Information

(a) Circulars — The Chamber keeps its members informed of important government notifications, trade policies, trade delegations and fairs and exhibitions through official circulars.

(b) Library — The Chamber maintains a collection of books on trade and commerce and also subscribes to various journals and periodicals of commercial interest. These publications are available to members for reference in the Chamber's library.

(c) Publications — The Chamber has, in the past, brought out useful publications on certain sectors of Hong Kong's manufacturing industries of interest to members, and also publications providing data on Hong Kong's major markets. It also issues, from time to time, a classified Directory of Members which gives an up-to-date list of names of the members, their addresses, the products they handle and the markets they deal with.

(d) Statistics — The Chamber maintains statistics, commodity-wise and country-wise, on the foreign trade of Hong Kong as well as statistics regarding Hong Kong's major markets for the use of members.[7]

Notes

1. *Trade Department Handbook 9th Edition*, 1999.

2. *Annual Report 1997–98, Who, What, How, Service Leaflets*, Hong Kong Trade Development Council.

3. Federation of Hong Kong Industries, Website information and recent updates.

4. The Chinese General Chamber of Commerce, Website information and recent updates.

5. The Chinese Manufacturers' Association of Hong Kong, Website information and recent updates.

6. The Hong Kong General Chamber of Commerce, Website information and recent updates.

7. Service notes from The Indian Chamber of Commerce.

9

Contractual Relationship of Various Parties in a Documentary Credit Operation

- ❏ Buyer vs Seller
- ❏ D/C Applicant vs Issuing Bank
- ❏ Issuing Bank vs Beneficiary
- ❏ Issuing Bank, Advising Bank and Beneficiary
- ❏ Issuing Bank, Confirming Bank and Beneficiary
- ❏ Beneficiary vs Negotiating Bank

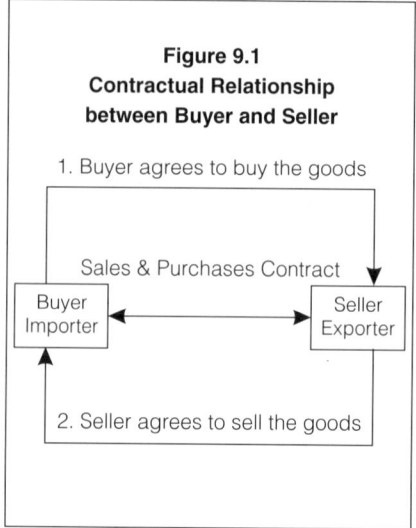

Figure 9.1
Contractual Relationship
between Buyer and Seller

1. Buyer agrees to buy the goods

Sales & Purchases Contract

Buyer Importer

Seller Exporter

2. Seller agrees to sell the goods

1 Buyer vs Seller (see Figure 9.1)

A Documentary credit (D/C) and a Sales and Purchase (S&P) contract constitute a "father and son" relationship. The D/C is born out of the underlying S&P contract, but as soon as the D/C has come into existence, it begins to lead its own life. Hence, a D/C once issued, will be separate from and independent of the S&P contract. This concept remains even if references to the content of a contract or the contract itself are included in the D/C.

1.1 Buyer's Rights and Duties

(a) Usually, among other terms in a contract, a buyer is required to issue a D/C in favour of a beneficiary. That means the buyer has the duty to arrange for the D/C to be issued within the agreed time frame. The issue of the credit is a condition for the execution of the sales contract. If the buyer fails to open the credit in a manner as stipulated in the contract, he may be considered to have breached the contract. Then, he has to seek seller's approval to extend the time to allow him to fulfil his obligation. If he does not seek approval, seller may claim damages from him.

(b) A D/C is a mechanism to provide the seller with a secured method of payment. If the seller does not make use of the mechanism, or does not utilize the D/C upon receipt of it, this does not mean that he has given up his right for payment. He has not surrendered his right for payment. The buyer is still obliged to pay him.

1.2 Seller's Rights and Duties

(a) If the credit he received consists of terms and conditions which are not the same as in the contract, he has the right to ask for amendment from the buyer within a reasonable time.

(b) Even if the credit terms appear the same as in the credit, amendment can be demanded by the seller provided that the buyer agrees to it.

(c) Deliver the goods as stipulated in the contract.

(d) Present documents strictly in compliance with the D/C before expiry date.

2 D/C Applicant vs Issuing Bank (see Figure 9.2)

This relationship builds on banker–customer relationships in general (Bills opening account mandate) and D/C application form in particular which contains detailed instruction given by the buyer to the bank.

The buyer in the D/C application form instructs his banker to issue a D/C that constitutes an independent and definite undertaking on the part of the issuing bank to pay the seller.

Conditions are inserted in the D/C so that the issuing bank will not pay the seller until the seller has fulfilled all the terms and conditions as stipulated in the D/C.

(a) As a D/C constitutes a definite and conditional undertaking on the issuing bank to pay the seller, the issuing bank would like to see that it has a right of recourse on the buyer for what it has

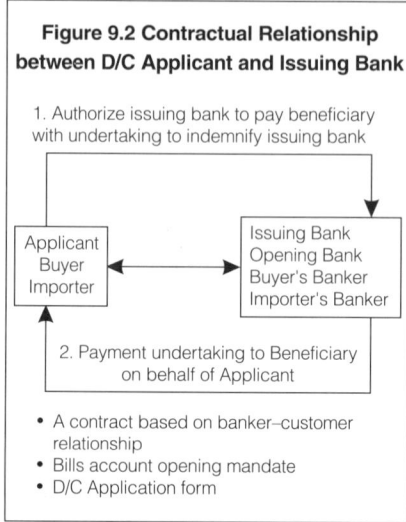

Figure 9.2 Contractual Relationship between D/C Applicant and Issuing Bank

1. Authorize issuing bank to pay beneficiary with undertaking to indemnify issuing bank

| Applicant Buyer Importer | Issuing Bank Opening Bank Buyer's Banker Importer's Banker |

2. Payment undertaking to Beneficiary on behalf of Applicant

- A contract based on banker–customer relationship
- Bills account opening mandate
- D/C Application form

paid to the seller. The right of recourse is incorporated in the account mandate or application form.

2.1 Applicant's Rights and Duties

(a) He has the right to insert in the D/C terms and conditions which he would like the seller to fulfil before payment (provided that the terms and conditions are acceptable to issuing bank).

(b) He has the right to take away documents after payment to (or against deposit of collateral) with the issuing bank.

(c) However, such instructions must be complete clear and precise.

(d) He is obliged to reimburse the issuing bank for payment of proceeds and charges.

(e) He is obliged to pay bank charges for the issue of the D/C.

2.2 Issuing Bank's Rights and Duties

(a) It has the right to receive commission.

(b) It should exercise professional care not to type the credit incorrectly nor change the buyer's instructions (once it accepts the buyers application).

(c) It must examine documents with reasonable care and make sure that documents appear to be in compliance with credit terms and conditions and not inconsistent among themselves.

(d) If documents are found to have discrepancies, it must take necessary action in accordance with UCP–500, e.g., notify discrepancies not less than seven banking days after the day of receipt of documents.

3 Issuing Bank vs Beneficiary (see Figure 9.3)

A D/C constitutes a conditional engagement by the issuing bank to pay beneficiary.

When a beneficiary accepts the credit, a payment undertaking between him and issuing bank exists. From that moment onwards and before expiry date, the beneficiary can demand payment from the issuing bank by means of drawing a set of drafts on the issuing bank provided that he has fulfilled all the terms and conditions under the D/C.

Turning to the issuing bank, its undertaking to pay the beneficiary depends on whether the beneficiary submits clean documents or not. If the beneficiary fails to meet the terms, the undertaking may be withdrawn. Even if documents presented are not in compliance with the D/C terms, the beneficiary still may get payment from the issuing bank provided the buyer accepts the discrepancies and instructs his banker to pay.

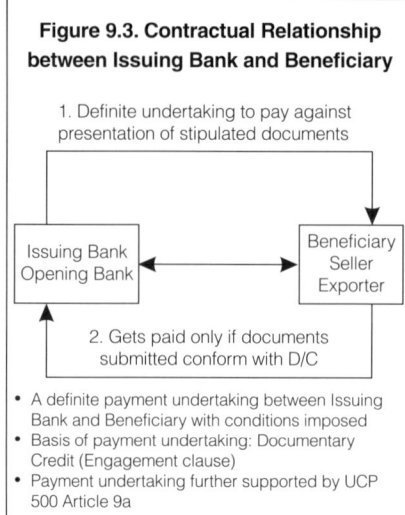

Figure 9.3. Contractual Relationship between Issuing Bank and Beneficiary

3.1 Rights and Duties of Issuing Bank

(a) The issuing bank has the right to refuse to pay if the beneficiary does not present complying documents.

(b) Issuing bank gives a conditional engagement to pay beneficiary.

(c) Issuing bank, however, cannot deny its undertaking if the credit applicant, after the issue of the credit, becomes insolvent.

3.2 Rights and Duties of Beneficiary

(a) The undertaking of the issuing bank to pay is without recourse on the beneficiary if the credit provides for negotiation and the beneficiary has submitted documents in compliance with D/C terms.

(b) He has the right to demand payment from issuing bank if he fulfils the instructions of the D/C.

(c) On the other hand, he must deliver goods as instructed and submit documents in strict compliance with D/C terms and conditions.

4 Issuing Bank vs Advising Bank (see Figure 9.4)

(a) This relationship is built on

(1) head office and branch
(2) branch to branch
(3) correspondent banking (principal and agent)

(b) To a certain extent, a type of principal and agent exists in which an issuing bank is a principal while the advising bank is acting in an agency capacity.

(c) In most cases, advising bank will not advise a D/C sent from the issuing bank with whom it has no relationship.

4.1 Rights and Duties of Issuing bank

(a) It has the right to be guaranteed by advising bank that if the latter chooses not to advise a credit, the advising bank must inform the issuing bank without delay.

(b) On the other hand, it has the duty to give clear and concise instructions to be acted on by the advising bank.

4.2 Rights and Duties of Advising Bank

(a) It has the right not to advise a D/C even if it is selected as an advising bank.

(b) It has no obligation to check the detailed contents of a D/C. Nor is it responsible for answering the beneficiary's queries as to the terms and conditions of the credit which it advises.

(c) On the other hand, it must take reasonable care to verify the authenticity of the credit which it advises by:

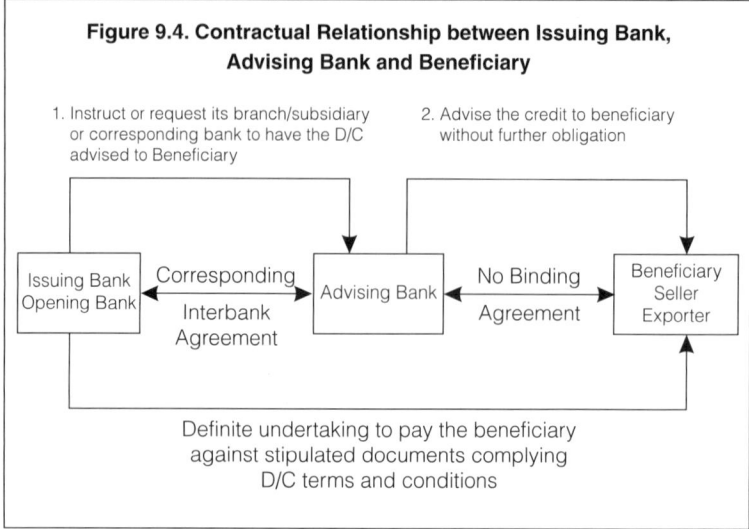

Figure 9.4. Contractual Relationship between Issuing Bank, Advising Bank and Beneficiary

(1) checking the test key / telex code / SWIFT in case the D/C is transmitted by a telex;

(2) checking the authorized signature(s) of the airmail credit in case the D/C is sent by mail.

(d) It must inform the issuing bank without delay if it chooses not to advise the D/C or if it cannot verify the test key / telex code / authorized signature(s) of the D/C.

4.3 Advising Bank vs Beneficiary

(a) Advising bank may not have any pre-determined and/or pre-defined legal relationship with beneficiary since the advising bank may not even know the beneficiary at all.

(b) It is the issuing bank, which gives a definite but conditional undertaking to pay the beneficiary through the advising bank, to pass on this undertaking. Theoretically, a D/C can be sent directly from issuing bank to beneficiary.

(c) However, the beneficiary may hold the advising bank liable to negligence by resorting to civil laws if the advising bank acts on the instructions sent from issuing bank carelessly.

4.4 Rights and Duties of Advising bank

(a) Basically, an advising bank reports to its instructing party which is the issuing bank.

(b) According to UCP–500, Article 7, an advising bank is given the option of advising or not advising the credit.

(c) However, if it elects to advise the D/C, it must exercise reasonable care to verify the signature(s) / incoming messages and advise the D/C without delay.

4.5 Rights and Duties of Beneficiary

(a) It has the right to receive the credit within reasonable time upon receipt of the credit by the advising bank. Otherwise, the beneficiary may sue the advising bank for damages arisen from delay and negligence of the advising bank (this seldom happens in real life).

(b) On the other hand, a beneficiary should give notice to the advising bank as to whether he accepts or rejects an amendment if it is stipulated in the D/C amendment that beneficiary should give such notification.

5 Issuing Bank vs Confirming Bank (see Figure 9.5)

(a) Issuing bank instructs advising bank to give a separate undertaking to pay the beneficiary. This advising bank, if it agreed, assumes an additional role to pay the beneficiary provided that the latter has submitted documents in compliance with the D/C terms.

(b) Unless confirming bank has a good correspondent relationship with issuing bank, (or some other relationship such as branch-to-branch) it may not be prepared to add confirmation to the D/C.

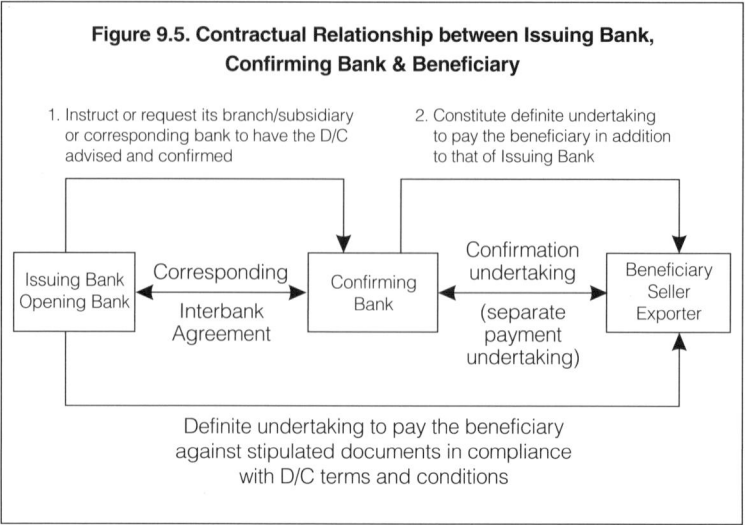

Figure 9.5. Contractual Relationship between Issuing Bank, Confirming Bank & Beneficiary

(c) Usually, a confirmation line of credit has been established between the two banks and agreed with the confirming bank.

(d) Under the confirmation agreement or corresponding bank agreement, issuing bank undertakes to reimburse confirming bank for rightful payment in connection with its confirmation.

5.1 Rights and Duties of Issuing Bank

(a) It has the right to be guaranteed that documents presented to confirming bank for payment have strictly complied with credit terms and conditions before payment.

(b) On the other hand, it is ultimately liable to reimburse confirming bank if the latter has rightfully paid the beneficiary on behalf of the issuing bank.

5.2 Rights and Duties of Confirming Bank

(a) It may refuse to be a confirming bank.

(b) It has a right of recourse on the issuing bank.

(c) On the other hand, once it accepts the role of a confirming bank and the acceptance has been communicated to the beneficiary, it is obliged to honour the D/C which complies with documents presented. This obligation remains even if issuing bank falls into bankruptcy before or after the time beneficiary presents documents to the confirming bank for payment.

5.3 Confirming Bank vs Beneficiary

(a) Having added a confirmation to a D/C, the advising bank becomes a confirming bank, taking up a dual role of being an agent for and on behalf of the issuing bank, as well as having engaged in a separate payment undertaking relationship with the beneficiary.

(b) Beneficiary has a double payment undertaking respectively given by issuing bank and confirming bank.

5.4 Rights and Duties of Confirming Bank

(a) It may refuse to be a confirming bank provided that in its covering letter accompanying the original D/C, it does not mention specifically that it has added a confirmation to it.

(b) On the other hand, once it adds its confirmation to the D/C, it gives an additional and independent commitment to the beneficiary. From that moment onwards, it acts not only as an agent but also enters into a contractual obligation to pay the beneficiary once the latter submits complying documents.

(c) It is often the case that a confirming bank also acts as a negotiating bank, that is, negotiation is restricted to the confirming bank stipulated in the credit. Even in the absence of such stipulation, the beneficiary's banker would present the documents to the confirming bank for negotiation on a without recourse basis. In that case, it should be noted that the confirming bank, having negotiated the documents, is without recourse to drawers (beneficiaries). If issuing bank falls into insolvency, confirming bank cannot ask for a refund from the drawers (sellers) (Art. 9 b iv. UCP–500).

5.5 Rights and Duties of Beneficiary

(a) He has the right to request the draft to be honoured by the confirming bank regardless of the position of issuing bank.

(b) He has a right of independent and definite payment undertaking from confirming bank in addition to that of issuing bank if he receives a confirmed D/C.

(c) On the other hand, he must submit stipulated documents strictly in compliance with D/C terms and conditions and not inconsistent among themselves.

6 Beneficiary vs Negotiating Bank

There exists a simple relationship between the banker and customer. Rights and duties between these two parties normally refer to whether or not a negotiating bank, after offering an advance to its customer (the beneficiary), has a right of recourse to the customer. This depends on various circumstances. Readers may refer to sections 2, 5 and 6 of Chapter 6 for details.

Part II

Practical Guide

10

Transferable Credit (Letter of Transfer)

1 Characteristics of a Transferable Credit

A transferable credit is a credit which can be transferred in whole or in part by the original beneficiary to one or more "second beneficiaries". It is normally used when the first beneficiary does not supply the goods himself, but acts as a middleman between the supplier and the ultimate buyer.

Transferor refers to the middleman who is the beneficiary of the original credit. He now applies for the issue of a transferable credit. Therefore, he is an applicant for the transferable credit. He is also known as the first beneficiary.

Transferee is the party who actually supplies goods. Therefore, he is known as the supplier. He is also known as the second beneficiary.

1.1 Characteristics

(a) A transferable credit must be an irrevocable credit.

(b) A transferable credit can only be transferred once. It cannot be transferred from the "second beneficiary" to a "third beneficiary/beneficiaries". However, it can be transferred to more than one "second beneficiary". For example, a transferor can transfer a D/C to Company A in USA, Company B in Europe, Company C in China. However, neither Company A, B nor C are allowed to transfer the credit further.

(c) The bank charges in respect of the transfer are payable by the first beneficiary.

(d) The transfer must be in accordance with the terms and conditions of the original credit, except that:

    (1) The name and address of the first beneficiary may be substituted for the name and address of the applicant for the credit;

    (2) The amount of the credit (and the unit price, if any) may be reduced, to allow the first beneficiary to take his profit;

    (3) The expiry date of the credit and shipment date may be shortened.

Figure 10.1 Diagrammatic Explanation of the Operation of a Transferable Credit

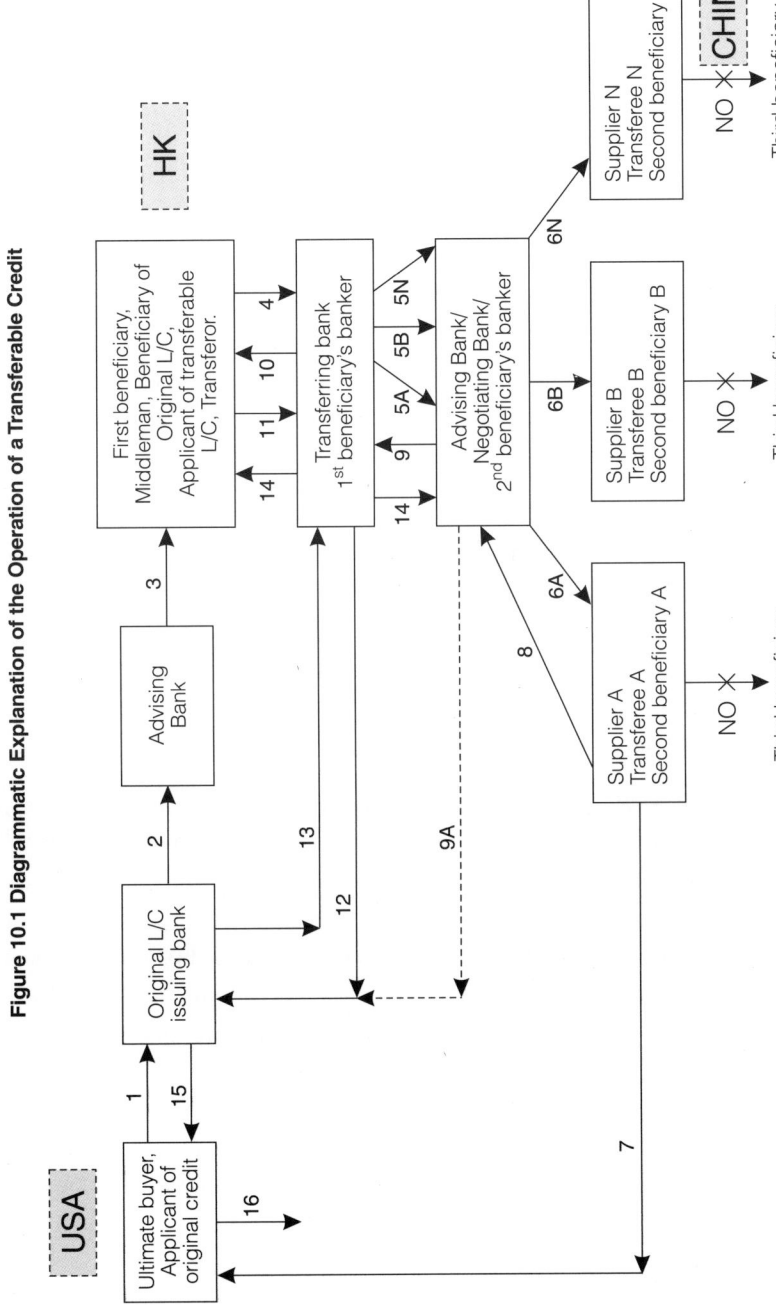

2 Explanation of the Operation of a Transferable Credit (see Figure 10.1)

(1) Ultimate buyer in USA applies for a transferable credit known as original credit from his banker.

(2) His banker, known as original L/C issuing bank, issued the L/C in USA and has it sent to its branch/ subsidiary/ corresponding bank in Hong Kong.

(3) The advising bank in Hong Kong advises the credit to the beneficiary who is usually a middleman. This middleman is the beneficiary under the original credit as well as the applicant under the transferable credit. He is also known as a transferor or first beneficiary.

(4) The transferor applies for a transferable credit (also known as letter of transfer) from his banker (or from the advising bank if it so happens that the advising bank is also his banker).

(5) The transferring bank effects the transfer and sends the transferable credit through its branch/ subsidiary/ corresponding bank in China for onward advising the transferable credit to a supplier or more than one suppliers.

Note that the transferable credit is effected without payment undertaking imposed on the transferring bank in Hong Kong. It is the undertaking of the original D/C issuing bank in USA to give a payment promise to the supplier in China. In the case of a partial transfer, the transferring bank will keep the original D/C at its premises and based on its contents, issue a separate D/C to the Chinese supplier. The separate D/C is usually a certified photostatic copy of the original D/C except that a few items are changed e.g., amount of credit, quantity of goods, unit price, if any. The transferable credit can even be a full telex message prepared by the Transferring bank if it finds it more convenient to do so.

In the case of a full transfer, the original D/C will be sent to the supplier. A letter issued by the Transferring bank is accompanied with the original D/C instructing that there should be no substitution of documents to be followed subsequently afterwards. It can be, perhaps, said that there are physically two credits involved in partial transfer and, one credit involved in fully transfer. And in both cases, the transferring bank effect the transfers without any payment obligation.

(6) The advising bank in China advises the transferable credit to the supplier, who is known as the transferee or second beneficiary. Note that there can be more than one "Second beneficiaries" who can be in the same country or different countries. Second beneficiaries, however, are not allowed to further transfer the credit to any third beneficiaries except in the case of retransfer back the letter of transfer to the first beneficiary. We consider supplier A only for simplicity reason.

(7) The supplier ships the goods to the ultimate buyer or his designated place.

(8) The supplier prepares documents which are submitted to his banker to have them sent to the Transferring bank for substitution of documents by the first beneficiary pending payment from DC issuing bank (in full transfer with no substitution stipulated, documents are sent direct to original D/C issuing bank for payment). Note that in most cases, unless a very good relationship has been established between the transferee and his banker, negotiation of transferee's documents will not happen.

(9) Transferee's banker (2nd beneficiary's banker) sends documents to the Transferring bank for substitution of documents (In case of full transfer, documents will be sent directly to original D/C issuing bank for payment, as shown in route 9A, bypassing routes 9–12).

(10) Transferring bank informs the first beneficiary to have documents substituted and fulfil the terms as per the original credit.

(11) Transferor submits substituted documents to the Transferring bank.

(12) Transferring bank, upon receipt of full set of documents, will send them to the original D/C issuing bank for payment. Also, unless a good relationship has been established between the transferor and his banker, there will not be negotiation.

(13) Issuing bank checks documents. It honours its payment undertaking if documents are found to be in order. Proceeds will be remitted to the Transferring bank.

(14) Payment by Transferring bank of the amount drawn by the second beneficiary and the difference of the transferred amount and original L/C amount paid to the first beneficiary as profit.

(15) Issuing bank releases documents to the ultimate buyer upon receipt of payment/against trust receipt.

(16) Ultimate buyer takes delivery of goods upon presentation of the transport document.

3 Types of Transfer: Partial Transfer, Full Transfer (Total Transfer)

There are two types of transfer, namely partial transfer and full transfer. Partial transfer means transfer part of the original DC amount to the second beneficiary(ies) with substitution of his (their) documents. Full transfer means transfer the full DC value to the second beneficiary(ies) normally without substitution of his (their) own documents.

In partial transfer, a transferor transfers part of the credit amount to a beneficiary or more than one beneficiaries. The remaining amount may be left for himself. For the portion being transferred, it is expected that substitution of the middleman's invoice for that of the supplier is required. Substitution of documents means the middleman is asked by the transferring bank to present his own invoice and draft (larger amount according to original credit) to replace those issued by the supplier's which, together with other shipping documents (submitted by supplier) will be sent to issuing bank for payment. In full transfer, a transferor simply requests his banker to have the credit wholly transferred to a supplier. This transferor may be an agent only, responsible for placing order for either the ultimate buyer or supplier. The amount in the letter of transfer is the same as that of the original credit. As such, no substitution of invoice will be followed. Also, it is expect that the transferee's banker should send documents directly to original credit issuing bank for payment, bypassing Transferring bank.

4 Checklist for the Transferring Bank in Transfer

(a) The original credit submitted by customers must be irrevocable and transferable.

(b) "Subject to UCP–500" must be shown in the credit.

(c) If transferor intends to have the credit transferred to more than one "Second beneficiary", L/C should allow partial shipment.

(d) Original credit requests third party document acceptable. Transferring bank being at the same time as the advising bank is advisable. Otherwise, ask for an amendment from credit applicant, nominating our bank (Transferring bank) as the second advising bank at the same time.

(e) In the case of a freely negotiable credit, our bank specifically authorized in the credit as the Transferring bank is necessary.

(f) It is advisable to add the following clause in the transferable credit to exempt our bank from payment liability clearly. "Upon receipt of fund from credit issuing bank, we shall pay to you according to your instruction".

(g) Care must be exercised to ensure that the issuing bank is informed about the details of transfer if it is stipulated in the original credit that in case of transfer, issuing bank must be notified about the details.

5 Checklist for the Transferring Bank upon Receipt of Supplier's Documents

(a) Upon receipt of supplier's documents, Transferring bank must immediately inform the first beneficiary to submit his documents for substitution as soon as possible. If this first beneficiary fails to react to the request of the Transferring bank, the Transferring bank has the right to send the supplier's documents to the issuing bank without further responsibility to the transferor.

(b) Only in rare occasion does a Transferring bank negotiate documents presented under letter of transfer. For example, the transferring bank has no doubt about the credit standing of the transferor and the issuing bank.

6 Possible Risks to the Transferring Bank in Effecting a Transfer

Transferring bank effects a transfer without payment obligation to the transferee. Therefore, it is obvious that a Transferring bank will expose to less extent of risk than a back-to-back credit issuing bank. However, a Transferring bank will easily expose to the kinds of risk which an agent will normally face. In effecting a letter of transfer, it may inadvertently fail to comply with the instructions stipulated in the original credit in transfer. Therefore, it runs into danger of negligence. Action may be taken against him by issuing bank, transferor or transferee.

7 Rights of the Transferring Bank

(a) A Transferring bank is not obliged to effect the transfer. Even if it is stipulated in the credit as the Transferring bank, a transferor cannot force this nominated bank to effect the transfer.

(b) If the first beneficiary does not substitute documents on first demand, a Transferring bank has the right to send the supplier's documents to issuing bank for payment without further responsibility.

8 Points to Note for the Ultimate Buyer

He made a contract with the middleman but the goods are not going to be shipped by the middleman but by a third party who may be unknown to him.

The quality of the goods is not assured unless they are inspected by the ultimate buyer himself or a public surveyor before departure.

9 Points to Note for the Supplier

His most concern is that:

He may be unable to be paid by issuing bank even if from his point of view, he has complied strictly with credit terms and condition. This can happen in the following circumstances:

Technical errors are made by either the transferor or Transferring bank in:

(a) Issue of letter of transfer — e.g., transferor fails to give clear instructions to Transferring bank in application. Transferring bank fails to inform issuing bank as specified in the original credit. For example, the transferring bank is required by the issuing bank to give detailed notice to it in case of transfer. However, the transferring bank fails to act as instructed.

(b) Substitution of document — error is made by Transferring bank or transferor which makes the document unclean (even if it was a clean document sent from the supplier's banker).

10 Sample of a Transferable Credit

Issuing Bank (in USA):	USA Bank, USA
Advising Bank (in Hong Kong):	A Bank Limited, Hong Kong (First Advising Bank in Hong Kong; City Bank, Hong Kong (Second Advising Bank)
Transferring Bank (in Hong Kong):	City Bank, Hong Kong
DC Applicant:	Ultimate Buyer Limited, USA
Transferor:	Middleman Limited, Hong Kong
Transferee:	Transferee Limited, Beijing, China
D/C Number:	12345
Transfer Credit Number:	T-67890

City Bank Limited

Check Sheet

Transferable Credit

Date :

Credit Number: 12345

Name of Issuing Bank: USA Bank, USA

Name of Applicant (Ultimate buyer): Ultimate Buyer Limited, USA

Name of our Transferor (Our customer): Middleman Limited, H.K.

Name of Transferee (Supplier): Transferee Limited, Beijing

	With substitution of documents	Without substitution of documents
Full Transfer		
Partial Transfer	√	

	Original Credit	Transferable Credit
Amount	USD 27,000.00	USD 21,900.00
Unit Price	USD 4.5/pc	USD 3.65/pc
Latest Shipment Date	15/6/1998	30/5/1998
Expiry Date	6/7/1998	10/6/1998
Presentation Period	21 days	11 days
Trade Term	CIF New York	CIF New York
Partial Shipments	allowed/not allowed	allowed/not allowed
Transhipments	allowed/not allowed	allowed/not allowed
Items (goods)	Men's Pyjamas, 18/6519	Men's Pyjamas 18/519

Other terms and condition:

Remarks:

Checker	Office	Manager	

Handled by: Mr/Miss _____

Ext.:   _____

A BANK LIMITED

HONG KONG

To: CITY BANK LIMITED   DATE: 10/04/98
      HONG KONG
                                                            OUR REF. NO: 1
ATTN.: L/C ADVISING DIVISION

LETTER OF CREDIT ADVICE

BENEFICIARY: MIDDLEMAN LIMITED, HONG KONG
L/C NO: 12345 FOR USD 126,000.00
ISSUING BANK: USA BANK, USA

AT THE REQUEST OF THE ABOVE-NAMED BANK, WE FORWARD HEREWITH, WITHOUT
ENGAGEMENT ON OUR PART THEIR IRREVOCABLE LETTER OF CREDIT AS INDICATED.

KINDLY NOTE THAT THIS LETTER OF CREDIT MUST ACCOMPANY THE DOCUMENTS AT THE
TIME OF PRESENTATION TO US FOR NEGOTIATION AND TO AVOID UNNECESSARY DELAY,
PLEASE MARK YOUR COVERING LETTER OUR REFERENCE NUMBER.

PLEASE ADVISE THE ATTACHED LETTER OF CREDIT TO BENEFICIARY AND ACKNOWLEDGE
RECEIPT QUOTING OUR REFERENCE.

BEFORE RELEASING THE L/C TO BENEFICIARY PLEASE COLLECT FROM THEM AND FAVOUR
US A CHEQUE FOR 200.00 COVERING OUR POSTAGE.

FOR AND ON BEHALF OF
A BANK
HONG KONG BRANCH

_____
AUTHORIZED SIGNATURE(S)

This is the Covering Letter issued by the first Advising Bank in Hong Kong.

CITY BANK LIMITED

HONG KONG

ADVICE OF DOCUMENTARY LETTER OF CREDIT   Date: 98 /4-15

	Our Ref.

Beneficiary:
    Middleman Limited,
    Hong Kong
	Transmitted To Beneficiary Through:

Issuing Bank:
    USA Bank,
    USA
	Transmitted To Us Through:
	A Bank Limited,
	Hong Kong Branch

L/C No. 12345	Advising Commission $250.00

We have pleasure in informing you that we have received an

(X)   authenticated

(   )   unauthenticated

(   )   original of

(   )   amendment to

(X)   teletransmission message opening the above L/C

(   )   teletransmission message amending the said document is enclosed herewith

(   )   confirmation of

(   )   confirmation of amendment to

(   )   brief cable advice of

(X)   Please note that this advice does not constitute our confirmation to the above L/C nor conveys any engagement or obligation on our part.

(X)   Please check the credit terms carefully. If you are unable to comply with the credit terms, it is suggested that you communicate direct with your buyers immediately with a view to arranging any desired amendments and thus avoid difficulties which would otherwise arise when documents are presented.

(X)   Kindly acknowledge receipt by signing and returning the duplicate of this advice.

CITY BANK LIMITED
HONG KONG BRANCH

_____
Authorized Signature(s)

This is the Covering Letter issued by the second Advising Bank in Hong Kong which is acting as the transferring bank..

form of documentary credit	:	IRREVOCABLE TRANSFERABLE
documentary credit number	:	12345
date of issue	:	980409
date and place of expiry	:	980706
applicant	:	ULTIMATE BUYER LIMITED, USA
beneficiary	:	MIDDLEMAN LIMITED, HONG KONG
currency code amount	:	
currency code	:	USD US Dollar
amount	:	#126,000.#
available with/by-name, address	:	AVAILABLE WITH ANY BANK IN HONG KONG BY NEGOTIATION
drafts at	:	DRAFT AT SIGHT
drawee - name and address	:	ISSUING BANK, USA
partial shipments	:	ALLOWED
on board/disp/taking charge	:	ANY HONG KONG PORTS / CHINESE PORTS
for transportation to	:	NEW YORK
latest date of shipment	:	980615
description of goods	:	MEN'S PYJAMAS
		18/6466-6,000 PCS AT USD 5.50/PC
		18/6467-6,000 PCS AT USD 5.50/PC
		18/6468-6,000 PCS AT USD 5.50/PC
		18/6519-6,000 PCS AT USD 4.50/PC
		C I F NEW YORK
charges	:	ALL CHARGES AND COMMISSIONS OUTSIDE L/C OPENING BANK ARE FOR ACCOUNT OF BENEFICIARY
period for presentation	:	21 DAYS
confirmation instructions	:	WITHOUT
instructions to pay/acc/neg bk	:	WE'LL REMIT PROCEEDS AS PER INSTRUCTIONS OF NEGOTIATING BANK. THE ADVICE TO THE BENEFICIARY MUST BE PRESENTED AT EACH NEGOTIATION. THE NEGOTIATING BANK MUST NOTE EACH NEGOTIATION ON THAT ADVICE
		DOCUMENTS ARE TO BE SENT BY COURIER OR REGISTERED AIRMAIL TO OUR ADDRESS P.O. BOX 8888 NEW YORK, USA IN 2 CONSECUTIVE LOTS
advise thru bank	:	CITY BANK, HONG KONG, G.P.O. BOX 8, HONG KONG
documents required	:	1. SIGNED COMMERCIAL INVOICES, 5-COPIES
		2. FULL SET CLEAN ON BOARD MARINE-OR COMBINED TRANSPORT OR FORWARDERS BILL OF LADING, MADE OUT TO ORDER AND BLANK ENDORSED, MARKED "FREIGHT PREPAID" - NOTIFY : MESSRS. ULTIMATE BUYER LIMITED, NEW YORK, USA
		3. INSURANCE POLICY OR - CERTIFICATE FOR AT ⌐ LEAST 110% OF CIF VALUE, BLANK ENDORSED, MARKED "PREMIUM PAID", COVERING ALL RISKS AS PER INSTITUTE CARGO CLAUSES "A" INSTITUTE WAR CLAUSES, INSTITUTE STRIKE CLAUSES, INCLUDING MALICIOUS DAMAGE CLAUSES
		4. PACKING - LIST, 2-FOLDS
		5. PHOTOCOPY OF EXPORT - LICENCE, ISSUED AND/OR SIGNED BY GOVERNMENT AUTHORITY
		6. PHOTOCOPY OF CERTIFICATE OF ORIGIN, ISSUED AND/OR SIGNED BY GOVERNMENT AUTHORITY
REMARK	:	THIS CREDIT IS TRANSFERABLE BY CITY BANK HK ONLY

This is the original D/C opened by Issuing Bank: USA Bank, USA.

As request by the prime beneficiary,
Middleman Limited, we transfer this credit
under our transfer no. T-67888 with
documents substitution.
    ORDER NO.:   18/6466-6,000 PCS
                   18/6467-6,000 PCS
                   18/6468-6,000 PCS

For and on behalf of
CITY BANK, HONG KONG

_____
Authorized Signature(s)

As request by the prime beneficiary,
Middleman Limited, we transfer this credit
under our transfer no. T-67890 with
documents substitution.
    ORDER NO.:   18/6519-6,000 PCS

For and on behalf of
CITY BANK, HONG KONG

_____
Authorized Signature(s)

This is the back side of the original D/C. The contents in the two boxes are endorsements made by the transferring bank evidencing that such items of the goods are respectively transfered.

APPLICATION FOR TRANSFER OF CREDIT

To : City Bank, Hong Kong   Date: April 30, 1998

       Credit No.: 12345   Date : APRIL 9, 1998

       Issued by : USA Bank, USA

       For account of Ultimate Buyer Limited, USA

1. (i) Please transfer the abovementioned credit to Transferee Limited, Beijing, China on the same terms and conditions except:-

    1. amount (in words and figures) USD21,900.00 (SAY US DOLLARS TWENTY-ONE THOUSAND NINE HUNDRED ONLY.)

    2. quantity of goods (if applicable) ORDER NO. 18/6519-6,000 PCS. AT USD 3.65/PC. CIF NEW YORK

    3. unit price (if applicable)

    4. latest shipment date MAY 30, 98.

    5. expiry date JUNE 10, 98 IN HONG KONG.

  (ii) Upon payment by you of any draft under the transferred Credit, or at some date prior to this payment we shall deliver to you our draft and commercial invoices drawn in accordance with the original Documentary Credit in order that these documents may be substituted for the transferee's draft and invoices, the latter of which are to be delivered to us together with your payment for the difference between the two invoices, less any charges due to you. In addition to our draft and invoices we also undertake to deliver to you any other documents which may be needed to substitute for any of the transferee's documents, which do not comply as regards value etc. with the requirements of the original Credit. Should we fail, upon your request, to hand to you immediately the new draft, invoices and other documents required as mentioned above, you are authorized to accompanying the draft of the transferee to your principals without any responsibility on your part for payment of any difference between the amount of the transferee's draft and the amount authorized to be paid under the original Documentary Credit.

  (iii) Alterations to the Credit may be notified to the new beneficiary after reference to us.

  (iv) We agree to be charged with interest for the period, if any, between the date of your payment to the transferee until the date of payment of the documents under the original Documentary Credit, and with any changes incurred by you or your correspondents in connection with this transferred Credit.

2. Neither you nor your Correspondents shall be responsible for the description, quantity, quality or value of the merchandise shipped under the transferred Documentary Credit, nor for the correctness, genuineness or validity of the documents, nor for any other cause beyond your or their control.

3. The transfer, if agreed to be made by you , shall be subject to the "UCP–500".

4. After the transfer (if agreed to be made by you), we shall/shall not retain the right to refuse to allow you to advise subsequent amendments to the said transfee. This instruction is given to you pursuant to Article 48(d) of UCP–500 and shall be irrevocable.

5. Notify the new beneficiary by   ❏ airmail ❏ brief cable ❏ full cable at our expense
                                     ❏ China courier

For and on behalf of
MIDDLEMAN LIMITED
HONG KONG

_____

Authorized Signature(s)

This is the application for the issue of a transferable credit given from the middleman to his banker.

CITY BANK

HONG KONG

To: Transferee Limited,
       Beijing,
       China

Dear Sirs,

Without any responsibility or engagement on the part of this bank, we wish to inform you that we have received an instruction from Transferor Limited, Hong Kong to transfer to you an Irrevocable Document credit No. 12345 issued by USA Bank, USA to the extent of USD21,900.00 (UNITED STATES DOLLARS TWENTY ONE THOUSAND NINE HUNDRED ONLY.)

All terms and conditions are as per our certified photostatic copies of the original credit attached hereto. All documents and drafts must be presented to Transferor's Bank Limited, HK's Counter, Central, Hong Kong in one cover for SUBSTITUTION. The remitting bank is required to indicate that documents are for substitution under transferred credit on their covering bill schedule quoting our transfer no. T-67890.

This transfer expires on 10TH JUNE 1998 in Hong Kong at our counter. All documents except drafts and invoice must not show value of goods and unit price.

Documents to be presented within 11 days after the issuance of the shipping documents but within the validity of this transfer.

Please note that this transfer is not valid unless accompanied by the aforesaid photostatic copy of the original credit. Transferring bank's handling commission and commission in lieu of exchange are for account of transferee.

SPECIAL INSTRUCTIONS TO REMITTING / NEGOTIATING BANK

PROVIDED ALL DOCUMENTS PRESENTED IN CONFORMITY WITH THE TERMS OF THIS CREDIT AND UPON RECEIPT OF PROCEEDS FROM THE CREDIT ISSUING BANK, WE SHALL REMIT THE PROCEEDS TO YOU ACCORDING TO YOUR INSTRUCTIONS. NEITHER TRANSFEROR NOR OUR BANK ASSUMES ANY RESPONSIBILITY FOR ANY DELAY PAYMENT/TRANSIT INTEREST, IF ANY, TO BE CLAIMED BY THE NEGOTIATING BANK.

For and on behalf of
CITY BANK, HONG KONG

_____
Authorized Signature(s)

This is the covering letter issued by the transferring bank. The letter should be accompanied with the next page to constitute a transferable credit.

form of documentary credit	:	IRREVOCABLE TRANSFERABLE
documentary credit number	:	12345
date of issue	:	980409
date and place of expiry	:	**980610 Hong Kong at transferring bank counter**
applicant	:	Ultimate Buyer Limited, USA
transferor	:	**Middleman Limited, Hong Kong**
currency code	:	USD US Dollar
amount	:	*21,900.00*
available with/by-name, address	:	AVAILABLE WITH ANY BANK IN HONG KONG BY NEGOTIATION
drafts at	:	DRAFT AT SIGHT
drawee — name and address	:	ISSUING BANK, USA
partial shipments	:	ALLOWED
on board/disp/taking charge	:	ANY HONG KONG PORTS / CHINESE PORTS
for transportation to	:	NEW YORK, USA
latest date of shipment	:	**980530**
description of goods	:	MEN'S PYJAMAS
		18/6519-6,000 PCS AT **USD 3.65/PC**
		C I F NEW YORK
charges	:	ALL CHARGES AND COMMISSIONS OUTSIDE L/C OPENING BANK ARE FOR ACCOUNT OF **TRANSFEREE**
period for presentation	:	**11 DAYS**
confirmation instructions	:	WITHOUT
documents required	:	1. SIGNED COMMERCIAL INVOICES, 5-FOLDS
		2. FULL SET CLEAN ON BOARD MARINE-OR COMBINED TRANSPORT OR FORWARDERS BILL OF LADING, MADE OUT TO ORDER AND BLANK ENDORSED, MARKED "FREIGHT PREPAID" - NOTIFY : MESSRS. ULTIMATE BUYER LIMITED, NEW YORK, USA
		3. INSURANCE POLICY OR - CERTIFICATE FOR **135.6164% OF CIF VALUE**, BLANK ENDORSED, MARKED "PREMIUM PAID", COVERING ALL RISKS AS PER INSTITUTE CARGO CLAUSES "A" INSTITUTE WAR CLAUSES, INSTITUTE STRIKE CLAUSES, INCLUDING MALICIOUS DAMAGE CLAUSES
		4. PACKING - LIST, 2-FOLDS
		5. PHOTOCOPY OF EXPORT - LICENCE, ISSUED AND/OR SIGNED BY GOVERNMENT AUTHORITY
		6. PHOTOCOPY OF CERTIFICATE OF ORIGIN, ISSUED AND/OR SIGNED BY GOVERNMENT AUTHORITY

This credit consists of TWO signed pages. This is a certified true copy which is not valid unless when used in conjunction with our Transfer No. T-2694 dated 2 May 98. As per article 48 of Uniform Customs & Practice for Documentary Credits (1993) Revision, no further transfer should be made under this instrument.

After the transfer, transferor will/will not retain the right to refuse to allow transferring bank to advise subsequent amendments to transferee. This instruction is given to you pursuant to Article 48(d) of UCP–500 and shall be irrevocable.

For and on behalf of
CITY BANK, HONG KONG

_____
Authorized Signature(s)

Bold letters represent the **changes in the "letter of transfer" from the "original letter of credit".**

11

Back-to-Back Credit and Bridge Credit

- ❏ Meaning of a back-to-back credit (B/B L/C)
- ❏ Various Steps in the Operation of a back-to-back credit
- ❏ Illustration of an issue of a back-to-back credit
- ❏ Risks to B/B credit issuing bank
- ❏ Considerations and precautions in the issue of a B/B credit
- ❏ Meaning, characteristics and risk in the issue of a bridge credit
- ❏ Illustration of an issue of a bridge credit
- ❏ Practical points to note in the issue of a bridge credit
- ❏ Similarities in and differences between a B/B credit and a transferable credit

1 Meaning of a Back-to-Back Credit (B/B Credit)

When a beneficiary receives a D/C which is not transferable and he cannot furnish the goods himself, he may arrange with his banker to issue a second credit, which is known as "Back-to-Back L/C", to a supplier to supply the goods.

In B/B credit transaction, there involves two separate credits. The first credit known as master credit, is issued by ultimate buyer's banker in favour of the middleman. The second credit (B/B credit) is issued by the middleman's banker in favour of the supplier. As the two credits cover the same goods, the Back-to-Back Credit must be issued in identical terms to the master credit except in smaller amount and that the expiry date is shortened (shipment date in the second credit can be the same as or earlier than that of the first credit).

Based on the deposit of the master credit as a proof of repayment, B/B credit issuing bank is assured of a source of repayment and is, therefore, willing to give an independent undertaking to pay the supplier. As long as his customer is able to fulfil all terms and conditions of the master credit, the repayment source is almost certain. B/B credit issuing bank must try to maintain control of the documents and hold them after payment to the supplier, pending receipt of its customer's invoices, draft and other documents which will be presented for payment under the master credit.

2 Various Steps in the Operation of a Back-to-Back Credit

In Figure 11.1, a Hong Kong middleman is buying goods from a USA supplier and selling them to an ultimate buyer in Hanzhou, Zhejiang, China.

(1) Ultimate buyer applies for a letter of credit known as master credit (original D/C, first credit) from his banker.

(2) This master credit is issued in the Hanzhou and sent to its overseas corresponding bank in Hong Kong.

(3) The advising bank in Hong Kong advises the credit to the beneficiary under the master credit who is also the applicant

under the Back-to-Back Credit (note that B/B L/C is also known as second credit, baby L/C).

(4) As the middleman he has no stock on hand or is simply acting as an agent, applies for another credit known as B/B L/C from his banker (or from the advising bank if it so happens that the advising bank is also his banker). Note that the second credit is an independent D/C and is legally separate from the first credit.

(5) The B/B L/C issuing bank in Hong Kong sends the second credit through its corresponding bank in USA for further advising the credit.

(6) The advising bank in USA advises the B/B L/C to the supplier who is known as the beneficiary of the B/B L/C.

(7) The supplier (beneficiary of B/B L/C) ships the goods to the ultimate buyer's country (or to places as stipulated in the B/B L/C).

(8) The supplier prepares documents which are submitted to his banker for negotiation.

(9) The supplier's banker negotiates the documents and pays the supplier.

(10) The negotiating bank sends documents to B/B credit issuing bank for reimbursement under the B/B L/C.

(11) The issuing bank under B/B transaction in Hong Kong pays the negotiating bank in USA if the documents are in order.

(12) The B/B L/C issuing bank informs its customer of the arrival of shipping documents and reminds him of the substitution of documents in accordance with those in the master credit.

(13) The applicant of the B/B L/C submits documents and fulfils all the terms and conditions as per the master credit.

(14) The B/B L/C issuing bank may negotiate the export documents under the master credit (in which case, the middleman will be paid, this is not shown in our diagram for simplicity reason) and then send the documents to the master credit issuing bank for reimbursement (or claim reimbursement from reimbursing bank).

Figure 11.1 Diagrammatic Explanation of
the Operation of a Back-to-Back Credit

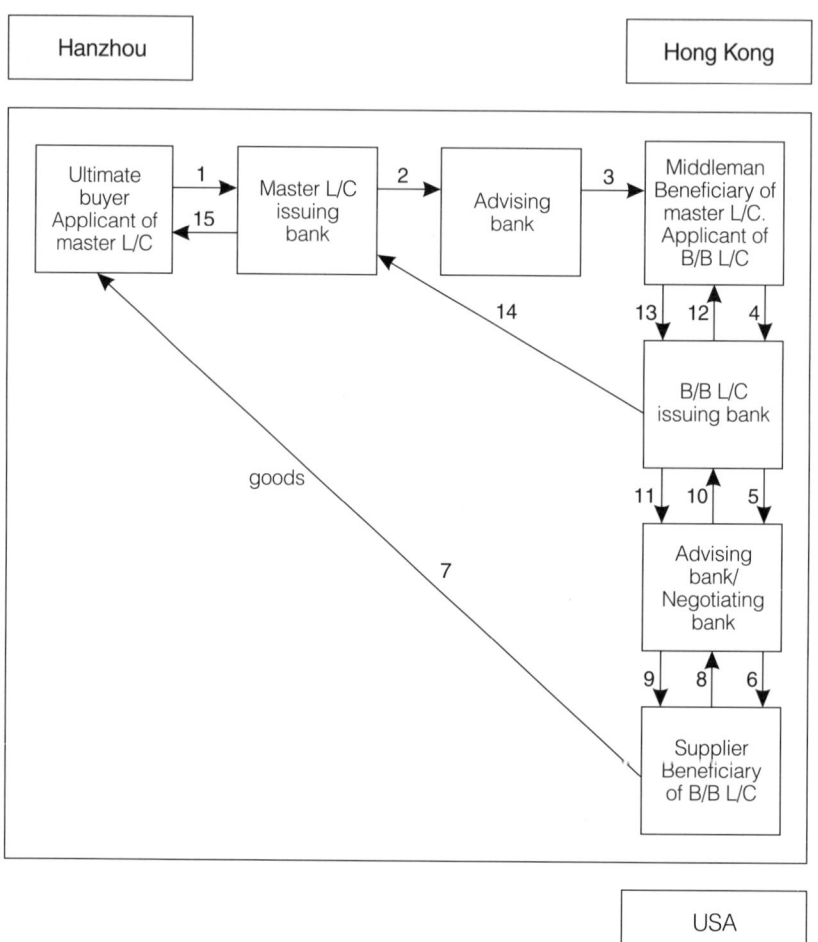

Note: In order to simplify the diagram, documents presented by the exporter
(middleman) here are treated to be in compliance with D/C terms and
conditions. If not, on the exporter's side, documents have to be (i) sent to
issuing bank on approval basis or (ii) negotiated under cable negotiation or
(iii) negotiated under exporter's Letter of Indemnity.

(15) The issuing bank under the master credit checks documents which are found to be in order. After honouring its undertaking to pay the negotiating bank (i.e., the BB credit issuing bank), the issuing bank releases documents upon receipt of payment from applicant who will then take delivery of goods.

On the importer's side, documents with discrepancies have to be referred to applicant for approval by the credit issuing bank.

3　Illustration of an Issue of a B/B Credit

Figure 11.2 shows a master credit issued by Bank of Zhejiang, Hanzhou Branch in favour of a Hong Kong Beneficiary. Details are as follows,

Figure 11.2
Master Credit Issued by Bank of Zhejiang

Master Credit Issuing Bank:	Bank of Zhejiang, Hanzhou
Ultimate Buyer:	China Import and Export Corporation, Zhejiang Branch
Advising Bank:	Citybank, Hong Kong
Middleman	City Import and Export Limited, Hong Kong
B/B L/C Issuing Bank:	Citybank, Hong Kong
Supplier:	USA Flexing Machine Limited, New York, USA

Note:　The extra terms inserted in the B/B credit to ensure that documents presented can comply with the requirement of master credit.

MASTER CREDIT (First Credit)

Bank of Zhejiang, Hanzhou Branch	Date: 1 May 1998

To Beneficiary: City Import and Export Limited Des Voeux Rd Central Hongkong	IRREVOCABLE DOCUMENTARY CREDIT NO. 1 valid for negotiation in Hong Kong until Aug 15, 1998
	Amount: USD5,300,000.00 (United States Dollars Five Million Three Hundred Thousand Only)
Advising Bank: Citybank, Hong Kong	Applicant: China Import and Export Corporation, Zhejiang Branch, Hangzhou, China

Dear Sir(s),

We hereby issue in your favour this documentary credit which is available by negotiation with City Bank Hong Kong against Beneficiary's draft(s) at — sight for 100% invoice value on us marked as drawn under this credit and accompanied by the following documents marked with numbers:

(1) Signed commercial invoice in 5 copies indicating contract No. and L/C No.
( ) Full set of clean on board ocean bills of lading made out to order and blank endorsed marked "Freight Prepaid" notifying China National Foreign Trade Transportation Corp at destination.
(2) Packing list/weight memo in 3 copies showing quantity/gross and net weight for each package.
(3) Certificate of quality in 3 copies issued by manufacturer.
(4) Clean Air Waybill consigned to issuing bank notifying the applicant marked "Freight Prepaid" and indicating freight amount.
(5) Copy of cable to applicant advising contract No., goods name, quantity, invoice value, packages, flight No., shipment date and place.

evidencing shipment of:

> One set of Whole Shoe Flexing Machine
> Model: WSFM/338
> As per contract number 12345, CFR Hangzhou, packing charges included.

Packing: In strong wooden cases, suitable for long distance air transportation.

Shipping Mark: 12345
            HANGZHOU CHINA

Shipment from USA Airport to Hangzhou Airport via Hong Kong not later than July 31, 1998	Partial shipments not allowed	Transhipment/not allowed

Special Instructions: 1. All banking charges in Hongkong are for beneficiary's account. 2. All documents must indicate contract No. 12345. Instruction to Negotiating Bank: 1. Please debit our account with you under telex advice to us. 2. All documents are to be presented to us in one lot by 1st available airmail. 3. This credit is subject to UCP–500.	We hereby undertake that all drafts drawn under and in compliance with the terms of this credit will be duly honoured on presentation at this office. for Bank of Zhejiang Hanzhou Branch _____ Authorized Signature

City Bank Limited
Check Sheet
Back-to-Back Credit

Date:

Name of applicant:	City I/E Limited
Amount of application form	USD 4,679,000.00[1]
☑ Back to Back letter of credit	❏ Bridge letter of credit
M/L/C no.:	Credit proposal no.:
Name of M/L/C issuing bank:	Bank of Zhejiang, Hangzhou Branch
Status of beneficiary:	❏ to be checked ❏ in processing ❏ checked

Master letter of credit	Application form
Shipment from USA Airport to Hangzhou Airport	Shipment from USA Airport to Hangzhou Airport [2]
Partial shipment: ❏ Yes ❏ No	Partial shipment:[3] ❏ Yes ❏ No
Transhipment: ❏ Yes ❏ No	Transhipment:[4] ❏ Yes ❏ No
Shipment date: 31 July 1998	Shipment date:[5] 19 July 1998
Validity date: 15 August 1998	Validity date:[6] 30 July 1998
Presentation date: Not Applicable	Presentation date:[7] 10 days
Master L/C: Discrepancies/points to note	Application: Discrepancies/points to note
1	1
2	2
3	3
4	4
5	5
6	6
7	7
8	8
9	9
10	10
11	11
12	12
13	13

Suggestions for credit proposal	Remarks

First Check	Second Check	Manager	Approve	Reject

Upon receipt of an application for issuing a Back-to-Back Credit, the bank staff may make use of the above Check Sheet to assess the application.

Notes:

1. Amount of application must be smaller than that of master credit to allow for profit.

2. Shipment route must be the same in both credits.

3. If partial shipment is not allowed in master credit, the same stipulation must appear in application form. If partial shipment is allowed in master credit, then, partial shipment may or may not be allowed in application form.

4. The same reason as in (3) above applies to transhipment.

5. In application form, shipment date may be earlier than that of the master credit. However, it can show the same date as that of the master credit since it should meet the latest shipment date and shipment port stipulated in the master credit only.

6. In application form, expiry date must be earlier than that of the master credit. Their differences are not the same in each case. In general, the following factors will be taken into account.

   (i) The postal distance between Hong Kong and the second beneficiary's country. More time should be allowed for shipping documents under the second credit to be sent from Europe to Hong Kong (long postal distance) than documents to be sent from Asia to Hong Kong (shorter postal distance).

   (ii) The complexity in substitution of documents.

   (iii) The postal distance between Hong Kong and Master Credit issuing bank if the expiry place under the first credit is at the counter of issuing bank.

   In practice, it is advisable to arrange to have the first and second credits to be made payable at the counter of the B/B credit issuing bank. Then, a difference of about fifteen days is allowed for substitution of documents and onward precontation.

7. If presentation period is stipulated in both credits, application form should shorten the presentation date by at least 7 days. Again, it is not the same in each case. Presentation period can be added in application form for protection even though no such period is required by master credit.

4 Risks to the B/B Credit Issuing Bank

(a) Credit risk of the master credit issuing bank. Assume that no discrepancies are found in the two sets of documents. It means B/B L/C issuing bank has to pay the second beneficiary but fails to be repaid under first credit.

(b) Country risk of the issuer of master credit prevents the movement of fund to B/B L/C issuing bank although the latter commitment remains valid.

(c) Supplier can fulfil all the terms under the second credit and so must be paid, whereas the middleman fails to comply with some terms under the first credit and so will not get paid.

(d) There is the possible risk that documents presented under the second credit may be delayed in the post on their way to Hong Kong so that documents cannot be presented on time for presentation under the first credit.

(e) Payments has to be made beforehand to the supplier under the second credit and the middleman will be paid under the first credit afterwards. There may be a delay in payment under the first credit (Middleman might require financial support from the B/B L/C issuing bank until receipt of the proceeds of the first credit).

(f) The sudden death or bankruptcy of the middleman does not allow substitution of documents.

(g) Middleman may not submit all the subsequent amendments of the master L/C. This may result that documents presented under the first credit can never comply with master credit.

(h) B/B L/C issuing bank may lose control over the amendments if the master credit is not advised by it.

(i) First credit is amended and accepted by middleman, but the supplier may refuse the amendment under the second credit.

(j) Fraudulent documents may be submitted by the supplier under the second credit.

City Bank Limited
Hong Kong

B/B Credit

ORIGINAL
PAGE 1

Date and Place of issue: 15 May 1998 Hong Kong	Irrevocable Documentary Credit Number 123
	Date and Place of Expiry: 30 July 1998 at issuing bank's counter
Applicant: City Import and Export Limited Des Voeux Rd Central Hong Kong	Beneficiary: USA Flexing Machine Limited, New York USA
Advising Bank: Bank of USA New York Branch New York USA	Amount: USD 4,679,000.00 (United States Dollars Four Million Six Hundred Seventy Nine Thousand only)
Partial Shipments are not allowed Transhipment is not allowed Shipment from USA Airport to Hangzhou Airport via Hong Kong Latest **19 July 1998**	Credit available by negotiation against presentation of the documents detailed herein and of your draft(s) at sight drawn on our bank for full invoice value

List of documents to be presented:

1. Signed commercial invoice in duplicate.
2. Clean Air Waybill consigned to Bank of Zhejiang, Hanzhou, China notifying the Applicant marked "Freight Prepaid" and indicating freight amount.
3. Packing list/weight memo in 3 copies showing quantity/gross and net weight for each package.
4. Certificate of quality in 3 copies issued by the manufacturer and **made out "To Whom It May Concern"**.
5. Beneficiary's certified copy of telex despatched to applicant advising contract no., goods name, quantity, invoice value, packages, flight no., shipment date and place after shipment effected.
6. **Beneficiary's certificate certifying that one set of N/N documents supported by relative courier receipt has been sent to applicant within 3 days after shipment.**

Evidencing shipment of:
    One set of whole shoe flexing machine
    Model: WSFM/338   (continue to next page)

We hereby issue this Documentary Credit in your favour. It is subject to the Uniform Customs and Practice for Documentary Credits (1993 Revision, International Chamber of Commerce, Paris, France, Publication N° 500) and engages us in accordance with the terms thereof, and especially in accordance with the terms of Articles 10 thereof. The number and the date of the credit and the name of our bank must be quoted on all drafts required. If the credit is available by negotiation, each presentation must be noted on the reverse of this advice by the bank where the credit is available.

For City Bank Limited, Hong Kong

_____
Authorized Signature(s)

City Bank Limited
Hong Kong

CONTINUATION OF IRREVOCABLE DOCUMENTARY CREDIT NUMBER	Credit number 123

Packing: In strong wooden cases, suitable for long distance air transportation.

Shipping mark: <u>12345</u>
                   Hangzhou China
CFR Hangzhou, packing charges included.

Other terms and conditions:

All documents except invoice, draft and telex copy must not show this credit number, value of shipment, name and address of L/C applicant and L/C issuing bank.

Documents must be presented within 10 days after shipment date but within credit validity.

All banking charges including advising, negotiation and reimbursement charges outside Hong Kong are for account of beneficiary.

All documents must indicate contract No. 12345.

Insurance to be covered by ultimate buyer.

Instructions to negotiating bank:

Please forward all documents to us in one lot by speedpost or courier service.

Upon receipt of documents in conformity with the terms of this credit we shall reimburse the negotiating bank according to their instructions.

* * * END OF L/C * * *

(Bold sentences represent the changes in the B/B credit)
(This credit consists of 2 pages)

Yours faithfully

For City Bank Limited Hong Kong

_____
Authorized Signatures

Pages 212 and 213 are the Back-to-Back Credit, also known as Second Credit.

5 Considerations and Precautions in the Issue of a B/B Credit

To safeguard against the above risks, a back-to-back credit issuing bank should take the following considerations and precautions before the issue:

(a) The creditworthiness of middleman — Make sure that the middleman is a trustworthy person.

(b) Credit standing of issuing bank of the master credit — Make sure that issuing bank is a reputable bank of a well-developed country. Otherwise, ask for the master credit to be confirmed by a reputable bank of the middleman's country.

(c) Creditworthiness of the supplier — Make sure the supplier is a well-known company with good credit standing. Check the supplier's status before issue if he is unknown to you.

(d) The political and economic condition of the country of master L/C issuing bank is an important consideration. There may be the case that even though ultimate buyer is willing to pay the middleman, his country may not allow movement of fund out of the country.

Steps taken by the B/B L/C issuing bank for protection are as follows:

(a) Arrange to have the first credit to be made payable to the middleman at the counters of the middleman's Hong Kong bank.

(b) Arrange to have the second credit to be expired at the counter's of the middleman's (B/B L/C) issuing bank so as to ensure that documents can arrive in Hong Kong as schedule ready for substitution of documents.

(c) Inform the advising bank in Hong Kong to submit any subsequent amendments to your bank if the master credit is not advised by your bank.

(d) Stipulate in the second credit that discrepant documents will not be accepted and that negotiation under Letter of Indemnity/or cable negotiation is not acceptable.

(e) Documents should be forwarded to B/B L/C issuing bank in Hong Kong in one lot by DHL or by the possible fastest means to allow for documents substitution and further presentation.

(f) Terms and conditions of the second credit should be similar to those of the first credit except:

(1) credit amount, unit price if any
(2) expiry date and presentation period
(3) insured amount
(4) shipment date may have to be shortened

(g) Provide sufficient time for substitution of documents.

(h) Take out a forward exchange contract if the two credits are in different currency.

6 Meaning, Characteristics and Risk in the Issue of a Bridge Credit

Bridge credit is a special type of back-to-back credit. However, it is more risky for a bank to issue a bridge credit than a B/B credit, as it involves two separate carriages and voyages with transhipment to be effected in the middleman's country.

In addition to the risks to be encountered in document substitution as in B/B credit, issuing bank has to arrange transhipment for its customer. The duration of time for the second carriage is usually very limited. Any carelessness or negligent on the part of either the issuing bank or its customer may easily fall into failure to comply with credit terms of the master credit.

To protect its own position, issuing bank of the bridge credit requires transhipment to be effected by the authorized forwarding agent when documents under the second credit arrives (the issue of a shipping guarantee in case documents have not yet arrive). Issuing bank will release the document of title to the approved forwarding agent to take care of the goods ready for transhipment. Then, the forwarding agent will deliver the goods to a shipping company for onward carriage to the final destination as specified by the ultimate buyer. A fresh set of bills of lading, issued by the shipping company, will be grouped together with other shipping documents as stipulated in the master credit for presentation to master L/C issuing bank for payment.

It must be noted that once the goods are taken delivery, any discrepancies in subsequent documents cannot be a reason to reject payment. Therefore, this type of credit is only suitable to customers with high integrity and trustworthy buyers and suppliers. Besides, bridge credit should be handled only by experienced staff.

7 Illustration of an Issue of a Bridge Credit

Master Credit Issuing Bank:	Bank of Shenzhen, Shenzhen
Ultimate Buyer:	Shenzhen I/E Limited
Advising Bank:	City Bank, Hong Kong
Middleman	City I/E Limited, Hong Kong
Second Beneficiary:	Hong Kong I/E Limited, Hong Kong
Shipment from:	Korea to Hong Kong

Notes: Besides the same considerations as in a B/B credit, a bridge credit should consider the time needed for the goods shipped from the supplier to Hong Kong. Hence, a bigger difference of shipment date in the two credits is found in goods to be shipped from Europe to Hong Kong. The time needed for taking delivering of goods and arrangement for onward carriage is an additional consideration.

In practice, a difference of at least 15 days should be taken into account.

In general, a difference of at least 15 days should be taken into account for master credit to be expired in Hong Kong. If master credit expires at the counter of issuing bank, an addition of 5 more days should be added. Again, the additional number of days depends on the expected time needed for shipping documents to be sent from Hong Kong to ultimate buyer's country.

Bank of Shenzhen, Shenzhen

To: City Bank, Hong Kong
Fm: Bank of Shenzhen, Shenzhen
Date: Dec 01, 1998

We hereby issue our irrevocable documentary credit No. 1

Amount USD151,405.80 in favour of City I/E Limited, Tat Chee Avenue, Yau Yat Chuen, Kowloon for account of Shenzhen I/E Limited, Shenzhen Road, Shenzhen, China

Available by beneficiary's draft(s) at sight for 100-0/0 invoice value drawn on US

Marked as drawn under this credit and accompanied by the following documents:

1. Signed commercial invoice in 3 copies indicating contract No. and L/C No.

2. Full set of clean forwarding agents' cargo receipts made out to order and blank endorsed marked "Freight Prepaid" notifying applicant.

3. Packing list/weight memo in 3 copies showing quantity/gross and net weight for each package.

4. Certificate of quality in 3 copies issued by manufacturer.

5. Insurance policy/certificate covering overland transportation risks for at least 110-0/0 of the invoice value.

Evidencing shipment of:

17" glass bulb
Model: 888
Quantity: 8554 pcs with 1 PCT spare free of charge
Unit price: USD 17.70
CIF Shenzhen
Goods under contract No DX-88019
Shipment from Hong Kong to Shenzhen not later than Dec 31 1998
This credit is valid for negotiation in Hongkong until Jan 14 1998
(*The correct date should be Jan 14 1999*)

Partial shipment permitted transshipment prohibited.

Special instructions:

1.   All banking charges outside Shenzhen are for the beneficiary's account
2.   All documents are to be presented to us in one lot by speed post.

We hereby undertake that all drafts drawn under and in compliance with the terms and conditions of this credit will be duly honored on presentation at this office.

Subject to Uniform Customs and Practice for Documentary Credits 1993 revision International Chamber of Commerce Publication N° 500.

This telex is an operative instrument no confirmation follows. Please advise beneficiary.

For Bank of Shenzhen, Shenzhen Branch

This is a sample of a Bridge Master Credit
Issuing bank: Bank of Shenzhen, Shenzhen
Applicant: Shenzhen I/E Limited
Advising bank: City Bank, Hong Kong
Beneficiary: City I/E Limited, Hong Kong

APPLICATION FOR IRREVOCABLE DOCUMENTARY CREDIT

To: City Bank, Hong Kong   Date: 3 Dec, 1998

Please establish by ❑ airmail❑ brief cable ❑ full cable   an Irrevocable Documentary Credit as follows:

Applicant: City I/E Limited, Tat Chee Avenue, Yau Yat Chuen, Kowloon	Expiry Date: 21/12/1998
	In the country or district of the beneficiary
	Beneficiary: Hong Kong I/E Limited, Wanchai, Hong Kong
Advising Bank (if blank, any correspondent at your option)	Amount (in figures and words) USD ONE HUNDRED THIRTY SEVEN THOUSAND AND SEVEN HUNDRED NINETEEN AND CENTS FORTY ONLY. USD 137,719.40

Partial shipments ❑ allowed ❑ not allowed	Transhipment ❑ allowed ❑ not allowed	This credit is available against presentation of the beneficiary's draft(s) at xxx sight drawn on your bank, your correspondent or us at your option for full invoice value accompanied by the documents detailed herein.
Shipment from KOREA to HONG KONG Latest 15/12/1998		

List of documents to be presented:

1. Signed commercial invoice in quadruplicate.
2. Packing list in quadruplicate showing the gross, net weight and measurement.
3. Clean delivery order issued by shipping company made out or endorsed to order of our bank for account of applicant dated not later than 15, Dec 1998.
4. Marine insurance policy or certificate in duplicate endorsed in blank for 110 PCT. of CIF value covering Institute Cargo Clauses (A) Institute War Clauses (Cargo) and Institute Strikes Clauses (Cargo) showing claims payable at destination.
5. Beneficiary's certificate certifying that one set of non-negotiable documents has been sent to applicant immediately after shipment.
6. Beneficiary's certified copy of cable/telex or shipment advice to applicant advising details of shipment immediately after shipment.
7. Certificate of quality in triplicate issued by manufacturer, made out to whom it may concern.

Evidencing Shipment of: 17" Glass Bulb

   Quantity: 8554 PCS Plus 1% spare free of charge (86PCS) spare.
   Unit Price: USD16.10/PC
   Model No: 898 (*Model no. should be 888 as per master L/C*)
   CIF Hong Kong

Other terms and conditions: (These shall prevail over all printed terms in case of any apparent conflict).

   ❑ All banking charges outside Hong Kong are for account of beneficiary.
   ❑ Documents must be presented within 6 days after date of issuance of delivery order but within validity of the credit.

                         City Import/Export Limited
                         Hong Kong

                         _____
                         Signature of Applicant

Check Sheet
Bridge Credit

Date:

Name of applicant:	City I/E Limited

Amount of application form	USD 137,719.40	Credit proposal No:
❏ Back-to-Back letter of credit		☑ Bridge letter of credit
M/L/C No.:	1	Amount: USD 151,405.80
Name of M/L/C issuing bank:	Bank of Shenzhen, Shenzhen, China	
Status of beneficiary:	❏ to be checked ❏ in processing	❏ checked

Master letter of credit	Application form
Shipment from Hong Kong to Shenzhen	Shipment from Korea to Hong Kong
Partial shipment: ❏ Yes ❏ No	Partial shipment: ❏ Yes ❏ No
Transhipment: ❏ Yes ❏ No	Transhipment: ❏ Yes ❏ No
Shipment date: 31 December 1998	Shipment date: 15 December 1998[1]
Validity date: 14 January 1998 should change to 1999	Validity date: 21 December 1998[2]
Presentation date: Not Applicable	Presentation date: 6 days
Master L/C: Discrepancies/points to note	Application: Discrepancies/points to note
1. Expiry date amended to 14 January 1999	1. Goods to be transshipped in Hong Kong forwarder being approved by us
2. Purchase of insurance by our bank	2. Model number not strictly complied with master L/C. (898 not equal to 888 under MLC)

Suggestions for credit proposal	Remarks

First Check	Second Check	Manager	Approve	Reject

Upon receipt of an application for issuing a Bridge Credit, the bank staff may make use of the above Check Sheet to assess the application.

Notes:

1. Besides the same considerations as in a B/B credit, a bridge credit should consider the **time** needed for the **goods** shipped from the supplier to Hong Kong. Hence, a bigger difference of shipment date in the two credits is found in goods to be shipped from Europe to Hong Kong. The time needed fro taking delivering of goods and arrangement for onward carriage is an additional consideration.

   In practice, a difference of at least 15 days should be taken into account.

2. In general, a difference of at least 15 days should be taken into account for master credit to be expired in Hong Kong. If master credit expires at the counter of MLC issuing bank, an addition of five more days should be added. Again, the additional number of days depends on the expected time needed for shipping documents to be sent from Hong Kong to ultimate buyer's country.

City Bank Limited
Hong Kong

B/B Credit

ORIGINAL
PAGE 1

Date and Place of issue: 6 December 1998 Hong Kong	Irrevocable Documentary Credit Number 12345 Date and Place of Expiry: 21 December 1998 at our counter
Applicant: City I/E Limited, Hong Kong Tat Chee Avenue, Yau Yat Chuen Kowloon, Hong Kong	Beneficiary: Hong Kong I/E Limited, Wanchai, Hong Kong
Advising Bank: City Bank Limited, Hong Kong	Amount: USD 137,719.40 (United States Dollars One Hundred Thirty Seven Thousand Seven Hundred Nineteen and 40/100 only)
Partial Shipments are not allowed Transhipment is not allowed Shipment from Korea to Hong Kong	Credit available by payment against presentation of the documents detailed herein and of your draft(s) at sight drawn on our bank for full invoice value

List of documents to be presented:

1. Signed commercial invoice in quadruplicate.
2. Clean delivery order issued by shipping company made out or endorsed to order of our bank for account of applicant dated not later than 15 December 1998.
3. Marine insurance policy or certificate in duplicate endorsed in blank for 110 PCT of CIF value covering Institute Cargo Clauses (A) Institute War Clauses (Cargo) and Institute Strikes Clauses (Cargo) showing claims payable at destination.
4. Packing list/weight memo in quadruplicate showing quantity, the gross weight, net weight and measurement of each package.
5. Certificate of quality in triplicate issued by manufacturer, made out to whom it may concern.
6. Beneficiary's certificate certifying that one set of non-negotiable documents has been sent to applicant immediately after shipment.
7. Beneficiary's certified copy of cable/telex to applicant advising details of shipment immediately after shipment.

Covering shipment of:
8,554 pcs, 17" glass bulb
with 1% spare free of charge
Model No. 888

Unit price :   USD16.10/PC

(continue to next page)

We hereby issue this Documentary Credit in your favour. It is subject to the Uniform Customs and Practice for Documentary Credits (1993 Revision, International Chamber of Commerce. Paris, France, Publication N° 500) and engages us in accordance with the terms therefor, and especially in accordance with the terms of Article 9 thereof. The number and the date of the credit and the name of our bank must be quoted on all drafts required. If the credit is available by negotiation, each presentation must be noted on the reverse of this advise by the bank where the credit is available.

For City Bank Limited, Hong Kong

_____
authorized signature(s)

City Bank Limited
Hong Kong

CONTINUATION OF IRREVOCABLE DOCUMENTARY CREDIT NUMBER	Credit number 123

Other terms and conditions:

1. Copy of cable/telex and certificate of quality must not show this L/C number, value of shipment, unit price, trade term, invoice/contract/order number and date, name and address of L/C issuing bank and L/C applicant.

2. Documents under this credit must be presented to our bank through your banker within 6 days after the date of delivery order but within credit validity.

3. This credit is payable:

   (1) In HKD at bank's O/D buying rate prevailing on the date of payment or payable in USD by demand draft on New York less commission in lieu of exchange: or

   (2) By TT reimbursement, in that case, commission in lieu of exchange, cable charges and transit interest are for account of beneficiary.

4. Delivery order must show shipment arrival date.

* * * END OF L/C * * *

(This L/C consists of 2 pages)

Yours faithfully
For City Bank Limited Hong Kong

_____
Authorized Signatures

This is the contiuation of a Bridge Credit issued by City Bank, HK in favour of a Hong Kong supplier.

8 Practical Points to Note in the Issue of a Bridge Credit

(a) Trade terms may be different.

(b) Make sure that your customer must be proficient in shipping practices.

(c) Upon receipt of documents, examine them before releasing bills of lading to forwarding agent for onward carriage.

(d) It is advisable in the bridge credit to call for a set of non-negotiable copy of shipping documents either to B/B L/C applicant or issuing bank so that B/B L/C issuing bank can have more time to check the documents before the issue of a shipping guarantee to take delivery of goods for onward carriage.

(e) Make sure that the appointed forwarding agent is a reliable party with high efficiency as the time allowed for document checking and transhipment arranged by us and onward carriage by forwarder is very limited.

9 Back-to-Back Credit vs Transferable Credit

9.1 Similarities

(a) Both credits involve a middleman as the initiator.

(b) Except in total transfer, both credits involve substitution of documents by the middleman.

(c) In both credits, the terms and conditions are about the same as their respective original credits except:

(1) Back-to-Back credit amount/transfer credit amount;

(2) expiry dates;

(3) latest shipment dates (can be the same as original credits);

(4) insured amount if any.

9.2 Differences

Back-to-Back Credit	Transferable Credit
1. Two separate credits are involved. Based on the deposit of the master credit as a source of repayment, B/B credit issuing bank gives an independent undertaking to pay the second beneficiary. This undertaking is independent of the underlying first transaction and remains valid irrespective of whether proceeds can be obtained from master credit issuing bank.	1. In total transfer, the original credit is endorsed by transferring bank and sent to second beneficiary. In partial transfer, the original credit is kept by transferring bank or its customer. Transferring bank transfers a credit usually by means of making a photostatic copy or a telex message of the original credit and have it sent to the transferee.
2. It can be issued by any bank at its own discretion.	2. Transfer is only restricted to the bank where the credit is available.
3. Subject to all rules under UCP–500.	3. Specifically covered by Article 48 UCP–500. Transferring bank must comply with Art 48 in transfer.
4. It will not be stipulated as "B/B credit allowed" in the master credit.	4. It is necessary to be designated as transferable in the original credit.
5. A long chain of transactions is allowed	5. Transfer is restricted to one time only. Further transfer from the transferee is prohibited.
6. The bank issuing the B/B credits is primarily liable to pay the supplier.	6. Transferring bank has no payment obligation to the supplier. It is the original credit issuing bank which undertakes to pay the supplier.
7. B/B credit allows to some extent flexibility in credit terms between the two credits; e.g. currency differences, extra documents submitted by supplier.	7. Less flexible and alterations are allowed only in areas strictly in accordance with Art 48 UCP–500. Especially, currency cannot be changed

12

Red Clause Credit, Revolving Credit and Standby Credit

❑ Meaning of a red clause credit

❑ Additional risks to issuing bank in the issue of a red clause credit

❑ Steps taken by issuing bank to protect its own interest

❑ Green clause credit

❑ Meaning of a revolving credit

❑ Meaning of a standby credit

❑ Possible protection to be added by the issuing bank in a standby credit

❑ International Standby Practices ISP 98 ICC Publication N° 590

1 Meaning of a Red Clause Credit

A red clause credit is a special type of credit with a clause inserted which authorizes the advising or confirming bank to make advances to the beneficiary before presentation of the documents.

The credit is so called because the clause was originally typed in red ink in the manual typewriter to draw the beneficiary's attention. The clause is added at the request of the DC applicant who instructs the issuing bank to incorporate such a clause in the credit. It specifies a certain percentage of the DC amount (or a fixed sum) to be given to the beneficiary before he delivers goods. This type of finance is known as pre-shipment finance, which is usually in the form of a loan from the advising/confirming bank to the beneficiary at the request of issuing bank.

Finance is given to the beneficiary against his undertaking to the financing bank (advising/confirming bank) that he promises to ship the goods and submit documents in strict compliance with DC terms and conditions. If he fails to ship the goods and default in payment of the pre-shipment finance, the financing bank has a right of recourse to the instructing bank (i.e., the issuing bank) for the amount advanced plus interest. The issuing bank, in turn, has a right of recourse against the applicant.

Sometimes, instead of asking the advising bank/confirming bank to finance the beneficiary on its behalf, the issuing bank may give a pre-shipment undertaking in an alternative way which is more popular in Hong Kong. The beneficiary is instructed to draw a set of draft on issuing bank, together with an undertaking to ship goods and present compliant documents. This set of draft and the undertaking are sent for payment (pre-shipment finance) to issuing bank, which then remits the proceeds to the beneficiary. Again, if the beneficiary fails to ship the goods and default in repayment, issuing bank has a right of recourse to the DC applicant. In most cases, issuing bank may have taken additional security to back up the amount of the pre-shipment finance.

The following example is a red clause credit commonly found in Hong Kong:

Credit Amount : HK$62,500
<u>List of Documents to be Presented</u>

Terms of Payment

Advance payment(s) up to 25 PCT, of total invoice value USD15,625. (Says US dollars) Fifteen Thousand Six Hundred Twenty Five Only) will be paid against presentation of the following documents:

1. Beneficiary's drafts at sight in duplicate drawn on our bank.

2. Beneficiary's undertaking certifying to deliver all of the goods within the delivery date and to present full set of document in full compliance with the terms and conditions of this credit.

Second payment upto USD 46,875. (Says US dollars Forty Six Thousand Eight Hundred Seventy Five Only) against presentation of the following documents:

1. Beneficiary's draft at sight drawn on our bank for 75PCT of invoice value.

2. Signed commercial invoice in quadruplicate.

3. Official cargo receipt issued and signed by authorised person of the applicant (whose signature must be in conformity with our file) certifying that the actual quantity of the goods had been received in good order and condition.

2 Additional Risks to the Issuing Bank in the Issue of a Red Clause Credit

(a) The beneficiary may misuse the funds advanced to him and may not make the shipment and present documents under the credit.

(b) Issuing bank is directly liable for the repayment of that advance plus interest to the advising bank.

(c) Beneficiary after obtaining the advance from the advising bank may negotiate the documents with another bank if the credit is available with any bank by negotiation.

(d) Applicant may go into insolvency/difficulty and may not be able to honour his commitment.

(e) Enforcement of the beneficiary's undertaking letter may be difficult and time consuming because issuing bank and beneficiary normally are in different countries.

3　Steps Taken by the Issuing Bank to Protect Its Own Interest

(a) Credit should be issued nominating a bank for negotiation. It is advisable to nominate the bank giving the advance being the negotiating bank. (i.e., restrict negotiation to advising bank)

(b) Should specifically mention the amount of the advance to be made by either specifying the percentage of the credit amount or a fixed sum.

(c) Should specify whether the interest for the advance is for account of the beneficiary or for account of the issuing bank (normally such charges are to be borne by beneficiary).

(d) Should specify if the advance is to be made in the currency of the credit or in the currency of the beneficiary's country (normally in the currency of the credit).

(e) Should incorporate an undertaking clause undertaking to pay the advising bank (or the issuing bank) the amount advanced plus the interest and bank charges should the beneficiary not export the goods.

(f) The portion of pre-shipment finance should be further supported by tangible security.

4　Green Clause Credit

(a) Sometimes, it may be very risky for a bank to issue a red clause credit for its customer as the issuing bank has no control over the goods.

(b) In green clause credit, the advances are made by the advising bank upon the beneficiary producing a warehouse receipt, thereby overcoming the weakness of a red clause credit.

(c) Warehouse receipts are made out in the name of the bank actually making the advance.

(d) Advising bank retains the control over the goods.

(e) Goods are released for shipment by the warehouse keeper on the instruction of the advising bank.

(f) Green clause credit is rarely seen in Hong Kong

5 Meaning of a Revolving Credit

A revolving credit is a credit which provides for the amount of the credit to be renewed (in practice known as reinstated) automatically after use without the need to renew the credit every time.

It can revolve with respect to either:

(a) time, or

(b) amount (i.e., total value of the credit).

A revolving credit "with respect to time" can be cumulative or non-cumulative.

A cumulative revolving credit allows any unused credit amount of a previous period to be carried forward to the next period.

A non-cumulative revolving credit, on the other hand, provides for a maximum amount of credit to be drawn for each period. If the exporter fails to use up the maximum amount allowed to be drawn for that period, the amount in that period (full amount or any utilized balance as the cases may be) will be forfeited automatically. "Period" is in terms of weekly, fortnightly, monthly, bi-monthly or quarterly. It is popular to see monthly revolving credit in Hong Kong. Table 12.1 is an illustration:

Table 12.1
Revolving with Respect to Time: (Cum vs Non-Cum)

Month	Each month	Cum	Non-Cum
1	100,000	100,000	100,000
2	100,000	60,000	60,000
3	100,000	140,000	100,000
4	100,000	100,000	20,000
5	100,000	100,000	100,000
6	100,000	100,000	100,000
7	100,000	100,000	100,000
8	100,000	100,000	100,000
9	100,000	100,000	100,000
10	100,000	100,000	100,000
11	100,000	80,000	80,000
12	100,000	120,000	100,000
Total	1,200,000	1,200,000	1,060,000

A revolving credit "with respect to amount" allows the credit amount to be renewed as soon as the exporter presents his shipping documents and uses up the credit amount. As the issuing bank theoretically may incur unlimited liability, this type of revolving credit is rarely seen unless some kinds of restriction are added (refer the following example).

Luk's Printing Company intends to import 10 tons of paper each month at USD10,000/ton (total USD 100,000) from a supplier in China for the next 12 months

Luk's Printing Company has to open one D/C each month (12 separate D/C) in order to import the same goods.

It can, as an alternative, open a revolving credit for USD100,000 in favour of the beneficiary to be revolved each month for same amount for the coming 12 months. Hence, at the start of each month, USD 100,000 is automatically available to the printing company.

5.1 Circumstances for Issuing a Revolving Credit

If an importer is trading with an overseas exporter and buying the same goods on a regular basis, with the same terms and conditions and at the same unit price, he can issue a revolving credit to this exporter instead of having to issue a credit with same terms and conditions every time.

This will save him time and the trouble of having to apply for many credits.

6 Revolving Credit: Steps Taken by the Issuing Bank to Protect the Applicant

(a) In order to ensure that beneficiary is going to ship goods up to standard in each shipment, the following clause can be added: "This is a revolving credit re-available to the beneficiary only upon your receipt of our authenticated telecommunication advice stating that the credit amount is re-available for drawing."

(b) In order to ensure minimum quantity of goods shipped in each shipment, the following clause can be added. "This credit is cumulative but if the credit is not drawn for a minimum amount of USD 80,000 in any calendar month, the credit ceases to be available for that month and for the remaining validity of the credit."

(c) In order to restrict the maximum liability in a revolving credit with respect to amount, issuing bank can add following clause:

> "This is a Revolving letter of credit with respect to amount which will be revolved for three times only with each shipment by amount of USD 83,200.00 (say, US dollars Eighty Three Thousand Two Hundred Only) covering 800 sets of goods and totally not exceeding USD 332,800.00 (say, US dollars Three Hundred Thirty Two Thousand Eight Hundred Only).

Each drawing must be for USD 83,200.00 covering 800 sets of goods. The total drawing under this credit must not exceed USD 332,800.00. Expiry date is 31 December 1998."

7 Meaning of a Standby Credit

A standby credit is a guarantee type of documentary credit. It might be in many forms such as pure loan form, bid bond and performance guarantee form, etc. The situation described below is a pure loan type standby credit.

A standby credit is opened at the request of the applicant in favour of a correspondent bank in a foreign country (the beneficiary) to provide a foreign customer with banking facilities under certain terms and conditions.

On receipt of the D/C, the correspondent bank notifies the foreign customer, stating that a credit line is available and at his disposal. Then, the foreign customer is instructed to sign an undertaking to the correspondent bank to the effect that he promises to repay the bank for the facility he has used and the amount remained unpaid. The correspondent bank is willing to grant the credit line as he has two undertakings to be repaid, one from the customer, the other one from the standby issuing bank.

At the expiry date, the bank is authorized draw under the credit for repayment of debts in the event of failure of the foreign customer to make good his payment. A signed statement from the correspondent bank is required to certify the sum unpaid in case of default by the foreign customer.

A standby credit can also be in another form with same effect as a guarantee against the default in payment of the applicant (see Chapter 13).

8 Possible Protection to be Added by the Issuing Bank in a Standby Credit

(a) Inclusion of a cancellation clause in the credit to the effect that if the applicant submits a certificate to state that he had fulfilled his obligation, then the credit will be cancelled automatically.

(b) Applicant to insist that the certificate of default issued by a public surveyor.

(c) Issuing bank restricts its undertaking to pay liquidated damage only in the sense that its liability is limited to the beneficiary's actual loss.

9 International Standby Practices ISP 98 ICC Publication N° 590

9.1 Introduction

In the past, many standby credits have been issued subject to the UCP. It has long been apparent that the UCP was not fully applicable to standby credits. More complex standby credits such as those involving longer terms or automatic extensions, requesting that the beneficiary to issue its own undertaking to another, etc., require more specialized rules of practice.

The long-awaited Rules on International Standby Practices (ISP 98) are published recently after five years in preparation. It reflects generally accepted practice, custom, and usage of standby letters of credit. Moreover, it provides separate rules for standby letters of credit in the same sense that the UCP–500 does for commercial letters of credit.

9.2 Similarity of ISP and UCP

The ISP 98, like the UCP–500 for commercial letters of credit, simplifies, standardizes, and streamlines the drafting of standbys, and provides clear and widely accepted answers to common problems. Even where the two rules overlap, however, the ISP 98 is more precise, stating the intent implied in the UCP rule, in order to make the standby more dependable when a drawing or honour is questioned.

9.3   Differences of ISP and UCP

The ISP 98 differs from the UCP in style and approach because it must receive acceptance not only from bankers and merchants, but also from a broader range of those actively involved in standby law and practice, corporate treasurers and credit managers, rating agencies, government agencies and regulators, and indenture trustees as well as their counsel.

Because standbys are intended to be available in the event of disputes or applicant insolvency, their texts are subject to a degree of scrutiny not encountered in the commercial letter of credit context. As a result, ISP 98 is also written to provide guidance to lawyers and judges in the interpretation of standby practice.

9.4   Uses and Various Types of Standby Credit

Standby credits are issued to support payment, when due or after default, of obligations based on money loaned or advanced, or upon the occurrence or non-occurrence of another contingency.

According to ISP 98, standby credits are classified into the following types based on their function in the underlying transaction or other factors not necessarily related to the terms and conditions of the standby itself:

(a)   Performance Standby Credit — it supports an obligation to perform other than to pay money including for the purpose of covering losses arising from a default of the applicant in completion of the underlying transactions.

(b)   Advance Payment Standby Credit — it supports an obligation to account for an advance payment made by the beneficiary to the Applicant.

(c)   A Bid Bond/Tender Bond Standby Credit — it supports an obligation of the applicant to execute a contract if the applicant is awarded a bid.

(d) Counter Standby Credit — it supports the issuance of a separate standby or other undertaking by the beneficiary of the counter standby credit.

(e) Financial Standby Credit — it supports an obligation to pay money, including an instrument evidencing an obligation to repay borrowed money.

(f) Direct Pay Standby Credit — it supports payment when due of an underlying payment obligation typically in connection with a financial standby without regard to a default.

(g) Insurance Standby Credit — it supports an insurance or reinsurance obligation of the applicant.

(h) Commercial Standby Credit — it supports the obligations of an applicant to pay for goods or services in the event of non-payment by other methods.

For the ISP to apply for a standby credit, an undertaking should be made subject to these Rules by including language such as:

"This undertaking is issued subject to the International Standby Practices 1998 or Subject to ISP 98."[1]

Note

1.   *International Standby Practices ISP 98*, International Chamber of Commerce.

The following two types of Standby Credit are popularly found in Hong Kong:

Sample of a Pure-Loan-Type Standby Credit

To: Bank of New York
Fm: City Bank, Hong Kong
For USD 150,000.00

We open irrevocable stand-by letter of credit no. 123 up to an aggregate amount of USD 150,000 in your favour for account of New York Company Limited, 470 Scott Ave. Brooklyn New York N.Y. 12345 U.S.A. applicant: Hong Kong Trading Ltd, 1/F, Block C, King Ford Bldg, 26-32 Kwai Hei St, Hong Kong available by negotiation of your right draft drawn on us. You are authorized to make advances in the form of various general banking facilities to New York Company Limited, New York Street, NY 12345 USA for a period not exceeding 31 January 1999. If New York Company Limited fails to repay the advance, you may draw under this credit accompanied by the following document:

Your signed certificate stating that the amount of such draft represents the unpaid balance of principal and interest on various general banking facilities made available by you to New York Company Ltd.

We hereby engage with the drawers and/or the bona fide holders that the draft so drawn and accompanied by the certificate shall be duly honoured by us upon presentation. This standby letter of credit will expire on 31 January 1999 at our counter in Hong Kong.

This standby letter of credit is subject to the Uniform Customs and Practice for Documentary Credits (1993 revision) I.C.C. Publication N° 500. This is an operative instrument and no confirmation will follow.

Sample of a Performance-Type Standby Credit

Applicant: Hong Kong City Development Co. Ltd.
Beneficiary:Guanzhou City Import and Export Corporation

Test 16 July 1998

> We open irrevocable standby D/C12345 for USD 85,033 favouring Guanzhou City import and export corporation Lianxin Road, Guanzhou, PRC for account of Hong Kong City Development Co. Ltd.

Available by negotiation of beneficiary's sight draft(s), drawn on us accompanied by the following documents:

> Beneficiary's certificate certifying that the applicant, Hong Kong City Development Co. Ltd. has received from beneficiary down payment of USD 85,033 but has not effected shipment of machinery for the production of needle punch non-wovens in accordance with documentary credit no. 67890 issued by Bank of Guanzhou, Guanzhou branch for the A/C of Guanzhou City import and export corporation in favour of Hong Kong City Development Co. Ltd.

Other Conditions:

1. This L/C is effective only if the beneficiary remits to the applicant's USD account no, 000888-8 opened at our bank on or before 25 July 1998, the sum of USD 85,033.00 being 25% of the invoice value for machinery for the production of needle punch non-wovens. To this effect a tested telex from our bank will be sent confirming that a remittance of USD 85,033 has been received by Hong Kong City Development Co. Ltd.

2. The beneficiary may collect interest on the sum of USD 85,033 at the rate of 5.25% per annum from the receipt date of the remittance to the date when the documents are presented for negotiation under this L/C.

3. The expiry date of this L/C is 15 Sept. 1998 at our counter.

13

Various Types of Bonds in International Trade

- ❑ Tender guarantee/bid bond/tender bond
- ❑ Characteristics of a tender guarantee
- ❑ Illustrations of tender guarantee
- ❑ Advance payment guarantee/advance payment bond
- ❑ Illustration of an advance payment guarantee
- ❑ Performance guarantee/Performance bond
- ❑ Illustration of a performance guarantee/performance bond
- ❑ Warranty bond
- ❑ Standby credit as an alternative to various bonds
- ❑ Illustrations of standby credit

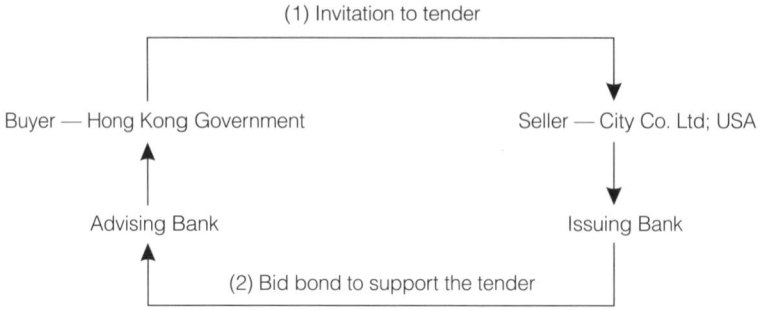

1 Tender Guarantee/Bid Bond/Tender Bond

Suppose HKSAR invites overseas companies to tender for a contract to build a new highway in Tung Chung, there will be at least several tendering companies for the Government to choose. What the Government worries are: if, for example, City Company Limited, USA is awarded the contract, it will not, for one reason or another, accept the contract. In that case, the Government is most likely to suffer losses in terms of time and administrative cost. Hence, the Government requests a bid bond (tender bond) issued by the bidder's banker against the risk that the bidder, once being awarded the contract, will not withdraw from it afterwards. If the bidder fails to proceed with the contracted work, the issuing bank (bid-bond giver, bid-bond issuer) will compensate the beneficiary of the bid bond (i.e., Government) for a certain percentage of the contract. Hence, it is the bond giver which stands in the shoes of the bidder to give a better promise to the Government that the bidder will proceed to sign the contract. Otherwise, the beneficiary can claim compensation from the bond giver.

Since a bid-bond issuer gives a definite promise to the beneficiary on behalf of its customer, he has no accompanying goods as security as in the case of a D/C. Hence, a bond giver will not issue a bid bond unless counter indemnity is taken from its customer. Usually, security in the form of full margin or other forms of tangible security is required from the customer. Meanwhile, the bond giver will reserve a right of recourse to its customer if the overseas beneficiary exercises his right to claim under the bond.

1.1 Characteristics of a Tender Guarantee (Bid Bond)

(a) This is a kind of service to the exporter who is going to tender for an export contract, usually involving a large project from an overseas buyer.

(b) As a condition of the tender, the overseas buyer demands a bid bond issued by the exporter's banker against the risk. The exporter (known as the contractor) who has been offered the contract, will accept it. If the exporter fails to accept it, then, the buyer can claim compensation from the bond giver, in which case, 2–5% of the value of the contract will be compensated to the overseas buyer.

(c) The bank, in effect, stands in the shoes of the exporter and gives support and evidence of the good standing of the contractor to the buyer who may be an overseas government).

(d) Since it is risky for the bank to issue a bid bond, counter-indemnity will be taken from the contractor, with a right of recourse to the contractor.

A good sample of a Tender Guarantee (Bid Bond) can be found in the following pages.

12 December 1998

Issuer	:	City Bank Company Limited, USA
Applicant	:	City Company Limited, USA
Beneficiary	:	Hong Kong Government, HK

Hong Kong Government,
Hong Kong Road,
Hong Kong

Re: Our Bid Security No. 1 for Bid No. 1
        HKG/HW No. 1 for Building a Highway in Tung Chung

This guarantee is hereby issued to serve as a Bid Security of City Company Limited, U.S.A. (hereinafter called the "Bidder") for Bid No. 1 for building a highway in Tung Chung for Hong Kong Government, Hong Kong Road, Hong Kong.

City Bank Company Limited, U.S.A. hereby unconditionally and irrevocably guarantees and binds itself, its successors and assigns to pay Company immediately without recourse, the sum of USD 2,021,196.00 (Say, United States Dollars Two Million Twenty One Thousand One Hundred and Ninety Six Only) representing two percent of the bid value, upon receipt of your written certification stating any of the following:

(a)   the Bidder has withdrawn his bid after the time and date of the bid opening and before the expiration of its validity period; or

(b)   the Bidder has failed to enter into Contract with you within thirty (30) calendar days after the notification of Contract award; or

(c)   The Bidder has failed to establish acceptable Performance Security within thirty (30) calendar days after receipt the Notification of Award. It is fully understood that this guarantee takes effect from the date of the bid opening, 20 November 1997, and shall remain valid for a period of 120 calendar days thereafter, and during the period of any extension thereof that may be agreed upon between you and the Bidder with notice to us, unless sooner terminated and or released by you.

This guarantee shall remain valid and in full force and effect until 20 March 1999 being the expiry date.

Any claims received by us after the expiry date will be treated as null and void whether this Guarantee is return to us for cancellation or not.

City Bank Company Limited
N.Y.
U.S.A

A seller's banker overseas issues a bid bond in favour of Hong Kong Government.

Our Bond No. 2

BY THIS BOND dated the 1st day of May 1998.

City Bank, Hong Kong Branch, whose registered office is at Tat Chee Avenue, Hong Kong, (the "Bondsman") is irrevocably and unconditionally bound to the Government of Hong Kong, together with its successors and assigns (the "Government") for payment of a sum of HKD1,380,000.00 (the "Bonded Sum") in accordance with the provisions of this Bond.

WHEREAS

(A) The Government has invited tenders for the supply, installation and commissioning of a Radiation System (hereinafter referred to as "the System").

(B) City Development Company Limited, Hong Kong ("the Tenderer") has submitted a response ("the Tender") to the Government's invitation.

(C) In consideration of the Government supplying to the Tenderer draft contract documents and agreeing to consider and examine the Tender, the Tenderer has agreed to keep the Tender open for acceptance without unilaterally varying or amending its terms for a period of 6 months and, if the Tender is accepted, to provide a performance bond as due security for due performance of the contract thereby formed in accordance with Conditions of Contract as set out in the tender document issued by the Government in connection with the System (together "the Tender Obligations") and to provide a Bond in the terms thereof.

(D) At the request and for the account of the Tenderer, the Bondsman has agreed to guarantee to the Government the due performance by the Tenderer of the Tender Obligations subject to the terms and conditions of this Bond and limits of the Bondsman's liability hereunder.

NOW THE TERMS AND CONDITIONS of this Bond are:

1. The Bondsman hereby irrevocably and unconditionally undertakes to pay to the Government the Bonded Sum upon receipt from the Government of a written demand accompanied by a Certificate signed by the Director of Radiation Supplies, or, in his absence, the person acting in his stead, on behalf of the Government stating that the Tenderer is in default of one or other of the Tender Obligations.

2. The Bondsman shall pay to the Government forthwith the amount thus demanded without requiring further evidence or proof of the default of the Tenderer.

3. The liability of the Bondsman under this Bond shall remain in full force and effect notwithstanding and shall not be affected or discharged in any way by and the Bondsman hereby waives notice of:

   (i)   any amendment to the Tender by agreement between the Government and the Tenderer or any concession or wavier by the Government in respect of the Tender Obligations;

   (ii)   any forbearance or wavier of any right of action or remedy the Government may have against the Tenderer or negligence by the Government in enforcing any such right of action or remedy;

   (iii) any other bond, undertaking, security or guarantee held or obtained by the Government for any of the Tender Obligations or under the contract formed by any acceptance of the Tender or otherwise pursuant to the Tender or any release or wavier thereof;

(continue to next page)

     (iv)   any act or omission of the Tenderer pursuant to any other arrangements with the Bondsman.

4.   The liability of the Bondsman under this Bond shall cease on whichever of the following events first occurs:

     (i)   notification in writing by the Government to the Tenderer of the termination of the tendering process for the System; or

     (ii)   acceptance by the Government of any other tender for the implementation of the System; or

     (iii) provision by the Tenderer of a performance bond in respect of its obligations under and in accordance with the terms of contract formed by acceptance of the Tender or otherwise pursuant to the Tender: or

     (iv) the expiry of 90 days after the end of the tender validity period specified in the Conditions of Tender as set out in the tender document issued by the Government in connection with the System or of such further period (after the expiry of such 90 days period) as the Bondsman may specify by notice in writing to the Government in the absence of prior service of a demand under this Bond.

     (v)   payment by the Bondsman of the Bonded Sum in full to the Government.

5.   The Government shall be entitled to assign the benefit of this Bond at any time without the consent of the Bondsman or the Tenderer being required.

6.   All documents arising out of or in connection with this Bond shall be served:

     (i)   upon the Government represented by the Director of Radiation Supplies at Hong Kong Street, Hong Kong, marked for the attention of the Director of Radiation Supplies.

     (ii)   upon the Bondsman at Tat Chee Avenue, Kowloon Tong, Hong Kong, the Government and the Bondsman may change their respective nominated addresses for service of documents to another address in Hong Kong by prior written notice to the other.

7.   All demands and notices must be in writing and must be served by hand or registered mail.

8.   This Bond shall be governed by and construed according to Hong Kong law.

IN WITNESS WHEREOF this Bond has been executed as a deed on the date first before written.

For and on behalf of
City Bank
Tat Chee Avenue Branch

in the presence of:

A local bank issues a bid bond in favour of Hong Kong Government for account of its customer for the supply, installation and commissioning of a Radiation System.

In bid bond/tender bond/tender guarantee, issuing bank should add at least the following clauses to protect itself and the applicant:

We hereby guarantee the payment to you on demand up to _____ in the event of your awarding the relative contract to the applicant and of its failing to sign the contract in the terms of its tender, or in the event of the applicant withdrawing its tender before expiry of this guarantee without your consent.

1. This guarantee shall come into force on (COMMENCEMENT DATE) being the closing date for tenders, and will expire at close of banking hours at this office on (EXPIRY DATE).

2. Any claim thereunder must be received in writing at this office before Expiry accompanied by your signed statement that the Applicant has been awarded the relative contract and has failed to sign the contract awarded in the terms of its tender or has withdrawn its tender before expiry date without your consent and such claim and statement shall be accepted as conclusive evidence that the amount claimed is due to you under this guarantee.

3. Upon Expiry this guarantee shall become null and void, whether returned to us for cancellation or not and any claim or statement received after expiry shall be ineffective.

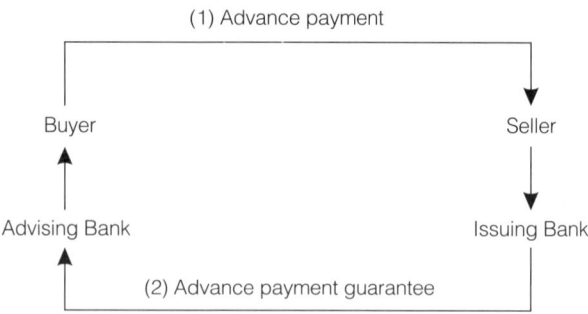

2   Advance Payment Guarantee/Advance Payment Bond

This is a kind of service to the exporter who has received a downpayment or an advance payment from an overseas buyer who is unwilling to depart with the downpayment without protection.

The overseas buyer requests a guarantee given by exporter's banker to refund advance payment that have already been made by the overseas buyer to the exporter. The guarantee is to provide against the risk that the exporter fails to fulfil the terms and conditions under the contract after he has received the advance payment. It is common for construction industry or companies selling machines to ask for a downpayment from buyers. The buyer under the bond can make a bond call if necessary to recover any advance payment already made to the exporter.

The following is a good sample of an advance payment bond/guarantee.

A seller in Hong Kong known as City Company Limited who receives an advance payment from Shanghai Industrial Corporation, Shanghai, applies an advance payment bond from his banker, City Bank, Hong Kong.

Date   3 February 1999

To: Shanghai Bank, Shanghai
From: CityBank, Tat Chee Avenue Branch, Hong Kong

Issuing Bank   :   City Bank, Tat Chee Avenue Branch, Hong Kong
Applicant   :   City Company Limited, Hong Kong, a seller who has received an
                     advance payment.
Advising Bank   :   Shanghai Bank, Shanghai, China
Beneficiary   :   Shanghai Industrial Corporation, Shanghai, China

Re: Advance Payment Guarantee No.
       For USD 45,000.00 in favour of Shanghai Industrial Corporation, Shanghai, China

We hereby issue a letter of guarantee no. 12345 up to USD 45,000.00 to undertake and indemnify Shanghai Industrial Corporation for any loss which may incur as a result of City Company Limited, Hong Kong, upon receipt of a downpayment, failed to deliver the goods to Shanghai Industrial Corporation before the end of May 1999 under contract no. 1 dated 24 November 1998. Payment under this guarantee will be effected against beneficiary's certificate certifying that City Company Limited has failed to deliver the goods to Shanghai Industrial Corporation, Shanghai before the end of May 1999 under contract no. 1 dated 24 November 1998.

This letter of guarantee will in every case expire on 15 June 1999 at our counter and it will automatically become null and void as soon as we received a non-negotiable bill of lading from City Company Limited evidencing that the goods have been delivered before the end of May 1999 according to contract no. 1 dated 24 November 1998.

This letter of guarantee shall be effective only upon our issue of a tested telex to you, Shanghai Bank, Shanghai confirming that we have received remittance USD 45,000.00 in favour of City Company Limited, Hong Kong from Shanghai Industrial Corporation, Shanghai.

This is an operative instrument and no confirmation follows please advise beneficiary.

The following sample is a special type of standby credit which serves the function as an advance payment guarantee. Note that a standby credit has the advantage that it is issued subject to UCP–500.

In advance payment bond or this type of standby credit, issuing bank should add the following clauses to protect itself and its applicant.

We hereby guarantee to refund to you (beneficiary) on demand up to _____ in the event of the applicant failing to fulfil the contract.

1. Claims and statements as aforesaid must bear the confirmation of your Bankers that the signatories thereon are authorized to sign.

2. This guarantee shall become operative only upon issue of a tested telex (may be in the form of an amendment) making it effective, which will be issued upon receipt by us of written confirmation from the Applicant that the latter has received the Advance Payment. (or as an alternative, the following clause is added: This guarantee shall become operative automatically upon receipt of the Advance Payment of (AMOUNT IN FIGURES) for the account of (APPLICANTS) at our office.

3. Upon Expiry, this guarantee shall become null and void, whether returned to us for cancellation or not and any claim or statement received after expiry shall be ineffective.

Date of issue   16 July 1999
Issuing Bank: City Bank, Hong Kong
Applicant: City Development Company Limited, Hong Kong
                     (seller who has received an advance payment from buyer)
Advising Bank: Bank of Guanzhou, Guanzhou
Beneficiary: Guanzhou Industry Corporation, Guanzhou, China

We open irrevocable standby DC 128 for USD 85,033.00 favouring Guangzhou Industry Corporation, Lianxin Road, Guangzhou, China Account City Development Co. Ltd, Hong Kong Road, Hong Kong, available by negotiation of beneficiary's draft(s) at sight drawn on us accompanied by the following documents:

1. Beneficiary's certificate certifying that the applicant, City Development Co. Ltd. has received an advance payment being USD 85,033 but has not effected shipment of machinery for the production of needle punch non-wovens in accordance with contract.

Other conditions:

1. This L/C is effective only if the beneficiary remits to the applicant's USD account no. opened at our bank on or before 25 July 1999 the sum of USD 85,033.00 being 25% of the invoice value for machinery for the production of needle punch non-wovens. To this effect a tested telex from our bank will be sent confirming that a remittance of USD 85,033.00 has been received by City Development Co. Ltd.

2. The beneficiary may collect interest on the sum of USD 85,033.00 at the rate of 5% per annum from the receipt date of the remittance to the date when the documents are presented for payment under this L/C.

3. The expiry date of this L/C is 15 September 1999 at our counter.
   The remitting bank is requested to send all documents to us in one registered airmail.

Reimbursement claim:
We shall credit your USD A/C with us.

This credit is subject to Uniform Customs and Practice for Documentary Credits (1993 revision) I.C.C. N° 500. This is an operative instrument and no confirmation follows Please advise beneficiary.

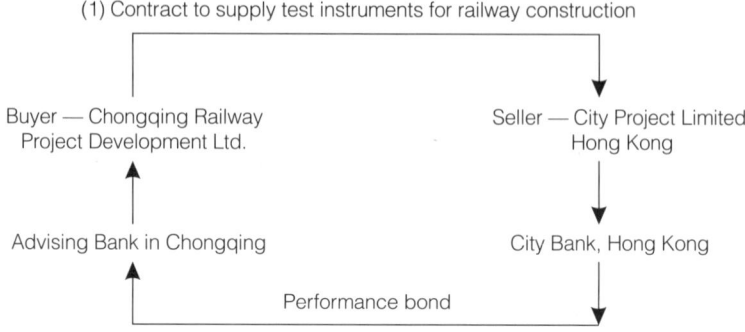

(1) Contract to supply test instruments for railway construction

Buyer — Chongqing Railway Project Development Ltd.

Seller — City Project Limited, Hong Kong

Advising Bank in Chongqing

City Bank, Hong Kong

Performance bond

3   Performance Guarantee/Performance Bond

(a) It is a written instrument, issued by a bank or a surety company (e.g., insurance company), stating that the exporter will comply with the terms of the contract with the buyer, or the performance is up to buyer's satisfaction. Otherwise, the buyer will receive compensation for any losses suffered as a result of the exporter's failure to perform under the contract.

(b) Usually, the tender of a performance bond is demanded by overseas/local buyers to replace a bid bond when the bid bond expires. This is common for the contractor who wants to bid for an overseas/local project. Among other terms, he is required to arrange a performance bond issued in favour of the relevant government department (overseas buyer) when the bid bond expires.

(c) If the contractor fails to carry out the responsibility of the contract, the bank will take up the responsibility to pay the government department.

(d) Usually, tangible security is required for the issue of the bond and in return, the bank will charge a fee for the risk taken and the service provided.

The following sample is a standard performance guarantee:

A Hong Kong exporter is going to supply test instruments for the construction of a railway project in Chongqing, China. This is a performance bond issued by City Bank, Hong Kong for the Hong Kong exporter in favour of the buyer in Chongqing, China.

In performance bond/performance guarantee, issuing bank may add the following clauses to protect itself and the applicant:

We hereby guarantee the payment to you on demand up to _____ in the event of the applicant failing to fulfil the contract against the following documents:

1. Your signed statement that the Applicant has failed to fulfil the Contract and
2. An independent third party's certificate, certifying that applicant has failed to fulfil the contract. Or
3. A public Surveyor's Report, certifying that applicant has failed to fulfil the contract.

---

1 January 1998

Chongqing Railway Project Development Limited,
Chongqing Road,
Chongqing, China

Gentleman:

Our performance Guarantee No. 3

This guarantee is hereby issued to serve as the Performance, Security of City Project Limited, Hong Kong (hereinafter called the "Seller") for Contract No.: 3 dated December 1997 between you and the Seller for supply of one lot of Test Instruments as detailed in the contract (hereinafter called the "Goods") for Chongqing Railway Project (hereinafter called the "Project").

City Bank, Hong Kong Branch (hereinafter called the "Bank") hereby unconditionally and irrevocably guarantees and binds itself, its successors and assigns to pay you, without recourse, up to the total amount of USD 1,000,000 (Say United States Dollars One Million Only) representing ten (10) percent of the Contract Price and accordingly covenants and agrees as follows:

(a)   On the Seller's failure of the faithful performance of all the Contract Documents and agreed modifications, amendments additions and alterations thereto that may thereinafter be made including replacement and/or making good of defective Goods (hereinafter called the "failure of performance") and determined by you and notwithstanding any objection by the Seller, the Bank shall immediately, on your demand in a written notification stating the failure of performance by the Seller, pay you such amount or amounts as required by you not exceeding the aggregate total amount of USD 1,000,000 (US Dollars One Million Only).

(b)   The covenants herein contained constitute an unconditional and irrevocable direct obligation of the Bank. No alteration in the terms of the Contract to be performed thereunder and no allowance of time by you or any other act or omission by you which but for this provision might exonerate or discharge the Bank shall in any way release the Bank from any liability hereunder.

(c)   This guarantee shall remain valid and in full force and effect until 30 June 1998 (the expiration of the guarantee period specified in the Contract signed by the Seller and Your corporation).

All claims made hereunder must be received on or before 30 June 1998, after which date, our liability hereunder will cease and this guarantee will be of no further effect whether returned to us for cancellation or not.

Yours faithfully,

City Bank
Hong Kong Branch

4 **Warranty Bond**

(a) When a contractor (an exporter) has completed a contract, he will expect to receive the retention money (a certain amount of money held by the buyer).

(b) However, this overseas buyer may be worried that the exporter will fail in after-sales services such as maintenance support if he is paid at once.

(c) To satisfy the buyer and reduce his worry, a warranty bond is issued in his favour.

(d) This type of bond is not so common as the previous types.

In warranty bond, issuing bank can add the following clauses to protect itself and its applicant:

---

1. In consideration of your releasing the sum of to the applicant we, City Bank Limited, Hong Kong hereby guarantee the repayment to you on demand of up to in the event of the Applicant failing to fulfil the Contract as agreed between buyer and seller.

2. This guarantee shall remain valid until close of banking hours at this office on (EXPIRY DATE) ("EXPIRY") Any claim thereunder must be received in writing at this office before Expiry accompanied by your signed statement that the Applicant has failed to fulfil the Contract, and such claim and statement shall be accepted as conclusive evidence that the amount claimed is due to you under this guarantee.

3. This guarantee shall become operative upon issue of our amendment making it effective, which will be issued upon receipt by us of written confirmation from the Applicant that the latter has received the Retention Monies.

4. Upon Expiry, this guarantee shall become null and void, whether returned to us for cancellation or not and any claim or statement received after Expiry shall be ineffective.

---

5 Conclusion: Types of Bond

Bonds can be issued in the form of conditional or unconditional. In conditional bond, the onus of proof lies on the beneficiary (buyer) to prove that the applicant fails to fulfil as specified. Meanwhile, the guaranteed amount may be limited to the beneficiary's actual loss.

In unconditional bond (also known as on demand bond), beneficiary can exercise his right at his sole discretion by means of the issue of a certificate of default. In other words, it can be called by the buyer for any reasons. Besides, compensation is not only limited to the buyer's actual loss. Therefore, this type of bond is in favour of the beneficiary and common in practice.

6 Standby Credit as an Alternative to Various Bonds

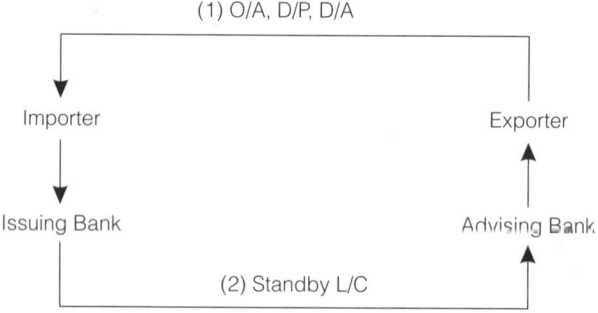

6.1 Standby Credit: Case 1

Standby credit, besides serving the function of a loan to the beneficiary, can in various circumstances replace a bond.

(a) This type of standby credit is to guarantee against an underlying shipment transaction between a buyer and a seller trading by means of open account (O/A) or collection (D/P, D/A).

(b) a buyer may receive regular shipment from a seller on open account basis. This seller, who may not feel comfortable with this payment method, may request protection. This can be effected by asking for the receipt of a standby credit issued by the buyer's banker.

(c) If the buyer default under open account, the exporter can draw under the standby credit for payment owed to him under open a/c by means of a set of draft and a certificate of default addressed to the issuing bank.

(d) In this type of standby credit, importer is the credit applicant.

6.2 Standby Credit: Case 2

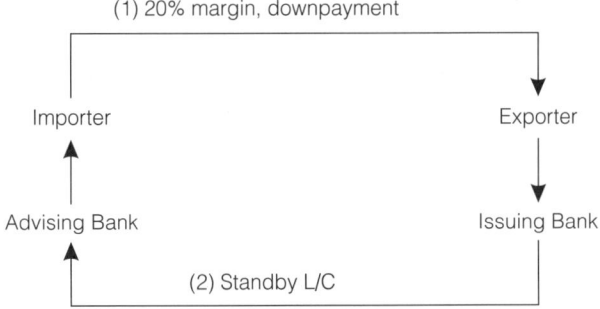

(1) 20% margin, downpayment

Importer   Exporter

Advising Bank   Issuing Bank

(2) Standby L/C

(a) Sometimes, in international trade, the buyer is required to make a deposit (e.g., 20% downpayment) to the exporter. This buyer, however, is not willing to depart with this amount which has been paid in advance. He may request a standby L/C issued by the receiver of the downpayment (the exporter) in favour of him.

(b) If the exporter fails to ship the goods, he (the buyer) may draw under the standby L/C and get back the downpayment.

(c) This type of standby credit is the same as advance payment guarantee, mentioned previously (For sample document and details, refer to the chapter on further considerations on various types of credit).

(d) In this type of standby credit, exporter is the credit applicant.

Further Reading

1. International Chamber of Commerce, *ICC N° 458 Uniform Rules for Demand Guarantees.*

2. International Chamber of Commerce, *ICC N° 510 Guide to ICC Uniform Rules for Demand Guarantees.*

3. International Chamber of Commerce, *ICC N° 503 Model Forms for Issuing Demand Guarantees.*

4. International Chamber of Commerce, *ICC N° 524 Uniform Rules for Contracts Bond.*

5. International Chamber of Commerce, *ICC N° 536 Guide to Uniform Rules for Contract Bonds and Model Forms.*

6. International Chamber of Commerce, *ICC N° 590 International Standby Practices ISP 98.*

14

Uniform Rules for Collections: ICC Publication N° 522

This Chapter is a summary of the main Articles of the Uniform rules for Collections: ICC Publication N° 522. Readers may refer to the original Articles for details.

Article 1

General Provision of Collection

Banks are not obliged to handle either a collection or any collection instruction. Even if banks have handled a collection or any collection instructions, they are not obliged to handle subsequent related instructions.

If a bank elects, for any reason, not to handle a collection or any related instructions, it must advise the "instructing party by telecommunication or, if that is not possible, by other expeditious means, without delay.

Article 2

Definition of Collection

(a) "Collection" means the handling by banks of documents (as defined in b), in accordance with instructions received, in order to:

i. obtain payment and/or acceptance,
ii. deliver documents against payment and/or against acceptance, or
iii. deliver documents on other terms and conditions.

(b) "Documents" means financial documents and/or commercial documents:

i. "Financial documents" mean bills of exchange, promissory notes, cheques, or other similar instruments used for obtaining the payment of money;
ii. Commercial documents mean invoices, transport documents or other similar documents excluding financial documents.

(c) "Clean collection" means collection of financial documents not accompanied by commercial documents.

(d) "Documentary collection" means collection of:

    i.   Financial documents accompanied by commercial documents;

    ii. Commercial documents not accompanied by financial documents.

Article 3

Parties to a Collection

(a) [The parties are:]

    i.   the "principal" who is the party entrusting the handling of a collection to a bank;

    ii. the "remitting bank" which is the bank to which the principal has entrusted the handling of a collection;

    iii. the "collecting bank" which is any bank, other than the remitting bank, involved in processing the collection;

    iv. the "presenting bank" which is the collecting bank making presentation to the drawee.

Article 4

Collection Instruction

(a) [Documents and instructions:]

    i.   All documents sent for collection must be accompanied by a complete collection instruction

    ii. Banks will not examine documents in order to obtain instructions.

    iii. Unless otherwise authorized in the collection instruction, banks will disregard any instructions from any party/bank other than the party/bank from whom they received the collection.

(b) A collection instruction should contain the following items of information:

   i.   Details of the bank from which the collection was received.

   ii.   Details of the principal.

   iii.   Details of the drawee.

   iv.   Details of the presenting bank, if any.

   v.   Amount and currency to be collected.

   vi.   List of documents enclosed and their numerical count.

   vii.   Terms of delivery of documents against: payment/acceptance/other terms & conditions.

   viii.   Charges to be collected and whether such charges may be waived or not.

   ix.   Interest to be collected, if applicable, indicating rate of interest, period covered, basis of calculation. Whether such interest may be waived or not.

   x.   Method of payment and form of payment advice.

   xi.   Instructions in case of non-payment, non-acceptance and/or non-compliance with other instructions.

(c) Collection instructions should bear the complete address of the drawee or of the domicile at which the presentation is to be made. If the address is incomplete or incorrect, the collecting bank may, without any liability and responsibility on its part, endeavour to ascertain the proper address.

Article 5

Presentation

(c) Unless otherwise instructed, banks may:

   i.   affix any necessary stamps,

   ii.   make any necessary endorsements,

   iii.   place any rubber stamps or other marks or symbol on documents at the expense of the "instructing party".

(e) Collection instruction may be sent directly by the remitting bank to the collecting bank or through another bank as intermediary.

Article 6

Sight/Acceptance

In case documents are payable at sight/at a tenor, the presenting bank must make presentation for payment/acceptance without delay/not later than the appropriate maturity date.

Article 7

Release of Commercial Documents (D/A vs D/P)

(a) Collections should not contain bills of exchange payable at a future date with D/P (documents against payment) as the payment instruction. (In other words, ICC discourages the use of D/P with a term bill)

(b) If a collection contains a bill of exchange payable at a future date, the collection instruction should state whether the commercial documents are to be released to the drawee against acceptance or against payment. In the absence of such statement, documents will be released only against payment.

(c) The collecting bank will not be responsible for any consequences arising out of any delay in the delivery of documents.

Article 8

Creation of Documents

If the remitting bank instructs the collecting bank/drawee to create documents (e.g., promissory notes, letters of undertaking, etc.), the form and wording of such documents shall be provided by the remitting bank. If not, the collecting bank shall create the documents at its own discretion without liability or responsibility for the form and wording of any such documents.

Article 10

Documents vs Goods/Services/Performance

(a) Goods should not be despatched directly to the address of a bank or consigned to or to the order of a bank without its prior agreement. If the above happens, such bank shall not be obliged to take delivery of the goods, which remain at the risk of the party despatching the goods.

(b) Banks have no obligation to take any action in respect of the goods to which a documentary collection relates, including storage and insurance of the goods. Even when specific instructions are given to do so, banks are not obliged to conform to it.

Banks will only take such action if, when, and to the extent that they agree to do so in each case. Notwithstanding the provisions of sub-Article 1c (a bank must advise the instructing party if it elects not to handle an instruction), this rule applies even in the absence of any specific advice to this effect by the collecting bank.

In other words, a collecting bank is **not obliged**:

i.   to take any actions in respect of the goods under a documentary collection;

ii.   such exemption from duty and responsibility remains even when specific instructions are given in the collection covering letter;

iii.   to inform the instructing party of its refusal to take action. (however, in practice, the collecting bank will inform the remitting bank of its refusal to take action)

If collecting banks elect to take action for the protection of the goods, they assume **no liability or responsibility** for:

i.   the fate and/or condition of the goods;

ii.   acts and/or omissions on the part of any third parties entrusted with the custody and/or protection of the goods.

However, the collecting bank **is obliged** to advise without delay the instructing party of any such action taken. This refers to the name of godown, insurance company etc.

(d) Any charges/expenses incurred by banks in connection with any action taken to protect the goods will be for account of the "instructing party".

(e) [Other provisions:]
  i.   When the collecting bank arranges for the release of the goods which are consigned to/ to the order of it, the remitting bank shall be deemed to have authorized the collecting bank to do so.

  ii.   Where a collecting bank arranges for the release of the goods, the remitting bank shall indemnify such collecting bank for all damages and expenses incurred.

Article 11

Disclaimer for Acts of an Instructed Party

(a) Banks utilizing the services of another bank or other banks for the purpose of giving effect to the instructions of the principal, do so for the account and at the risk of such principal.

(b) Banks assume no liability or responsibility should the instructions they transmit not be carried out.

(c) The "instructing party" is obliged to indemnify the "instructed party" against all liabilities incurred by foreign laws and usages.

Article 12

Disclaimer on Documents Received

(a) Banks must determine that the documents received appear to be as listed in the collection instruction and must advise by

telecommunication or other expeditious means, without delay the "instructing party", of any documents missing/found
to be other than listed.

(b) If the documents do not appear to be listed, the remitting
bank shall be precluded from disputing the type and number
of documents received by the collecting bank.

Article 13

Disclaimer on Effectiveness of Documents

Banks assume no liability or responsibility for the form,
sufficiency, accuracy, genuineness, falsification or legal
effect of any documents. Nor do they assume any liability or
responsibility for the description and contents of any
documents.

Article 14

Disclaimer on Delays, Loss in Transit and Translation

(a) Banks assume no liability or responsibility for the
consequences arising out of delay and/or loss in transit of any
messages, letters, or documents or for delay, mutilation or
other errors in translation and/or interpretation of technical
terms.

(b) Banks will not be liable or responsible for any delays
resulting from the need to obtain clarification of any
instructions received.

Article 15

Force Majeure

Banks assume no liability or responsibility for consequences
arising out of the interruption of their business by Acts of
God, riots, civil commotions, insurrections, wars, or any
other causes beyond their control or by strikes or lockouts.

Article 16

Payment Without Delay

Amounts collected (less charges and/or disbursements and/or
expenses where applicable) must be made available without

delay to the party from whom the collection instruction was received (i.e., the instructing party) in accordance with the terms and conditions of the collection instruction.

Article 17

Payment in Local Currency

If a set of documents (import) is to be payable in the currency of the country of payment (local currency), the presenting bank must release the documents to the drawee against payment in local currency only if such currency is immediately available for disposal in the manner specified in the collection instruction.

Article 18

Payment in Foreign Currency

If a set of documents (import) is to be payable in a currency other than that of the country of payment (foreign currency), the presenting bank must release the documents to the drawee against payment in the designated foreign currency only if such foreign currency can immediately be remitted in accordance with the instructions given in the collection instruction.

Article 19

Partial Payments

(a) In respect of clean collection, partial payments may be accepted if and to the extent to which and on the conditions on which partial payments are authorized by the law in force in the place of payment.

The financial documents will be released only when full payment has been received.

(b) In respect of documentary collection, partial payments will only be accepted if specifically authorized in the collection instruction.

The presenting bank will release the documents only after full payment has been received and the presenting bank will not be responsible for any consequences arising out of any delay in the delivery of documents.

Article 20

Interest

If the collection instruction specifies that interest is to be collected and the drawee refuses to pay such interest, the presenting bank may deliver the document(s) against payment or acceptance or on other terms and conditions as the case may be, without collecting such interest, unless sub-Article 20 c applies. (Article 20 a)

If the collection instruction expressly states that interest may not be waived and the drawee refuses to pay such interest, the presenting bank will not deliver documents and will not be responsible for any consequences arising out of any delay in the delivery of documents. (Article 20 c)

When payment of interest has been refused, the presenting bank must inform by telecommunication or other expeditious means without delay the "instructing party".

Where such interest is to be collected, the collection instruction must specify the rate of interest, interest period and basis of calculation. (Article 20 b)

Article 21

Charges and Expenses

If the collection instruction specified that collection charges and/or expenses are to be for account of the drawee and the drawee refuses to pay them, the presenting bank may deliver the documents against payment or acceptance or on other terms and conditions as the case may be, without collecting such charges and/or expenses, unless sub-Article 21 b applies.

Where the collection instruction expressly states that charges and/or expenses may not be waived and the drawee refuses to pay such charges/expenses, the presenting bank will not deliver documents and will not be responsible for any consequences arising out of any delay in the delivery of documents.

However, the presenting bank must inform by telecommunication or other expeditious means without delay the "instructing party".

In all cases where disbursements/expenses/collection charges are to be borne by the principal, the collecting bank shall be entitled to recover promptly outlays in respect of such charges from the "instructing party" (i.e., the remitting bank). The remitting bank shall be entitled to recover promptly from the principal such charges, regardless of the fate of the collection.

Banks reserve the right to demand payment of charges/and expenses in advance from the "instructing party" to cover costs in attempting to carry out any instructions, and pending receipt of such payment also reserve the right not to carry out such instructions.

Article 22

Acceptance

The presenting bank is responsible for seeing that the form of the acceptance of a bill appears to be complete and correct, but is not responsible for the genuineness of any signature or for the authority of any signatory to sign the acceptance.

Article 23

Promissory Notes and Other Instruments

The presenting bank is not responsible for the genuineness of any signature or for the authority of any signatory to sign a promissory note, receipt, or other instruments.

Article 24

Protest

In the absence of specific instructions, banks have no obligation to have the documents protested for non-payment or non-acceptance. The collection instruction should give specific instructions regarding protest. Any charges/expenses incurred by banks with respect to such protest will be for account of the "instructing party".

Article 25

Case-of-Need

If the principal nominates a representative to act as case-of-need in the event of non- payment/non-acceptance, the collection instruction should clearly and fully indicate the powers of such case-of-need. Otherwise, bank will not accept any instructions from the case-of-need.

Article 26

Advices

Collecting banks are to advise fate in accordance with the following rules:

(a) Form of Advice

All advice from the collecting bank to the remitting bank ("instructing party") must bear the latter bank's reference.

(b) Method of Advice

The remitting bank shall give instruction to the collecting bank about the methods of:

   i. advice of payment
   ii. advice of acceptance
   iii. advice of non-payment and/or non-acceptance

In the absence of such instructions, the collecting bank will send the relative advice at its own choice at the expense of the "instructing party".

(c) Advice of non-payment/non-acceptance
The presenting bank should endeavour to ascertain the reasons for non-payment and/or non-acceptance and advise accordingly without delay the "instructing party" (i.e., the remitting bank).

On receipt of such advice the remitting bank must give appropriate instructions as to the further handling of the documents. If such instructions are not received by the presenting bank within 60 days after its advice of non-payment and/or non-acceptance, the documents may be returned to the bank from which the collection instruction was received (i.e., the "instructing party") without any further responsibility on the part of the presenting bank.

Revision Questions

True or False

1. Unless otherwise authorized in the collection instruction, banks will disregard any instructions from any party/bank other than the party/bank from whom they received the collection.

2. Collections cannot contain bills of exchange payable at a future date with instructions that commercial documents are to be delivered against payment.

3. Goods cannot be despatched directly to the address of a collecting bank or consigned to or to the order of a collecting bank without prior agreement on the part of that bank.

4. Collecting banks have no obligation to take any action in respect of the goods to which a documentary collection relates, including storage and insurance of the goods unless specific instructions are given to do so.

5. Nevertheless, in the case that banks take action for the protection of the goods, whether instructed or not, they assume no liability or responsibility with regard to the fate and/or condition of the goods and/or for any acts and/or omissions on the part of any third parties entrusted with the custody and/or protection of the goods. The collecting bank is not obliged to advise the bank from which the collection instruction was received of any such action taken.

6. Where the goods are consigned to or to the order of the collecting bank and the drawee has honoured the collection by payment, acceptance or other terms and conditions, and the collecting bank arranges for the release of the goods, the collecting bank shall be deemed to have authorised the presenting bank to do so.

7. If the documents do not appear to be listed, the collecting bank shall be precluded from disputing the type and number of documents received.

8. Amounts collected (less charges and/or disbursements and/or expenses where applicable) by the remitting bank must be made available without delay to the party from whom the collection instruction was received in accordance with the terms and conditions of the collection instruction.

9. In respect of documentary collections, partial payments may be accepted if and to the extent to which and on the conditions on which partial payments are authorized by the law in force in the place of payment.

10. If the collection instruction specifies that interest is to be collected and the drawee refuses to pay such interest, the presenting bank may deliver the document(s) against payment or acceptance or on other terms and conditions as the case may be, without collecting charges and/or expenses, unless sub-Article 21(b) applies.

11. Prosperity Trading Company Ltd. has been importing male underwear from Aberdeen Ltd. in London on 60 days L/C term.

    Today, Mr. Frank Chan, the financial controller calls and tells you that as letters of credit are costly, their imports will be covered on a 60 days sight D/A or 60 days sight D/P basis. All presentations are apparently routed through banks.

    Required

    Write brief notes on:

    (a) Any international regulations your bank may have to be aware of when handling documents in the terms mentioned above.

    (b) Your advice to Mr. Chan with particular emphasis on the difference in operating procedure of your bank's Imports Department when handling 60 days sight D/A as opposed to 60 days sight D/P bills. Give reasons by citing relevant international regulations and local legislations, if any.

    (c) Any aspects you can foresee which might cause problem between you and your customer and your responsibilities to the parties involved in overcoming the difficulties.

    Banking Practice in Hong Kong, HKIB Associateship Examination, May 1999.

Answers

1. T (Article 4iii)
2. F (Article 7a)
3. F (Article 10a)
4. F (Article 10b)
5. F (Article 10c)
6. F (Article 10e)
7. F (Article 12b)
8. T (Article 16a)
9. F (Article 19b)
10. F (Article 20a)

Further Reading

1. *International Chamber of Commerce, ICC Uniform Rules for Collections Publication N° 522*
2. *International Chamber of Commerce, ICC Uniform Rules for Collections A Commentary 522*

15

Uniform Customs and Practice for Documentary Credit: ICC Publication N° 500

This Chapter is a summary of the main Articles of the Uniform Customs and Practice for Documentary Credits: ICC Publication N° 500. Readers may refer to the original Articles for details.

Article 1

Application of UCP

The Uniform Customs and Practice for Documentary Credits, 1993 Revision, ICC Publication N°500, shall apply to all Documentary Credits (including to the extent to which they may be applicable, Standby Letter(s) of Credit) where they are incorporated into the text of the Credit.

Article 2

Meaning of Credit

For the purpose of these Articles, the expressions "Documentary Credit" and "Standby Letter of Credit" mean any arrangement, however named or described, whereby a bank (the "Issuing Bank") acting at the request and on the instructions of a customer (the "Applicant") or on its own behalf,

i. is to make a payment to or to the order of the "Beneficiary" or is to accept and pay bills of exchange drawn by the Beneficiary, or

ii. authorizes another bank to effect such payment, or to accept and pay such bills of exchange, or

iii. authorizes another bank to negotiate against stipulated document(s), provided that the terms and conditions of the Credit are complied with.

Article 3

Credits vs Contracts

(a) Credits, by their nature, are separate transactions from the sales or other contract(s) on which they may be based and banks are in no way concerned with or bound by such contract(s), even if any reference whatsoever to such contract(s) is included in the Credit.

Article 4

Documents vs Goods

In Credit operations all parties concerned deal with documents, and not with goods, services.

Article 6

Revocable vs Irrevocable Credits

(a) A Credit may be either

    i.   revocable, or

    ii. irrevocable

(b) The Credit, therefore, should clearly indicate whether it is revocable or irrevocable.

(c) In the absence of such indication the Credit shall be deemed to be irrevocable.

Article 7

Advising Bank's Liability

(a) Advising Bank shall take reasonable care to check the apparent authenticity of the Credit which it advises.

(b) If it elects not to advise the Credit, it must inform the Issuing Bank without delay.

Article 9

Liability of Issuing and Confirming Banks

(a) An irrevocable Credit constitutes a definite undertaking of the Issuing Bank,

i.   **to pay at sight**; if the Credit provides for sight payment.

ii.   **to pay on the maturity date(s)** determinable in accordance with the stipulations of the Credit; if the Credit provides for deferred payment.

iii. a) **to accept Draft(s)** drawn by the Beneficiary on the Issuing Bank and pay them at maturity, if the Credit provides for acceptance by the issuing bank.

   b) **to accept and pay at maturity Draft(s)** drawn by the Beneficiary on the Issuing Bank in the event the drawee bank stipulated in the Credit does not accept Draft(s) drawn on it, if the credit provides for acceptance by another drawee bank.

iv.   **to pay without recourse to drawers** and/or bona fide holders Draft(s) drawn by the Beneficiary, if the Credit provides for negotiation.

*provided that the terms and conditions of the credit are complied with

(b) A confirmed credit constitutes a definite undertaking of the confirming bank, in addition to that bank, provided that the stipulated documents presented are complied with DC: The different forms of undertaking by the confirmation is similar to those by the issuing bank as in Article 9(a).

(d) [Amendment:]

i.   An irrevocable credit can neither be amended nor cancelled without the agreement of the issuing bank, confirming bank, if any and the beneficiary. (except in transferable credit)

ii.   The issuing bank shall be irrevocably bound by an amendment issued by it from the time of issuance of such amendment. A confirming bank shall be irrevocably bound as if the time of its advice of the amendment. A confirming bank may, however, choose to advise an amendment without extending its confirmation. In that case, it is obliged to inform the issuing bank and beneficiary accordingly without delay.

iii. The terms of the original credit will remain in force for the beneficiary until he communicates his acceptance of the amendment to the advising bank. Beneficiary should give notification of acceptance or rejection of amendment. If he fails to give such notification, the tender of documents to the nominated bank or issuing banking, that conform to the credit and to not yet accepted amendment, will be deemed to be notification of acceptance of such amendment and as of that moment the credit will be amended.

Article 10

Types of Credit

(b)

i. Unless the Credit stipulates that it is available only with the Issuing Bank, all Credits must nominate the bank authorized to pay, to incur a deferred payment undertaking, to accept Draft(s) or to negotiate. In a freely negotiable Credit, any bank is a Nominated Bank.

ii. Negotiation means the giving of value for Draft(s) and/or document(s). Mere examination of documents without crediting the customer's account (e.g., without giving value) does not constitute a negotiation. Nomination by the issuing bank does not constitute any undertaking by the the nominated bank to pay, to incur any payment undertaking/accept/negotiate unless the nominated bank is the confirming bank.

Article 11

Teletransmitted and Pre-Advised Credits

(a) [Mode of transmission:]

i. Full Cable — When an Issuing Bank instructs an Advising Bank by an authenticated teletransmission to advise a Credit or an amendment to a Credit, the teletransmission will be deemed to be the operative Credit instrument or the operative amendment and no mail confirmation should be sent. If sent, advising bank has no obligation to verify it against the telex message.

ii.   Brief cable — If the teletransmission states "full details to follow" or states that the mail confirmation is to be the operative Credit instrument or the operative amendment, then the teletransmission will not be deemed to be the operative Credit instrument or the operative amendment.

(b)   Issuing bank must use the same advising bank for advising amendment, if any.

(c)   A preliminary advice of the issuance or amendment of an irrevocable Credit (pre-advice), shall only be given by an Issuing Bank if such bank is prepared to issue the operative Credit instrument or the operative amendment. Issuing Bank having given such pre-advice shall be irrevocably committed to issue or amend the Credit, in terms not inconsistent with the pre-advice, without delay.

Article 13

Standard for Examination of Documents

(a)   Banks must examine all documents stipulated in the Credit with reasonable care, to ascertain whether or not they appear, on their face, to be in compliance with the terms of the Credit.

Documents not stipulated in the Credit will not be examined by banks.

(b)   The Issuing Bank, shall have a reasonable time, not to exceed seven banking days following the day of receipt of the documents to examine the documents.

(c)   If a Credit contains conditions without stating the document(s), banks will deem such conditions as not stated. (non-documentary condition)

Article 14

Discrepant Documents and Notice (applicable to issuing bank, confirming bank, and nominated bank)

(a) Upon receipt of the documents the Issuing Bank must determine **on the basis of the documents alone** whether or not they appear on their face to be in compliance with the terms of the Credit.

(b) If the Issuing Bank determines that the documents appear on their face not to be in compliance with the terms and conditions of the Credit, it may **in its sole judgement** approach the Applicant for a waiver of the discrepancy(ies).

(c) If the Issuing Bank decides to refuse the documents, it must state whether it is holding the documents at the disposal of, or is returning them to, the presenter.

(d) If the Issuing Bank fails to act in accordance with the provisions of this Article and fails to hold the documents at the disposal of, or return them to the presenter, the Issuing Bank shall be precluded from claiming that the documents are not in compliance with the terms and conditions of the Credit.

(e)

    i.   If the remitting bank draws the attention of the Issuing Bank, to any discrepancy(ies) in the document(s) or advises such banks that it has paid, incurred a deferred payment undertaking, accepted Draft(s) or negotiated under reserve or against an indemnity in respect of such discrepancy(ies), the Issuing Bank shall not be relieved from any of their obligations under any provision of this Article.

    ii.   Such reserve of indemnity concerns only the relations between the remitting bank and the beneficiary.

Article 15

Effectiveness of Documents

Banks are not responsible for the accuracy, genuineness of documents nor for the descriptions of goods stated in them, the good faith, solvency of consignors, carriers, insurers, forwarders, the consignees, etc.

Article 16

Transmission of Messages

Banks are not responsible for consequences arisen from delays, loss in transit of messages/letters/documents, nor for delay, errors in telecommunication or mistranslations of technical terms.

Article 17

Force Majeure (Acts of God)

Banks are not responsible for consequences arisen from matters out of the bank's control such as interruption of business by Acts of God, war riots, strikes, etc.

Banks will not, upon resumption of their business, pay, accept Draft(s) or negotiate under Credits expired during such interruption of their business.

Article 18

Acts of an Instructed Party

(a) Banks are not responsible for the actions of another banks or other banks, even though they have taken the initiative in the choice of these banks. It is for the account and risk of the Applicant.

(b) Banks assume no liability should the instructions not be carried out, even if they have themselves taken the initiative in the choice of such other bank(s).

(c) [Charges:]

    i.   A party instructing another party to perform services is liable for any charges in connection with its instructions.

    ii.   Where a Credit stipulates that such charges are for the account of a party other than the instructing party, and charges cannot be collected, the instructing party remains ultimately liable.

(d) The Applicant shall be bound by and liable to indemnify his bank.

Article 19

Bank-to-Bank Reimbursement

(a) Issuing Bank should provide Reimbursing Bank in good time with the proper instructions or authorization to honour reimbursement claims.

(b) Issuing Banks shall not require a Claiming Bank to supply a certificate of compliance with the terms and conditions to the Reimbursing Bank.

(c) An Issuing Bank shall not be relieved from any of its obligations to provide reimbursement if reimbursement is not received by the Claiming Bank from the Reimbursing Bank

(d) The Issuing Bank shall be responsible to the Claiming Bank for any loss of interest if reimbursement is not provided by the Reimbursing Bank on first demand.

(e) Reimbursing bank's charge, if the credit is drawn under, and stipulating for account of beneficiary, should be collected from the claiming bank. Such charge, however, should be borne by issuing bank if the credit is not drawn.

Article 20

Ambiguous Issuers

(a) Issuers such as first class, well known, qualified, independent, official, competent, can be constructed as any parties except beneficiary.

(b) Banks will also accept as an original document(s) — a document(s) produced or appearing to have been produced:

    i.   by reprographic, automated or computerized systems;

    ii. as carbon copies;

provided that it is marked as original and, where necessary, appears to be signed.

A document may be signed by handwriting, by facsimile signature, by perforated signature, by stamp, by symbol, or by any other mechanical or electronic method of authentication.

(c) [Copies:]

    i.   a copy is labelled copy or not marked as an original — a copy(ies) need not be signed.

    ii. Duplicate, two fold, two copies can be interpreted as one original and the remaining in copies.

Article 21

Unspecified Issuers

The credit should stipulate by whom documents are to be issued (except transport documents, insurance documents, invoices). If not, banks will accept documents by any issuers including beneficiary provided that their content is not inconsistent with the other stipulated documents presented.

Article 22

Issuance Date of Documents vs Credit Date

Documents dated prior to the credit are acceptable.

Article 23–33*

Marine/Ocean Bill of Lading

Banks will accept a document, however named, under a port-to-port shipment:

(a) Unless otherwise stipulated in the credit, transport documents should have been issued by a named carrier, or a named agent for the carrier, or the master, or a named agent for the master. (article 23a, i)

(b) It must indicate that the goods have been loaded on board, or shipped on a named vessel and indicate the port of loading and the port of discharge as stipulated in the credit. (article 23a, iii)

(c) Loading on board may be indicated by pre-printed wording on the bill of lading in which case, the date of issue is deemed to be the date of loading on board the ship.

In all other cases, the date of the onboard notation will be deemed to be the date of shipment.

If the bill of lading contains "intended vessel", loading on board must be evidenced by an on board notation, with the date evidencing loaded on board and the name of the vessel.

If the bill of lading indicates a place of receipt or taking in charge different from the port of loading, on board notation must also include the port of loading, the name of the vessel, even if the goods have been loaded on the vessel named in the bill of lading.

This applies whenever loading on board the vessel is indicated by preprinted wording on the bill of lading.

Indicates the port of loading and the port of discharge notwithstanding that it indicates a place of taking in charge different from the port of loading, and/or a place of final destination different from the port of discharge. (article 23a, ii)

*Articles 23 through 33 are rearranged under six themes. Specific sections of the ICC articles are indicated.

Consists of a sole original bill of lading or, if issued in more than one original, the full set as so issued. (article 23a, iv)

(d) The following bills of lading are acceptable unless stipulated otherwise:

Short form or blank back transport documents. (article 23a, v)

(e) The following bills of lading are not acceptable unless stipulated otherwise:

i. Charter party bill of lading.
ii. Bill of lading indicating that the vessel is propelled by sail only. (article 23a, vi)

(f) Even if transhipment is not allowed in the credit, banks will accept a bill of lading which indicates that:

i. Transhipment will take place so long as the relevant cargo is shipped in container(s), etc. and the entire carriage is covered by the same bill of lading. (article 23d, i)
ii. The carrier reserves the right to tranship. (article 23d, ii)

Air Transport

The date of issuance of air transport document is deemed to be the date of shipment unless the D/C stipulates an actual flight date in which case the date of despatch will be deemed to be the date of shipment. (article 27a, iii)

Accept the Following Transport Documents Issued by Freight Forwarders

i. Transport documents issued by freight forwarders indicating the name of the freight forwarder as the carrier or multimodal transport operator and duly signed is acceptable. (article 30, i)
ii. Transport documents issued by freight forwarders indicating as agent for or on behalf of a named carrier or named multimodal transport operator. (article 30, ii)

"On Deck", "Shipper's Load and Count", Name of Consignor

Banks will accept a transport document which:

(a) Indicate that the goods may be carried on deck, provided it does not specifically state that they are or will be loaded on deck. (article 31, i)

(b) Bears a clause "shipper's load and count" or "said by shipper to contain" or words of similar effect. (article 31, ii)

(c) Third party as shipper — The shipper of the goods (consignor) can be a party other than the beneficiary of the credit. (article 31, iii)

Clean Transport Documents

(a) A clean transport document bears no clause or notation expressly declaring a defective condition of the goods and/or the packaging. (article 32a)

(b) Banks will not accept transport documents bearing such clauses. (article 32b)

Freight Payable/To be Prepaid vs Freight Prepaid

(a) "Freight prepayable" and "Freight to be prepaid" are not the same as "Freight prepaid" and are not acceptable. (article 33c)

(b) Banks will accept transport documents bearing reference by stamp or otherwise costs additional to the freight, such as costs of loading, unloading or similar operations, unless the Credit specifically prohibit such reference. (article 33d)

Article 34

Insurance Documents

(a) Insurance documents are to be issued by an insurance company, its agent or an underwriter.

(b) All the originals must be presented unless stipulated otherwise.

(c) Cover notes will not be accepted, unless otherwise stipulated.

(d) Bank will accept insurance policy if L/C calls for insurance certificate.

(e) In practice, bank will not accept insurance certificate if calling for policy.

(f) Insurance documents must be dated on or before the shipment date unless stipulated otherwise. (e.g., the effective date of the cover must be on or before the date of shipment unless stipulated otherwise. Also note the difference between the effective date and date of issue)

(g) Insurance document must be in the same currency as the credit, and for a minimum of 110% of CIF or CIP value unless stipulated otherwise.

Article 35

Type of Insurance Cover

(a) Credits should specify the type of insurance and any additional risks covered. Imprecise terms such as "usual risks" or "customary risks" shall not be used; if used, banks will accept insurance documents as presented, without responsibility for any risks not being covered.

(b) Unless otherwise stipulated in the Credit, banks will accept an insurance document which indicates that the cover is subject to a franchise or an excess (deductible).

Article 36

All Risks Insurance Cover

Where a Credit stipulates "insurance against all risk", banks will accept an insurance document which contains any "all risks" notation or clause.

Article 37

Commercial Invoices

(a) [Commercial invoices must be:]
   i.   issued by the Beneficiary named in the Credit (except as provided in Article 48),
   ii. made out in the name of the Applicant (except as provided in sub-Article 48(h)), but
   iii. need not be signed.

(b) Banks may refuse commercial invoices issued for amounts in excess of the amount permitted by the Credit. Nevertheless, if a bank authorized to negotiate under a Credit accepts such invoices, its decision will be binding upon all parties, provided that such bank has not negotiated for an amount in excess of that permitted by the Credit.

(c) The description of the goods in the commercial invoice must correspond with the description in the Credit. In all other documents, the goods may be described in general terms which are consistent with other documents.

Article 39

Allowances in Credit Amount, Quality and Unit Price

(a) "about" and similar words to be construed as allowing $\pm$ 10% of the Credit amount, or the quantity or unit price.

(b) Quantity of goods shipped has a tolerance of $\pm$ 5% provided that drawings do not exceed credit amount but quantity of goods in terms of a stated number of packing units or individual terms are excluded.

Article 40

Partial Shipments/Drawings

(a) Allows partial drawings and/or shipments, unless the Credit prohibits them.

(b) Transport documents which indicate that shipment has been made on the same means of conveyance and for the same journey, same destination, will not be regarded as covering partial shipments, even if the transport documents indicate different dates of shipment and/or different ports of loading, places of taking in charge, or despatch.

(c) Shipments made by post or by courier will not be regarded as partial shipments if the post receipts or certificates of posting or courier's receipts appear to have been stamped, signed or otherwise authenticated in the place from which the Credit stipulates the goods are to be dispatched, and on the same date.

Article 41

Instalment Shipments/Drawings

In case of shipment/drawing by instalement, the credit creases to be operative if a drawing and/or shipment is not made as scheduled.

Article 42

Expiry Date and Place

All Credits must state an expiry date and an expiry place.

Article 43

21 Days

Banks will not accept transport documents presented to them more than 21 days after shipment, if no presentation period is specified. (the so-called 21 days rule).

Article 44

Extension of Expiry Date

(a) If the bank is closed for bank holiday or for reasons other than Article 17 (i.e., by Acts of God), then the credit's expiry date or the last date to present documents shall be extended to the first following business day.

(b) The latest date for shipment shall not be extended by reason of the extension of the expiry date and/or presentation of documents in accordance with sub-Article (a) above.

(c) The bank to which presentation is made on such first following business day must provide a statement that the documents were presented within the time limits extended in accordance with sub-Article 44(a).

Article 45

Hours of Presentation

Banks are not obliged to accept presentations of documents outside their banking hours.

Article 46

"On or About" Shipment Date

"On or about" means 'from the five days before to five days after the specified date.

Article 47

Date Terminology for Periods of Shipment

(a) "To", "until", "till", "from" etc. relating to a date or period will be construed to include the date in question. 'After' excludes the date mentioned.

(b) "First half" of a month means 1st to 15th inclusive."Second half" means 16th and onwards.

(c) "Beginning" includes the 10th of the month. 'Middle' means from the 11th to 20th inclusive.'End' means the 21st and onwards.

Article 48

Transferable Credit

(a) The beneficiary may request the bank authorized to pay, incur a deferred payment undertaking, accept or negotiate to effect the transfer.

(b) Or in the case of a freely negotiable credit, the bank specifically authorized in the credit as a transferring bank, to make the credit available in whole or in part to one or more other beneficiary(ies) (i.e., the following wordings must appear in a freely negotiable credit: this credit is transferable by, for example, City Bank)

(c) A credit is transferable only if specified 'transferable'. Other words such as 'divisible' do not make the credit transferable.

(d) Transferring bank is not obliged to effect the transfer except to the extent and in the manner expressly consented by such bank.

(e) The first beneficiary must irrevocably instruct the transferring bank whether he retains the right to refuse to allow the transferring bank to advise amendments to the second beneficiary(ies). (in practice, the first beneficiaries normally are not allowed to retain the right)

(f) One or more second beneficiaries may refuse an amendment but this does not invalidate the agreement of other second beneficiaries to accept this amendment.

(g) Transferring bank charges are payable by the first beneficiary.

Credits cannot be transferred to subsequent third beneficiary(ies) with the exception of retransfer back to the first beneficiary by second beneficiary.

(h) Can be transferred only according to the terms & conditions of the original credit except:

i.   Amount of the credit

ii. Its expiry date

iii. Any unit prices stated in the credit

iv   The last date for presenting documents in accordance with Article 43

v.   The period for shipment

vi. The percentage for which insurance cover must be effected may be increased, so as to ensure that insurance cover is sufficient to meet the stipulations of the original credit.

vii. The name of the first beneficiary can be substituted for that of the applicant.

viii. Invoice(s) and draft(s) of the first beneficiary can also be substituted for those of the applicant.

ix. Can ask for a transferable credit to be transferred to a second beneficiary in either the same country or a different country.

(i) The First Beneficiary has the right to substitute his own invoice(s) (and Draft(s)) for those of the Second Beneficiary(ies), for amounts not in excess of the original amount stipulated in the Credit.

If the First Beneficiary is to supply his own invoice(s) (and Draft(s) for substitution but fails to do so on first demand, the Transferring Bank has the right to deliver to the Issuing Bank the documents received under the transferred Credit.

First beneficiary has the right to request that payment or negotiation should be effected to the second beneficiary at the place to which the credit has been transferred.

Revision Questions

True or False

1. Documentary Credits, are separate transactions from the sales and purchases contract(s).
2. In Documentary Credit operations, all parties concerned deal with documents only.
3. The advising bank has the right not to advise the credit even though it is nominated by the issuing bank as the advising bank.
4. Advising Bank, if it elects to advise the Credit, should take reasonable care to check the apparent authenticity of the Credit which it advises.
5. An unauthenticated D/C can never be advised to the beneficiary.
6. A D/C with the clause "this credit is available with advising bank by deferred payment" is a deferred payment credit.
7. A D/C with the clause "this clause is available with advising bank by acceptance" is an acceptance credit.
8. If an advising bank is authorized by the issuing bank to add its confirmation to a credit, it must do so since it is acting as the agent of the issuing bank.
9. Documents which are not called for in the credit will not be examined by banks.
10. Documents which are not called for in the credit shall be returned to the party from which they were received OR passed on without any responsibility imposed on the part of the issuing bank.
11. Upon receipt of the documents, the issuing Bank must determine on the basis of the documents alone whether or not they appear on their face to be in compliance with the terms and conditions of the Credit.
12. Notice of discrepancy(ies) from issuing bank to negotiating bank must also state whether issuing bank is holding the documents at the risk of and pending further instruction form negotiating bank OR returning the documents to negotiation bank.

13. If D/C calls for "Inspection Certificate issued by competent authority", beneficiary can submit "Inspection Certificate issued by any party as long as it is not issued by the beneficiary himself and meets the requirement of the other terms and conditions of the credit.

14. If D/C calls for "Inspection Certificate" without mentioning the name of the issuers, beneficiary can submit "Inspection Certificate" issued by any party except the beneficiary himself when its data content is consistent with any other stipulated document presented.

15. Loading on board on a named vessel may be indicated by pre-printed wording on the bill of lading that the goods have been loaded on board a named vessel or shipped on a named vessel, in which case the date of issuance of the bill of lading will be deemed to be the date of loading on board and the date of shipment.

16. Loading on board on a named vessel may be evidenced by notation on the bill of lading, in which case the date of the on board notation will be deemed to be the date of shipment.

17. If the words "intended vessel: Maersk Line 888" is indicated in B/L, loading on-board a named vessel must be evidenced by an on board notation specifying the date of loading on board and the name of vessel.

18. Even if transhipment is prohibited, the following bill of lading is acceptable: that the carrier reserves the right to tranship.

19. Even if transhipment is prohibited, the following bill of lading is acceptable: that the it indicates that transhipment will take place but the cargo is shipped in container and the entire ocean carriage is covered by the same bill of lading.

20. If D/C calls for a multimodal transport bill of lading, bank will accept a document, however named, provided that it meets all other requirements as stipulated in the credit.

21. Banks will not accept a transport document which indicate that the goods are or will be loaded on deck unless otherwise stipulated in the credit.

22. Banks will not accept a transport document which indicate that the goods may be carried on deck unless otherwise stipulated in the credit.

23. The words "freight prepayable" or "freight to be prepaid" will be accepted as constituting evidence of the payment of freight.

24. If a Credit specifically calls for an insurance certificate or a declaration under an open cover, banks will accept, in lieu thereof, an insurance policy.

25. If a credit specifically calls for an insurance policy, banks will accept, in lieu thereof, an insurance certificate or a declaration under an open cover.

26. Cover notes issued by brokers will be accepted, unless specifically authorized in the Credit.,

27. If the insurance document indicates that it has been issued in more than one originals, all the originals must be presented even though D/C doses not mention that full set must be submitted.

28. Unless otherwise stipulated in the Credit, the insurance document may be expressed in a currency other than the D/C.

29. Unless otherwise stipulated in the Credit, banks will accept an insurance document which indicates that the cover is subject to a franchise of an excess (deductible).

30. If D/C calls for "commercial invoice in duplicate", beneficiary may submit one original and one copy without any signature.

31. If D/C calls for "signed commercial invoice in triplicate", beneficiary may submit one original and two copies without any signature because according to Art 37 a iii, commercial invoice need not be signed.

32. Unless other wise stipulated in the Credit, banks may refuse commercial invoices issued for amounts in excess of the amount permitted by the Credit.

33. Nevertheless, if a bank authorized to negotiate under a Credit accepts such invoices, its decision will be binding upon all parties, provided that such bank has not negotiated for an amount in excess of that permitted by the Credit.

34. Partial shipments are not allowed if D/C does not mention whether partial shipments are allowed of not.

35. A bill of lading which appears on their face to indicate that shipment has been made on the same means of conveyance or the same journey, same destination, will not be regarded as covering partial shipments, even if the B/L indicates different

dates of shipment, different ports of loading, places of taking in charge, or despatch.

36. Shipments made by post will not be regarded as partial shipments if the post receipts appear to have been stamped, signed or otherwise authenticated in the place from which the Credit stipulates the goods are to be dispatched, and on the same date.

37. If shipments by instalments within given periods are stipulated in the Credit and an instalment is not shipped within the period allowed for that instalment, the Credit is still to be available for that and subsequent instalments, unless otherwise stipulated in the Credit.

38. In the case of a freely negotiable Credit, the bank specifically authorized in the Credit as a Transferring Bank is to make the credit available in whole or in part to the transferee(s).

39. Terms such as "divisible", "fractionable", "assignable", and "transmissible" do not render the Credit transferrable.

40. The advising bank is under an obligation to effect the transfer if it is the only nominated bank to effect the transfer.

41. At the time of making a request for transfer, the First Beneficiary must irrevocably instruct the Transferring Bank whether or not he retains the right to refuse to allow the Transferring Bank to advise amendments to the Second Beneficiary(ies). If the Transferring Bank consents to the transfer under these conditions, it must, at the time of transfer, advise the Second Beneficiary(ies) of transfer, advise the Second Beneficiary(ies) of the First Beneficiary's instructions regarding amendments.

42. A transferable Credit can be transferred to many parties once only.

43. Credit cannot be transferred at the request of the Secondary Beneficiary to any subsequent Third Beneficiary.

44. Retransfer to the First Beneficiary from Secondary Beneficiary does not constitute a prohibited transfer.

45. The Credit can be transferred on the terms and conditions specified in the original Credit, with the exception of:
     —the amount of the Credit.
     —any unit price stated therein.
     —the expiry date.

—the last date for presentation of documents in accordance with Article 43.

—the period for shipment.

any or all of which may be reduced or curtailed.

46. When a Credit has been transferred and the First Beneficiary is to substitute his own documents but fails to do so on first demand, the transferring bank has the right to deliver to the Issuing Bank the documents received under the transferred Credit.

47. The First Beneficiary may request that payment or negotiation be effected to the Second Beneficiary(ies) at transferring bank's counter.

48. If the issuing bank opens details of a D/C by cable without mentioning "full details to follow", the cable advice is not considered to be an operative credit instrument.

49. If the issuing bank opens a D/C by brief cable mentioning "full details to follow", the teletransmission can be deemed to be the operative credit instrument.

50. If the issuing bank advises a D/C by brief cable mentioning "full details to follow", it is not obliged to issue the mail letter (cable confirmation).

Answers

No	Answer	Article No.	No	Answer	Article No.
1	T	3	26	F	34c
2	T	4	27	T	34b
3	T	7a	28	F	34f(i)
4	T	7a	29	T	35c
5	F	7b	30	T	37a
6	T	9a(ii)	31	F	37a(ii)
7	T	9a(iii)	32	T	37b
8	F	9c	33	T	37b
9	T	13a	34	F	40a
10	T	13a	35	T	40b
11	T	14b	36	T	40c
12	T	14d(ii)	37	F	41
13	T	20a	38	T	48a
14	F	21	39	T	48b
15	T	23a(ii)	40	F	48c
16	T	23a(ii)	41	T	48d
17	T	23a(ii)	42	T	48g
18	T	23d(ii)	43	T	48g
19	T	23d(i)	44	T	48g
20	T	26a	45	T	48h
21	T	31(i)	46	T	48i
22	F	31(i)	47	T	48j
23	F	33c	48	F	11a(ii)
24	T	34d	49	F	11a(ii)
25	F	34d	50	F	11a(i)

16

Uniform Rules for Bank-to-Bank Reimbursement: ICC Publication N° 525

❏ Summary

❏ Diagrammatic explanation of a reimbursement process

❏ Revision Questions

This Chapter is a summary of the main Articles of the Uniform rules for Bank-to-Bank Reimbursement (URBBR) ICC Publication N° 525. Readers may refer to the original Articles for details.

Article 1

Application of URR

This Issuing Bank is responsible for indicating in the DC that Reimbursement claims are subject to these Rules. Reimbursing Bank acts on the instructions of the issuing bank.

A General Provisions and Definitions

Article 2

Definitions

(a) "Issuing Bank" shall mean the bank that has issued a Credit and the Reimbursement Authorization under that Credit.

(b) "Reimbursing Bank" is the bank instructed to provide reimbursement pursuant to a Reimbursement Authorization issued by the Issuing Bank.

(c) "Reimbursement Authorization" is an instruction issued by an Issuing Bank to a Reimbursing Bank to :

  i.   reimburse a Claiming Bank, or,

  ii. to accept and pay a time draft(s) drawn on the Reimbursing Bank. This instruction is independent of the Credit.

(d) "Claiming Bank" is:

  i.   a bank that pays, incurs a deferred payment undertaking, accepts draft(s), or negotiates under a Credit and presents a Reimbursement Claim to the Reimbursing Bank.

  ii. a bank authorized by the negotiating bank to present a Reimbursement Claim to the Reimbursing Bank.

(f) "Reimbursement Claim" is a request for reimbursement from the Claiming Bank to the Reimbursing Bank.

(g) "Reimbursement Undertaking" is a separate irrevocable undertaking of the Reimbursing Bank to the Claiming Bank to honour that bank's Reimbursement Claim.

(h) "Reimbursement Undertaking Amendment" is an advice from the Reimbursing Bank to the Claiming Bank stating changes to a Reimbursement Undertaking.

Article 3

Reimbursement Authorizations vs Credits

A Reimbursement Authorization is separate from the Credit to which it refers.

B Liabilities and Responsibilities

Article 4

Honour of a Reimbursement Claim

Reimbursing Bank is not obligated to honour a Reimbursement Claim. (except with reimbursement undertaking)

C Form and Notification of Authorizations, Amendments and Claims

Article 6

Issuance and Receipt of a Reimbursement Authorization or Reimbursement Amendment

(a) Reimbursement Authorizations and Amendments must be in the form of an authenticated teletransmission or a signed letter. When a Credit is issued by teletransmission, the Issuing Bank should advise its Reimbursement Authorization or Reimbursement Amendment by authenticated teletransmission. The teletransmission will be deemed the operative Reimbursement Authorization or the operative Reimbursement Amendment.

(b) Issuing Banks must not send to Reimbursement Banks :

    i.   a copy of the Credit or any part thereof

    ii. multiple Reimbursement Authorizations under one teletransmission or letter.

(c) Issuing Banks shall not require a certificate of compliance with the terms and conditions of the Credit in the Reimbursement Authorization.

(d) Reimbursement Authorizations must state:

    i.   Credit number;

    ii. currency and amount;

    iii. amounts more or less;

    iv. Claiming Bank if any;

    v. parties responsible for Claiming Bank's and Reimbursing Bank's charges.

(e) In a usance credit, Reimbursement Authorization must indicate the following additional information:

    i.   tenor of draft;

    ii. drawer;

    ii. party responsible for acceptance and discount charges.

(g) If Reimbursing Bank is not prepared to act under the Reimbursement Authorization or Reimbursement Amendment, it must inform the Issuing Bank without delay and not responsible for the consequences resulting from non-reimbursement and/or delay.

Article 7

Expiry of a Reimbursement Authorization

Reimbursement Authorization must not have an expiry date or latest date for presentation of a claim.

Reimbursing Banks take no responsibility for the expiry date of Credits.

Issuing Bank must inform the Reimbursing bank for cancellation of any unutilized portion of the Credit without delay.

Article 8

Amendment or Cancellation of Reimbursement Authorizations

(a) Issuing Bank may issue a Reimbursement Amendment or cancel a Reimbursement Authorization at any time after issue (except with the issue of Reimbursement undertaking).

(b) Issuing Bank must send notice of any amendment to a Reimbursement Authorization to the nominated bank or, the advising bank. In the case of cancellation of the Reimbursement Authorization prior to expiry of the Credit, the Issuing Bank must provide the nominated bank or the advising bank with new reimbursement instructions.

(c) Issuing Bank must reimburse the Reimbursing Bank for any Reimbursement Claims honoured prior to the receipt by it of notice of cancellation or Reimbursement Amendment.

Article 9

Reimbursement Undertakings

(b) Authorization by the Issuing Bank to the Reimbursing Bank to issue a Reimbursement Undertaking is irrevocable and must contain the following:

    i.   Credit number;

    ii. currency and amount;

    iii. amounts more or less;

    iv. full name and address of the Claiming Bank;

    v.   latest date for presentation of a claim;

    vi. parties responsible for charges.

(c) In a usance credit, Reimbursement Authorization must also indicate the following additional information :

    i.   tenor of draft;

    ii. drawer;

    iii. party responsible for acceptance and discount charges.

(d) If the Reimbursing Bank is authorized to issue its Reimbursement Undertaking but is not prepared to do so, it must so inform the Issuing Bank without delay.

(e) Reimbursement undertaking must contain:

    i.   Credit number and Issuing Bank;

    ii. currency and amount of the Reimbursement Authorization;

    iii. amounts more or less;

    iv. currency and amount of the Reimbursement Undertaking;

    v.   latest date for presentation of a claim;

    vi. party to pay Claiming bank's, Reimbursing Bank's and Reimbursement Undertaking fees.

(f) If the latest date for presentation of a claim falls on a day on which is closed for reasons other than those mentioned in Article 15, it shall be extended to the first following business day.

(g) [Provision i. omitted]

    ii. When an Issuing Bank has amended its Irrevocable Reimbursement Authorization, a Reimbursing Bank which has issued its Reimbursement Undertaking may amend its undertaking to reflect such amendment.

If a Reimbursing Bank chooses not to issue its Reimbursement Undertaking Amendment, it must so inform the Issuing Bank without delay.

iii. An Issuing Bank which has issued its irrevocable Reimbursement Authorization Amendment, shall be irrevocably bound as of the time of its advice of the Irrevocable Reimbursement Authorization Amendment.

iv. The terms of the original Irrevocable Reimbursement Authorization will remain in force for the Reimbursing Bank until it communicates its acceptance of the amendment to the Issuing Bank.

v. A Reimbursing Bank must communicate its acceptance or rejection of an Irrevocable Reimbursement Authorization Amendment to the Issuing Bank.

(h) i. A Reimbursing Bank is not required to accept or reject an Irrevocable Reimbursement Authorization Amendment until it has received acceptance or rejection from the Claiming Bank to its Undertaking Amendment.

ii. A Reimbursement Undertaking cannot be amended or cancelled without the agreement of the Claiming Bank.

iii. A Reimbursing Bank which has issued it Reimbursement Undertaking Amendment shall be irrevocably bound as of the time of its advice of the Undertaking Amendment.

iv. The terms of the original Reimbursement Undertaking will remain in force for the Claiming Bank until it communicates its acceptance of the Undertaking Amendment to the Reimbursing Bank.

v. A Claiming Bank must communicate its acceptance or rejection of a Reimbursement Undertaking Amendment to the Reimbursing Bank.

Article 10

Standards for Reimbursement Claims (claiming bank must)

(a) The Claiming Bank's claim for reimbursement:

    i.   must be in the form of a teletransmission, or an original letter;

A Reimbursing Bank has the right to request that a Reimbursement Claim be authenticated and shall not be liable for any consequences resulting from any delay incurred;

If a Reimbursement Claim is made by teletransmission, no mail confirmation is to be sent and Claiming Bank will be responsible for the consequences arisen from duplicate reimbursement;

    ii.   must clearly indicate the Credit number and Issuing Bank;

    iii. must stipulate the principal amount and charges;

    iv. must not be a copy of the Claiming Bank's advice of payment;

    v.   must not include multiple Reimbursement Claims under one message;

    vi. must in the case of a Reimbursement Undertaking, comply with the terms and conditions of the Reimbursement Undertaking.

(b) In usance credit Claiming Bank must forward the draft with the Reimbursement Claim to the Reimbursing Bank for processing, and include the following :

    i.   general description of the goods

    ii.   country of origin;

    iii. place of destination/performance; and if the transaction covers the shipment of merchandise.

    iv. date of shipment;

    v.   place of shipment.

(c) Claiming Banks must not indicate in a Reimbursement Claim that negotiation was made under reserve or against an indemnity.

Diagrammatic Explanation of a Reimbursement Process

Note: Reimbursement undertaking may be involved in the process when the reimbursement authorization requests reimbursing bank to issue a Reimbursement Undertaking to the claiming bank, as shown in the dotted lines.

Assumption of the case:

1. Issuing bank is in Hong Kong.

2. Claiming bank is in Singapore.

3. Reimbursing bank is in New York.

4. D/C Currency is US Dollars.

Reimbursement procedures:

1. A D/C is issued in Hong Kong and sent via an advising bank in Singapore.

2. Advising bank in Singapore advises the D/C to the beneficiary.

3. After having shipping the goods the beneficiary submits all the documents to a negotiating bank which also acts as a claiming bank.

4. Claiming bank sends a reimbursement request to the reimbursing bank for payment (4a). Meanwhile, shipping documents are sent to issuing bank for disposal (4b).

5. Reimbursing bank processes and honours claims.

Article 11

Processing Reimbursement Claims

(a) [Time and delay:]
    i.   Reimbursing Banks shall have a reasonable time, not to exceed three banking days following the day of receipt of the Reimbursement Claim, to process claims.
    ii. If the Reimbursing Bank determines not to reimburse for any reason whatsoever, it shall give notice to that effect by telecommunication or, other expeditious means, without delay, but no later than the close of the third banking day following the day of receipt of the claim.
(b) Reimbursing Banks will not process requests for back value.

Article 12

Duplications of Reimbursement Authorizations

Issuing Bank must not, upon receipt of documents, give a new Reimbursement Authorization, or additional instructions.

If the Issuing Bank does not comply with the above and a duplicate reimbursement is made, it is the responsibility of the Issuing Bank to obtain the return of the amount of the duplicate reimbursement.

Reimbursing Bank assumes no liability or responsibility for any consequences that may arise from any such duplication.

D Miscellaneous Provisions

Article 13

Foreign Laws and Usages

Issuing Bank shall be bound by and shall indemnify the Reimbursing Bank against all obligations imposed by foreign laws and usages.

Article 14

Disclaimer on the Transmission of Messages

Reimbursing Banks assume no liability or responsibility for the consequences arising out of delay and/or loss in transit of any message(s), and for errors in translation.

Article 15

Force Majeure

Reimbursing Banks assume no liability for the consequences arising out of the interruption of their business by Acts of God, riots, civil commotions, insurrections, wars or causes beyond their control, or by any strikes or lockouts.

Article 16

Charges

In cases where the Reimbursing Bank's charges are for the account of another party, they shall be deducted when the Reimbursement Claim is honoured. If a Reimbursement Claim is never presented to the Reimbursing Bank, the Issuing Bank remains liable for such charges.

Article 17

Interest Claims/Loss of Value

All claims for loss of interest, loss of value due to any exchange rate fluctuations, revaluations or devaluations are between the Claiming Bank and the Issuing Bank (exception non-performance of Reimbursing bank in confirmed Reimbursement).

Revision Questions

True or False

1. Reimbursing Bank is obligated to honour a Reimbursement Claim once it is nominated as a reimbursing bank.

2. Reimbursement Authorizations and Amendments must be in the form of an authenticated teletransmission or a signed letter. When a Credit is issued by teletransmission, the Issuing Bank should advise its Reimbursement Authorization or Reimbursement Amendment by authenticated teletransmission.

3. Issuing Bank must send to Reimbursing Bank a copy of the Credit or any part thereof when it sends a reimbursement authorization.

4. Issuing bank may send to Reimbursing bank multiple Reimbursement Authorizations under one teletransmission or letter.

5. Issuing Banks shall require a certificate of compliance with the terms and conditions of the Credit in the Reimbursement Authorization.

6. Reimbursement Authorizations must state:

    i.   Credit number;
    ii.   currency and amount;
    iii. amounts more or less acceptable
    iv.   Claiming Bank if any;
    v.   parties responsible for Claiming Bank's and Reimbursing Bank's charges.

7. In a usance credit, Reimbursement Authorization must indicate the following additional information:

    i.   tenor of draft;
    ii.   drawer;
    iii. party responsible for acceptance and discount charges.

8. If Reimbursing Bank is not prepared to act under the Reimbursement Authorization or Reimbursement Amendment, it is not obliged to inform the Issuing Bank and not responsible for the consequences resulting from non-reimbursement and/or delay.

9. It is impossible to find an expiry date or latest date for presentation of a claim in a Reimbursement Authorization.

10. Reimbursing Banks take no responsibility for the expiry date of Credits.

11. It is the responsibility of the Issuing Bank to inform the Reimbursing bank for cancellation of any unutilized portion of the Credit when the credit expires.

12. Issuing Bank may issue a Reimbursement Amendment or cancel a Reimbursement Authorization at any time after its issue unless with Reimbursement undertaking.

13. Reimbursing Bank must reimburse the Issuing Bank for any Reimbursement Claims honoured prior to the receipt by it of notice of cancellation or Reimbursement Amendment.

14. Authorization by the Issuing Bank to the Reimbursing Bank to issue a Reimbursement Undertaking is irrevocable.

15. Authorization to issue a Reimbursement undertaking must contain:
    i. Credit number;
    ii. currency and amount;
    iii. amounts more or less;
    iv. full name and address of the Claiming Bank;
    v. latest date for presentation of a claim;
    vi. parties responsible for charges.

16. In a usance credit, Reimbursement Authorization must also indicate the following additional information:
    i. tenor of draft;
    ii. drawer;
    iii. party responsible for acceptance and discount charges.

17. If the Reimbursing Bank is authorized to issue its Reimbursement Undertaking but is not prepared to do so, it is not obliged to so inform the Issuing Bank.

18. Reimbursement undertaking must contain :
    i. Credit number and Issuing Bank;
    ii. currency and amount of the Reimbursement Authorization;
    iii. amounts more or less acceptable;
    iv. currency and amount of the Reimbursement Undertaking;
    v. latest date for presentation of a claim;
    vi. party to pay charges.

19. If the latest date for presentation of a claim falls on a day on which is closed because of heavy flood, it shall be extended to the first following business day.

20. If the latest date for presentation of a claim falls on Sunday, it shall be extended to the first following business day.

21. An Issuing Bank which has issued its irrevocable Reimbursement Authorization Amendment, shall be irrevocably bound as of the time of its advice of the Irrevocable Reimbursement Authorization Amendment.

22. The terms of the original Irrevocable Reimbursement Authorization will remain in force for the Reimbursing Bank until it communicates its acceptance of the amendment to the Issuing Bank.

23. A Reimbursing Bank must communicate its acceptance or rejection of an Irrevocable Reimbursement Authorization Amendment to the Issuing Bank.

24. A Reimbursing Bank is not required to accept or reject an Irrevocable Reimbursement Authorization Amendment until it has received acceptance or rejection from the Claiming Bank to its Undertaking Amendment.

25. A Reimbursement Undertaking can be amended or cancelled without the agreement of the Claiming Bank.

26. A Reimbursing Bank which has issued it Reimbursement Undertaking Amendment shall be irrevocably bound as of the time of its advice of the Undertaking Amendment.

27. The terms of the original Reimbursement Undertaking will remain in force for the Claiming Bank until it communicates its acceptance of the Undertaking Amendment to the Reimbursing Bank.

28. A Claiming Bank is not obliged to communicate its acceptance or rejection of a Reimbursement Undertaking Amendment to the Reimbursing Bank.

29. The Claiming Bank's claim for reimbursement : must be in the form of a teletransmission.

30. A Reimbursing Bank has the right to request that a Reimbursement Claim be authenticated and shall not be liable for any consequences resulting from any delay incurred.

31. If a Reimbursement Claim is made by teletransmission, no mail conformation is to be sent and Claiming Bank will not be

responsible for the consequences arisen from duplicate reimbursement.

32. A claim for reimbursement must, among other requirement, clearly indicate the Credit number and Issuing Bank; stipulate the principal amount and charges; not be a copy of the Claiming Bank's advice of payment; not include multiple Reimbursement Claims under one message.

33. In usance credit Claiming Bank must forward the draft with the Reimbursement Claim to the Reimbursing Bank for processing, and include the following :

    i.   general description of the goods
    ii. country of origin;
    iii. place of destination/performance; and if the transaction covers the shipment of merchandise.
    iv. date of shipment;
    v.   place of shipment.

34. Claiming Banks may indicate in a Reimbursement Claim that negotiation was made under reserve or against an indemnity.

35. Reimbursing Banks shall have a reasonable time, not to exceed three banking days following the day of issue of the Reimbursement Claim, to process claims.

36. If the Reimbursing Bank determines not to reimburse for any reason whatsoever, it shall give notice to that effect by telecommunication or, other expeditious means, without delay, but no later than the close of the third banking day following the day of receipt of the claim.

37. Reimbursing Banks will not process requests for back value.

38. Issuing Bank must not, upon receipt of documents, give a new Reimbursement Authorization, or additional instructions.

39. If the Issuing Bank does not comply with the above and a duplicate reimbursement is made, it is the responsibility of the Claiming Bank to obtain the return of the amount of the duplicate reimbursement.

40. Reimbursing Bank assumes no liability or responsibility for any consequences that may arise from any such duplication.

41. Issuing Bank shall be bound by and shall indemnify the Reimbursing Bank against all obligations imposed by foreign laws and usages.

42. Claiming Banks assume no liability or responsibility for the consequences arising out of delay and/or loss in transit of any message(s), and for errors in translation.

43. Issuing Banks assume no liability for the consequences arising out of the interruption of their business by Acts of God, riots, civil commotions, insurrections, wars or causes beyond their control, or by any strikes or lockouts.

44. In cases where the Reimbursing Bank's charges are for the account of another party, they shall be deducted when the Reimbursement Claim is honoured. If a Reimbursement Claim is never presented to the Reimbursing Bank, the Issuing Bank remains liable for such charges.

45. All claims for loss of interest, loss of value due to any exchange rate fluctuations, revaluations or devaluations are between the Claiming Bank and the Issuing Bank. (exception non-performance of Reimbursing bank in confirmed Reimbursement).

Answers

No.	Answer	Article No.	No.	Answer	Article No.
1	F	4	24	T	9g(v)
2	T	6a	25	F	9h(i)
3	F	6b(i)	26	T	9h(ii)
4	F	6b(ii)	27	T	9h(iii)
5	F	6c	28	F	9h(iv)
6	T	6d	29	F	10a(i)
7	T	6e	30	T	10a(i)
8	F	6g	31	F	10a(i)
9	F	7	32	T	10a(i)
10	T	7	33	T	10b
11	T	7	34	F	10c
12	T	8a	35	F	11a(i)
13	F	8c	36	T	11a(ii)
14	T	9b	37	T	11b
15	T	9b	38	T	12
16	T	9c	39	F	12
17	F	9d	40	T	12
18	T	9e	41	T	13
19	F	9f	42	F	14
20	T	9f	43	F	15
21	T	9g(iii)	44	T	16c
22	T	9g(iv)	45	T	17
23	T	9g(v)			

17

Questions
and
Answers

1. What is the main value of a documentary credit to the exporter?

A: The exporter has the assurance that provided he presents the documents in accordance with the terms and conditions of the credit, he will receive payment from the issuing bank.

   The financial standing of the importer is replaced by that of the issuing bank who gives a conditional undertaking to pay, accept or negotiate against presentation of the documents. The financial standing of a bank is normally better than that of an individual importer.

2. Is there any value of a documentary credit to the importer?

A: The importer will receive the documents which were specified by him when the credit was issued.

   He can control approximately the arrival of the goods by including in the D/C a latest shipment date. He is assured that he will only be debited with the value of the credit provided all the credit instructions have been carried out in accordance with his specifications.

3. If the exporter is doubtful about the credit standing of the D/C issuing bank, what additional protection is available to him from his banker? Briefly describe this service.

A: The exporter can request the buyer to issue a confirmed letter of credit. If a letter of credit is confirmed by a bank (the advising bank), this means that, in addition to the definite undertaking of the issuing bank to honour the commitment, the advising bank also adds its promise to pay the beneficiary. Such confirmation by the advising bank not only confirms the undertaking of the issuing bank but also constitutes an additional promise on the part of the advising bank (which becomes a confirming bank).

A confirmed D/C is normally requested by the beneficiary if the D/C applicant's country is facing political instability or if the credit standing of the issuing bank is in doubt.

4.   If an importer is trading with an exporter for the first time and he is quite concerned about the quality of the goods to be shipped, what precaution can he take?

A: The precaution can be:

    i.   He can include in the D/C the following term that the beneficiary is to ship the goods in accordance with the sales contract, i.e., "goods shipped in accordance with contract no. ... dated ...". He should also call for a beneficiary's certificate to certify it, as non-documentary condition can be disregarded by the exporter if he so intends, according to UCP–500 article 13 c, or/and

    ii.   provide for additional security by calling for documents such as a certificate of inspection issued by an independent party. A surveyor's report is most suitable, or/and

    iii.   ask for samples of the goods from the beneficiary before shipment, or/and

    iv.   try to find out the credit-standing of the supplier before making the contract.

5.   What are the differences between a Back-to-Back credit and a transferable credit?

A: Back-to-Back Credit:

    i.   Two separate credits are involved.

    ii.   The bank issuing the second credit (B/B L/C) makes a definite undertaking to pay the second beneficiary upon certain condition.

    iii.   Will not be stated as a Back-to-Back credit.

    iv.   Not specifically covered in article 48 of UCP–500 as in transfer credit.

    v.   It is possible for the second credit to have a currency different from the first credit.

    iv. In theory, a long chain of transactions can happen. The first beneficiary under the master credit can issue a Back-to-Back credit to a second beneficiary, who may issue another D/C to a third beneficiary based on the second credit as security etc.

Transferable Credit:

    i.   Only one credit is involved.

    ii. Transferring bank transfers the credit without taking responsibility (except negligence). It is the issuing bank which is obliged to honour beneficiary's draft.

    iii. Has to be stated as transferable.

    iv. Specifically covered in article 48 of UCP–500.

    v. Currency cannot be changed in case of transfer.

    vi. Can be transferred once only. The second beneficiary cannot transfer the D/C to a third party.

6. **What are the differences between D/P sight and D/P 30 days sight (D/P usance)?**

A: Under D/P, the banks may be instructed to release the commercial documents of title to the buyer against immediate payment for the goods. This form of collection is referred to as D/P or documents against payment.

When a bill of exchange is the financial document, it will be a sight bill.

The buyer must make immediate payment to the presenting bank in return for the shipping documents to take delivery of goods.

D/P usance, e.g., D/P 30 days sight, means payment is due 30 days after presentation of documents to the drawee (importer). But documents will only be released to the drawee on payment.

For instance, a Hong Kong importer is trading with a UK exporter on documents against payment basis. As we know, the documents can reach Hong Kong in a week, but shipment of goods takes more than a month. If the importer is required to honour payment immediately upon presentation of draft which is long before the arrival of goods, it will be unfair to him from his point of view. So, he can ask for a D/P 30 days sight in which case he is obliged to make payment 30 days after presentation of documents pending arrival of the goods. But he may make payment earlier in order to take delivery upon arrival of goods.

7. You have received a documentary collection for $100,000 directly from Shanghai, China, and the bill of exchange is drawn at 90 days sight on your customers, Luk's printing company.

Among other things, the collection order states:

i.   Release documents against acceptance.
ii. Protest if unpaid.
iii. In case of need, refer to City Consultant Company.

(a) What are the purposes and powers of a case-of-need?
(b) State what action you would take if the accepted bill was unpaid at maturity because customers claimed the goods to be unsatisfactory and not in accordance with the contract. Customers offer payment of $50,000 as they are negotiating fresh terms with the sellers.

A:

(a) A case-of-need is a person nominated by the seller to act on his behalf should any need arise. The only time that he might be called upon is on the dishonour of a bill, either on acceptance or payment.

If a case-of-need is nominated, the collection order should state precisely what his powers are. If the collection order states that he has the full powers of the seller, then, the bank will obviously abides by his instructions.

If the powers of the case of need are not indicated clearly and fully, then, the bank will refuse to take instructions from him.

(b)

    i.   accept the $50,000 and hold it on a suspense account pending receipt of further instructions from the remitting bank;

    ii. instruct a notary public to protest the bill having advised him that 50% had already been paid (protest if unpaid);

    iii. send an advice to the case of need, City Consultant Company, but no instructions should be accepted and acted upon from them;

    iv. send cable advice of the circumstances to the remitting bank asking for further instructions.

8.   **What are the main requirements of invoice in accordance with Uniform Customs and Practice for Documentary Credits UCP–500?**

A: Unless otherwise specified in the credit, the commercial invoice:

    i.   must be made out in the name of the applicant and issued by the beneficiary (article 37 a);

    ii. the description of goods in invoice must correspond with that on the credit although the description in other documents may be shown in general terms of the goods (article 37 c); e.g., Description of goods in D/C is:
        100,000 pcs (pieces) Men's Pyjamas at USD 3.65/pc.

If such was the case in the D/C, then invoice must show the same description:
100,000 pcs (pieces) Men's Pyjamas at USD 3.65/pc.

In other shipping documents such as bills of lading, insurance documents etc., the mere description of "Men's Pyjamas" is acceptable.

9. **What are the main requirements of a bill of lading in relation to UCP–500?**

A: Unless the D/C stipulates otherwise, a bill of lading must be:

    i.   clean,

    ii. shipped on board,

    iii. a full set (3/3 or 2/2),

    iv. issued by a carrier or a named agent for the carrier, or the master or a named agent for the master (article 23 a i),

    v. "freight prepaid": which must appear if D/C call for CIF term,

    vi. consistent with the description of goods in the invoice.

10. **An exporter known as City Company has been supplying toys to a Chinese buyer for several years, payment of which being always effected by letters of credit. Recently, the company received a complain from the importer on the increasing commission charged and time involved in this method of payment. On the other hand, City Company would not like to accept open account terms.**

    i.   **Suggest other methods of payment that may be used by City Company.**

    ii. **Compare the methods you suggested in (a) above in terms of time needed and protection to an exporter.**

    iii. **If the Chinese buyer insists on trading under open account terms, what other method related to D/C can City Company suggest to protect his position?**

A:

    i.   Other methods of payments:

       Cash in Advance

       (a) exporter receives full payment before making delivery of shipment,

       (b) gives exporter the greatest protection,

       (c) allows the exporter to avoid tying up its own funds,

(d) useful when the importer's country is facing political instability, or

(e) when there are exchange controls in the importer's country,

(f) probably, this payment method is unlikely to be accepted by the importer.
Documentary Collection
The exporter shipped the goods and arranges with his bank for the documents to be dispatched to an appropriate overseas correspondent bank for collection of payment

Types of collection:

(a) Clean collection — a collection of financial documents not accompanied by commercial documents

(b) Documentary collection — a collection involving commercial documents

(c) Document against payment — commercial documents are released to the importer upon payment

(d) Document against acceptance — documents are released upon the importer's acceptance of the bill of exchange

Probably, City Company may prefer to use collection.

ii. Comparison of different methods of payment.

In terms of time needed (in an ascending order):

(a) payment in advance (shortest)
(b) clean collection
(c) documents against payment
(d) documents against acceptance (longest)

In terms of protection to an exporter (in a descending order):

(a) payment in advance greatest protection
(b) documents against payment
(c) documents against acceptance
(d) clean collection least protection

iii. City Company can request a standby letter of credit issued by the Chinese buyer in its favour and at the same time accepts open account term.

Under the open account term, the Chinese buyer may receive regular shipments before paying the seller.

Meanwhile, the exporter, City Company can ask the Chinese buyer to arrange a standby credit opened in his favour, in case of default on a payment.

If the buyer happens to be default, the supplier, City Company can present a signed statement to the effect that payment has not been received under the open account term and claim payment under the standby credit. Hence standby D/C provides a guarantee against default of payment under open account term.

11. **Your customer, City Company (CC), imports antique furniture from China and resells to European companies. Recently, the company received a substantial order from a new European buyer. In view of the substantial amount, CC insists to have payment in some form of undertaking by a bank. CC also received similar request from its China supplier.**

   i. **Name and describe a suitable method of providing security of payment to CC.**
   ii. **How will the method you suggested in (a) above provide assistance to secure payment to the China supplier? Name and describe those methods.**

A:

   i. The appropriate method of payment is documentary credit.

   It is a written undertaking by a bank to make payment to the exporter, up to a certain sum of money, within a designated time period and against any stipulated terms and documents.

   Parties involved:
   (a) applicant (importer) European buyer

(b) issuing bank European buyer's bank

(c) beneficiary (exporter): CC

(d) advising bank: CC's bank

CC now gets an undertaking from the European buyer's bank to make payment in future, even if the buyer is insolvent, CC can still obtain payment from the issuing bank.

ii. Payment to China supplier may be effected by:

(a) Transferable credits

Can be transferred in whole or in part by the original beneficiary to one or more "second beneficiaries".

Normally used when the first beneficiary does not supply the goods himself.

Characteristics:

—irrevocable,
—transferred once,
—in accordance with the term and conditions of the original credit, except the name and address of the first beneficiary, the amount, the expiry date.

Ask the European buyer to apply for a transferable L/C.

The advising bank on receiving the L/C may transfer part of it to the China supplier.

(b) Back-to-Back credit

When a beneficiary receives a D/C which is not transferable, he may arrange with his banker to issue a B/B L/C.

The bank issuing the Back-to-Back credit will obtain repayment through the master D/C which is deposited to the issuing bank.

The issuing bank must ensure that the terms and conditions of the B/B L/C is the same as the original D/C, except the names of the beneficiary, shipment dates, etc.

12.   What is a confirmed letter of credit?

A: If a letter of credit is confirmed by a bank (the advising bank), this means that, in addition to the definite undertaking of the issuing bank to honour beneficiary's draft, the advising bank also adds its promise to pay the beneficiary. Such confirmation by the advising bank not only confirms the undertaking of the issuing bank but also constitutes an additional promise on the part of the advising bank (which becomes a confirming bank).

A confirmed D/C is normally requested by the beneficiary if the D/C applicant's country is facing political instability.

When the confirming bank has honoured its obligation under the terms of the credit, it has a right of recourse against the issuing bank.

In practice, the issuing bank must have arranged a line of confirmed credit with the advising bank before opening a confirmed D/C for its customers.

13.   State two circumstances under which a Back-to-Back credit is most appropriate.

A: A trader may be a middleman who cannot supply the goods himself. He has to arrange either a transfer credit or Back-to-Back credit issued to a supplier.

i.   If the ultimate buyer of the goods from the middleman is willing to issue a D/C but not a transferable D/C (due to a greater risk), a Back-to-Back credit is appropriate.

ii.   If the supplier of the goods is doubtful about the creditworthiness of the issuing bank and the ultimate buyer's country risk, he may not be prepared to accept a transfer credit. In this case, a Back-to-Back credit issued separately by the middleman's banker is most appropriate.

14. What do you understand by a red clause credit?

A: A red clause credit is a special type of credit with a clause which authorizes the advising or confirming bank to make advances to the beneficiary before presentation of the documents.

The clause is added in the credit at the request of the applicant for the credit. In other words, it is a pre-shipment finance in the form of a loan from the advising/confirming bank to the beneficiary, with payment of principal and interest guaranteed by the issuing bank of the credit, which in turn has the right of recourse to the applicant if beneficiary fails to perform under the credit.

The credit specifies the amount of the advance to be given to the beneficiary, which can be in the form of a percentage or a fixed sum.

Finance is given against undertaking from the beneficiary certifying that he promises to submit documents to advising bank.

15. Give a situation where it is most suitable to issue a revolving credit.

A: If an importer is trading with an overseas exporter and buying the same goods on a regular basis, with the same terms and conditions and at the same unit price, he can issue a revolving credit to this exporter instead of having to issue a credit with same terms and conditions every time.

This will save him time and the trouble of having to apply for many credits.

e.g., Luk's Printing Co. intends to import 10 tons of paper each month of USD 100,000 from a supplier in China for the next 12 months.

Luk's Printing Co. has to open one D/C each month (12 separate D/Cs) in order to import the same goods.

It can, as an alternative, open a revolving credit for USD 100,000 to be revolved each month for the same amount for the coming 12 months.

16. **What additional risks will an applicant of a transferable credit have to bear?**

A: He will have to deal with an unknown supplier since the integrity of the second beneficiary is not known.

Besides, the quality of the merchandise is not assured as it is shipped by an unknown party.

Amendment may not be advised to the ultimate supplier, so documents will never comply with D/C terms even though the second beneficiary presents documents in compliance with D/C.

17. **Explain two import facilities available to the importer.**

A: The facilities are:
  i.   Trust receipt (T/R):

       It is a document executed by a customer who is the pledgor of the goods or the documents of title thereto when they are released to him by a bank, in order that he may sell the goods and pay the proceeds to the bank.

  ii. Loan against goods (produce loan):

       This is a form of advance to importers based on the goods as security. Produce loan comes from the idea that importers usually buy goods in bulk and sell them quickly. Hence, provided the goods are not easily perishable and are marketable, banks are ready to give finance to the importers against goods.

(note: other facilities like letter of credit, overdraft are also acceptable)

18. **List two facilities available to an exporters.**

A: An exporter may use:
    i.   Negotiation of export bills.
    ii. Collection of export bills.

Appendix

- ❏ Blank Forms
    - ❏ Documentary Credit
    - ❏ Collection Order
    - ❏ Commercial Invoice
    - ❏ Bill of Lading
    - ❏ Certificate of Insurance
    - ❏ Certificate of Origin
- ❏ Authenticated Documents
    - ❏ Sample Documentary Credit
    - ❏ Bill of Exchange
    - ❏ Invoice
    - ❏ Packing List
    - ❏ GSP Form A
    - ❏ Bill of Lading
    - ❏ Insurance Policy
    - ❏ Beneficiary's Statement

Documentary Credit

Cable Confirmation	Airmail	
Date of Issue:	Credit Number of Issuing Bank #...	Credit number of Advising Bank #...
Advising Bank:	For Account of:	
To Beneficiary:	Amounts (in figures and words)	
	Expiry date: in: for negotiation	

Gentlemen:

We hereby open our irrevocable documentary letter of credit in your favour available by your drafts at .... drawn on .... for full invoice value clearly indicating the No. and date of this LC accompanied by documents specified below:

1. Full set of clean on board Marine Bills of Lading made to the order of ABC Bank marked "Freight Prepaid" notify ....
   Clean Air waybills consigned to ABC Bank, marked freight prepaid
2. Signed commercial invoices in ..... fold.
3. Marine insurance to be covered by accountee.
4. Weight and packing list in ..... fold.
   Covering shipment of: (name of goods) CFR Hong Kong
   Latest shipment date

Dispatch: To: Partial Ship: Transhipment:

SPECIAL CONDITIONS: INSTRUCTIONS TO NEGOTIATING BANK	
We hereby engage with drawers and/or bona fide holders that draft drawn and negotiated/paid in conformity with the terms of this credit will be duly honoured on presentation and that draft accepted within the terms of the credit will be duly honoured at maturity. The advising bank is requested to notify the beneficiary without adding their confirmation. Subject to the Uniform Customs and Practice for Documentary Credit (1993 Revision) ICC publication N° 500. Yours faithfully ABC Bank Auth. Signature	Advising bank's notification:

Collection Order

Drawer/Exporter	Drawer's/Exporter's reference (to be quoted by banks in all correspondence)						
Consignee	Drawee (if not Consignee)						
To your corresponding bank	Designated bank:						
FORWARD DOCUMENTS ENUMERATED BELOW BY AIRMAIL. FOLLOW SPECIAL INST AND THOSE MARKED X.							
Bill of Exchange	Comm'l Invoice	Cert/Cons Inv	Cert of Origin	Ins'ce/ Pol Cert	Bill of Lading	Parcel Post Rec	Airway Bill
Combined Trans Doc		Other doc and whereabouts of any missing original Bills of Lading					
RELEASE DOC AGAINST	ACCEPT- ANCE	PAY- MENT	If unaccepted and advise reason by			Protest	Don't
If unpaid/unaccepted	Store the goods	Do not Store				Cable	Airmail
	Insure the goods	Do not Insure	If unpaid and advise reason by			Protest	Don't
Collect all charge		Waive the charge/do not waive					
Collect cor'd corresponding change		Waive/do not waive	Advise due date by			Cable	Airmail
Return Account Bill by Airmail			Remit proceeds by			Cable	Airmail
In case of need, refer to			For Guidance			Accept their Instruct- ions	

SPECIAL INSTRUCTIONS:	
Date of Bill of Exchange:	Bill of Exchange Value/Amount of coll'n
Tenor of Bill of Exchange	Please collect the above mentioned Bill and/ or Doc subject to .... or delay however caused ....
Bill of Exchange Claused:-	
Payment instructions: Please credit proceeds to our account no. Others:	
	Date & Signature:

Commercial Invoice

GOODS CONSIGNED FOR ACCOUNT AND RISK OF MESSRS.		INVOICE NO.		DATE	
Carrier	Form	Marks & Numbers			
Port (Discharge)	Destination	Departure Date	Order No.	Total Pkgs	
Description		Quantity	Unit Price	Amount	
Payment term: (e.g., 90 days signed under DC) Shipping term: (e.g., CFR Hong Kong)					

Bill of Lading

BILL OF LADING FOR COMBINED SHIPMENT OR PORT TO PORT SHIPMENT

Shipper

B/L No ....
Booking Ref: ....
Shipper's Ref: ....

Consignee ....

Notify Party/Address	Place of Receipt ....
Intended Vessel and Voy. No.	Place of Delivery ....

Intended Port of Loading

....

Intended Port of Discharge loaded on Board the vessel on:

Marks and nos.	Quantity And Kind of Packages	Description	Weight and Measurement

ABC shipping company
AS carrier

Certificate of Insurance

CERTIFICATE OF INSURANCE

Issued at the request of and for the convenience of the assured and to have the same force and effect as the Company's usual form of Cargo Policy and always subject to the terms thereof.

Date ....

THIS IS TO CERTIFY that XYZ INSURANCE COMPANY LTD has insured in Hong Kong the following shipment under and subject to the conditions of Open Policy No .... in favour of RTG (Holdings) LTD and/or their Subsidiary and/or Associated Companies.

Certificate Issued for the Account of

	INTEREST
Sum Insured (figures)	
Sum Insured (words)	
....	
Vessel	
Sailing Date	
Voyage at and from	
a	
Conditions As per Open Policy No	
Inaccordance with CLAUSES	
Settling Agents	Survey Agents
....	....
....	....
....	....
	....
	....

KEY TO CLAUSE NUMBERS

1. All risks, Institute Cargo Clauses (A) S.R.C.C. and war
2. W.A., Institute Cargo Clauses (B) S.R.C.C. and war
3. F.P.A., Institute Cargo Clauses (C) S.R.C.C. and war
4. Air Cargo, all risks, S.R.C.C. and war
5. Parcel Pose, all risks, S.R.C.C. and war
6. Airmail, all risks, S.R.C.C. and war
7. Miscellaneous conditions

This certificate is not valid unless
Countersigned by RTG(Holdings) LTD.

Countersigned ....

All matters relating to the Certificate shall be referred to the XYZ INSURANCE COMPANY LTD. P.O. BOX 11102.

Certificate of Origin

1. Goods consigned from (exporter's business name, address, country)	Reference No .... Generalized system of Preferences CERTIFICATE OF ORIGIN (Combined declaration & certificate) FORM A Issued in .... (country) see note over
2. Goods consigned to (consignee's name, address, country)	
3. Means and transport and route (as far as known)	4. For official use

5. Item No.	6. Marks & No. of pkg	7. No. and kind of pkg; description of goods	8. Origin criterion	9. Gross weight or other quality	10. No. & date of invoice

11. Certification It is hereby certified, on the basis of control carried out, that the declaration by the exporter is correct. .... Place, date, signature, stamp of certificate authority	12. Declaration by exporter The undersigned hereby declares that the above details and statement are correct; the all goods were produced in .... (country) and that they comply with the origin requirements specified for those goods in the Generalized System of Preference for goods exported to .... (importing country) .... Place, date, and signature

Sample Documentary Credit issued by City Bank, NY, USA L/C No. 1234

Issuing bank	:	City Bank, New York, USA
Applicant	:	City I/E Company Limited, 1 New York Road, NY, USA
Beneficiary	:	Hong Kong Co Ltd
Amount	:	USD 12,500.00

We open an irrevocable documentary credit number 1234 dated 26 September 1998 in favour of Hong Kong Co Ltd for account of City I/E Co Ltd NY USA.

With the following terms and conditions:

To be accompanied by:

1. Signed commercial invoice in quadruplicate.
2. Packing list in duplicate.
3. Certificate of origin (GSP FORM A)
4. Duplicate copies of freight forwarder's charges.
5. Beneficiary's statement certifying that copies of all documents plus one non-negotiable copy have been mailed direct to buyer.
6. Full set clean on Board Ocean bill of lading and 1 copy issued to the order of City I/E Co Ltd, 1, New York Road, NY, USA marked "Freight Collect" and to notify applicant at 487-0075.
7. Insurance policy covering all risks and war risks.

Covering:

"Basket ware and housewares"   SHIPPING MARKS: Ever Good

Latest shipment date 22/3/1999
Expiry date 6/4/1999
Partial shipments allowed   MADE IN CHINA
Transhipments allowed

Special Conditions:

1. Drawings under this letter of credit may be negotiated through any bank in Hong Kong.
2. All banking charges other than our own are for account of beneficiary.
3. All documents to be sent to us in one lot by registered mail.
4. CFS charges are accepted.
5. Shipment C & I USA from Hong Kong to USA.
6. Please notify beneficiary at telep.

_____

Authorized Signature(s)

Bill of Exchange

No ____70818____

Exchange for _____USD12,500.-_____   *Hong Kong,* ____19 MAR 1999_____

         *At*_____   *after sight of this* FIRST *of*

Exchange (Second of the same tenor and date being unpaid)

Pay to the order of **Bank of Hong Kong Ltd.**

US DOLLARS TWELVE THOUSAND FIVE HUNDRED ONLY ******

Value received ___100 sets of BASKET WARE_____

*To*__City Bank, NY USA_____   For and on behalf of

                                          HONG KONG CO LTD.

Hong Kong Company Limited
ADDRESS: Middle Road, Far East Mansion
Tsimshatsui, Kowloon, P O Box 1, G P O Hong Kong

I N V O I C E

Invoice No_____6_____   Hong Kong _____1 Mar 1999_____

TO: City I/E Co Ltd, 1 New York Road, NY, USA

MARKS & NUMBERS	QUANTITY	DESCRIPTION	UNIT PRICE	AMOUNT
◇ EVER GOOD ◇ MADE IN CHINA CTNS 1–30	100 sets	BASKET WARE C & I USA DRAWN UNDER City Bank, NY, USA L/C NO. 1234 DATED 26 SEPT, 1998 For and on behalf of Hong Kong Company Limited ——————————— Manager	@125 per set	USD 12,500.-

Hong Kong Company Limited
ADDRESS: Middle Road, Far East Mansion
Tsimshatsui, Kowloon, P O Box 1, G P O Hong Kong

PACKING LIST

Invoice No____6_____   *Hong Kong _____1 Mar 1999_____*

Shipping Mark & Nos.	Number of CTN	Containing		Weight		Measurement CM
		Quantity	Description of Article	Net Kg	Gross Kg	
◇EVER GOOD◇ MADE IN CHINA CTNS 1-30	30 CTNS	50 doz	Primula cluster w/18 ivs & 66 flowers Item no. 1 Fty no. 1 Colour: 48 doz Salmon 48 doz Lavender	90 Kgs	100 Kgs	12 x 12 x 12 CM
		75 doz	Hoya Vine x 32/42 flowers & 47 lvs. Item no. 2 Fty no. 2 Colour: 36 doz White Red 36 doz Pink Red			
		100 doz	Episicia vine x 5 w/226 lvs & 16 flowers Item no. 3 Fty no. 3 Colour: Rose Red			
		125 doz	Calathea Zebrina plant x 18 lvs Item no. 4 Fty no. 4 Colour: 2 Tone Green			
		75 doz	Streptocarpus x 8 lvs, 5 flrs & 3 buds Item no. 5 Fty no. 5 Colour: 24 doz purple 24 doz Light Ping			

For and on behalf of
Hong Kong Company Limited

Manager

G.S.P. Form A

1. Goods consigned from (Exporter's business name, address, country) LUCKY Trading Co Ltd., Shenzhen, China	Reference No. SN 41/99/013 GENERALIZED SYSTEM OF RREFERENCES CERTIFICATE OF ORIGIN (Combined declaration and certificate) FORM A
2. Goods consignee to (Consignee's name, address, country) City I/E Co Ltd. 1, New York Road, NY, USA	Issued in <u>PEOPLE'S REPUBLIC OF CHINA</u> (country) See Notes overleaf
3. Means of transport and route (as far as known) BY TRUCK FROM SHENZHEN TO HONG KONG ON/AFTER 28 JAN 1999 AND TRANSHIPPED TO FRANCE BY SEA.	4. For official use

5. Item number	6. Marks and numbers of packages	7. Number and kind of packages; description of goods	8. Origin criterion (see Notes overleaf)	9. Gross weight or other quantity	10. Number and date of invoices
5	◇EVER GOOD◇ MADE IN CHINA 1–30	20 CTNS BASKET WARE TOTAL TWENTY CTNS ONLY	"W"	100 SETS	#89/006 26 JAN 99

11. Certification It is hereby certified on the basis of control carried out, that the declaration by the exporter is correct.	12. Declaration by the exporter The undersigned hereby declares that the above details and statements are correct: that all the goods were produced in <u>The People's Republic of China</u> (country) and that they comply with the origin requirements specified for those goods in the Generalized System of Preferences for goods exported to USA.
	For & on behalf of LUCKY Trading Co Ltd., Shenzhen, China
<u>SHENZHEN, 26 JAN 1999</u> Place and date, signature and stamp of certifying authority	

Bill of Lading

Shipper		B/L No. H K 888
JOY AND GAY CO LTD. Merry Building, Happy Road, Kowloon, Hong Kong.		

ScanCity

Europe/Far East – Far East/Europe
Operated by the Line's detailed on the reverse of this Document

Consignee of Order	Carrier
City I/E Co Ltd., 1, New York Road, NY, USA	NEDLLOYD

Notify Party/Address	It is agreed that no responsibility shall attach to the Carrier or his Agents for failure to notify (See Clause 20 on reverse of this Bill of Lading)	Place of Receipt	(Applicable only when this document as used as a Combined Transport Bill of Lading)
City I/E Co Ltd., 1, New York Road, NY, USA			HONGKONG CFS

Vessel and Voy. No.		Place of Delivery	(Applicable only when this document is used as a Combined Transport Bill of Lading)
EVER HIGH v/170	522		
	Port Loading HONG KONG		New York, USA
Port of Discharge LOS ANGELES			

Marks and Nos: Container Nos:	Number and kind of Packages: description Goods	Gross Weight (kg)	Measurement (cbm)
	20 CTNS BASKET WARE	100 Kgs	12 x12 x12cm

⟨EVER GOOD⟩

MADE IN CHINA
CTNS 1–30

CONTAINER NO. 88888

ONE OF THREE PARTS CARGO. DELIVERY IS TO BE MADE WHEN COMBINING B/L NO. HK0549 & HK0550

SHIPPED ON BOARD
20 MARCH 1999

ABOVE PATICULARS AS DECLARED BY SHIPPER

* Total No. ofContainers/Packages 20	RECEIVED by the Carrier from the Shipper in apparent good order and condition (unless otherwise noted herein) the total number or quantity of Containers or other packages or units indicated * stated by the Shipper to comprise the Goods specified above for Carriage subject to all the terms herof (INCLUDING THE TERMS ON THE REVERSE HEREOF AND THE TERMS OF THE CARRIERS APPLICABLE TARIFF) from the Place of Receipt or the Port of Loading whichever is aplicable to the Port of Discharge or the Place of Delivery whichever is applicable. One original Bill of Lading must be surrendered duty endorsed in exchange for the Goods in accepting this Bill of Lading the Merchant expressly accepts and agrees to all its terms conditions and exceptions whether printed stamped or written or otherwise incorporated notwithstanding the non-signing of this Bill of Lading by the Merchant.	
Movement LCL/FCL		
Freight and Charges (Indicate whether prepaid or collect):		
Origin Inland Handling Charge		
Origin Terminal Handling/LCL Service Charge P	Freight payable at HONG KONG	Place and Date of Issue HONG KONG
Ocean Freight C	Number of Original Bills of Lading THREE (03)	IN WITNESS whereof the number of original Bills of Lading stated opposite have been issued one of which being accomplished the other(s) to be void
Destination Terminal Handling/LCL Service Charge C		
Destination Inland Handling Charge		
	ORIGINAL	For the Carrier For and on behalf ot Far East Shipping Co as agent for ScanCity — the carrier

Insurance Policy

INSURANCE COMPANY OF AMERICA   ORIGINAL
(INCORPORATED IN USA WITH LIMITED LIABILITY)

Hong Kong Service Office
G.P.O. Box 123
Hong Kong.
Telephone: 852-1234567
Facsimile: 123 HK 456789

SPECIAL MARINE POLICY

(This policy is issued in Duplicate, one of which being accomplished the other to be null and void.)

No. HOC 0 22

Declaration under Open Policy
No. 87 HK 12

FOR THE ACCOUNT OF

HONG KONG CO LTD.

Producer KNI

Consignee / Buyer

DATE: Hong Kong 21 MAR 1999

This Company, in consideration of a premium as agreed and subject to the Terms and Conditions printed or stamped hereon and/or attached hereto, insures, lost or not lost, the following shipment.

Pre-Carriage From	Port of Loading	
	Hong Kong	Please note, this document may require to be stamped within a given period in order to conform with the laws of the country of destination. Holders are therefore advised to ascertain the amount of stamp duty that is required and act according.
Conveyance	Date of Departure	
EVER HIGH	20 Mar 1999	
Port of Discharge	Place of Delivery if on-carriage	Insured Value (state currency)
LOS ANGELES		USD13,700.00

Marks and Numbers	Interest	
◇ EVER GOOD ◇ MADE IN CHINA CTNS 1–30	20 CTNS BASKET WARE	**Claims:** Surveys to be conducted by CIGNA Worldwide Inc., Akasaka Eight-One Bldg., HONG KONG Claims (if any) payable in the currency of the draft at HONG KONG by:- the above to the order of:- on surrender of the Policy. **IMPORTANT:** **YOUR ATTENTION IS DRAWN TO THE INSTRUCTIONS TO CLAIMANTS ON THE BACK OF THIS POLICY.**

Conditions of Insurance – Institute Cargo Clauses (A) – applying to this Policy (Nominate either A, B or C) see over.

Delete if not required – Including War, Strikes and Malicious Damage as per Institute Clauses.
Institute Replacement Clauses, Labels Clause, Institute Dangerous Drugs Clause.
NOTE: Institute Clauses referred to herein are those current at date of issue of this Policy.

This Policy is subject to the provisions of the Marine Insurance Act, 1909, except as modified or altered by the terms of this Policy or any endorsement attached hereto.

In Witness Whereof, this Company has caused these presents to be signed by its Hong Kong Service Office General Manager

Not valid or negotiable unless countersigned by

Beneficiary's Statement

Hong Kong Company Limited
ADDRESS: Middle Road, Far East Mansion
Tsimshatsui, Kowloon, P O Box 1, G P O Hong Kong

BENEFICIARY'S STATEMENT

Invoice No ____6____   *Hong Kong* ____*1 Mar 1999*____
TO: City I/E Co Ltd, 1, New York Road, NY, USA

MARKS & NUMBERS	QUANTITY	DESCRIPTION	UNIT PRICE	AMOUNT
EVER GOOD MADE IN CHINA CTNS 1–30	100 sets	BASKET WARE C & I USA DRAWN UNDER City Bank, NY, USA L/C NO. 1234 DATED 26 SEPT, 1998	@125 per set	USD12,500.-

We certify that copies of all documents plus one non-negotiable copy have been mailed direct to buyer.

For and on behalf of
Hong Kong Company Limited

Bibliography

1. Charles del Busto (1994). *ICC Guide to Documentary Credit Operations*. Paris: International Chamber of Commerce.

2. Joseph Chan (1994). *An Analysis of UCP–500*, BOC Group Training Centre (in Chinese). Hong Kong: Bank of China.

3. Taylor Dan (1997). *ICC Guide to Bank-to-Bank Reimbursements under Documentary Credits*. Paris: International Chamber of Commerce.

4. T. K. Ghose (1993). *Export Credit Insurance–A Hong Kong Perspective*. Division of Commerce, City Polytechnic of Hong Kong , monograph co-ordinated by Dr. T. Oswald Siu, City University of Hong Kong.

5. Gutteridge, H. C. and Maurice Megrah (1984). *The Law of Bankers' Commercial Credits*. London: Europa Publications Limited.

6. William Hedley (1994). *Bills of Exchange and Bankers' Documentary Credits*. London: Lloyd's London Press Ltd.

7. HSBC (1994). *The ABC Guide to Trade Services*. Hong Kong: HSBC.

8. International Chamber of Commerce (1997). *DOCDEX Rules for Documentary Credit Dispute Resolution Expertise*. Paris: International Chamber of Commerce.

9. _____ (1995–99). *Documentary Credit Insight*. Various Volumes. Paris: International Chamber of Commerce.

10. _____ (1998). *International Standby Practices, ISP98*. Paris: International Chamber of Commerce.

11. _____ (1998). *The Official Commentary on the International Standby Practices, ISP98*. Paris: International Chamber of Commerce.

12. _____ (1997). *Opinions of the ICC Banking Commission ICC Publication N° 434 and N° 565*. Paris: International Chamber of Commerce.

13. _____ (1993). *Uniform Customs and Practice for Documentary Credits Publication N° 500*. Paris: International Chamber of Commerce.

14. _____ (1995). *Uniform Rules for Collections Publication N° 522 and Its Commentary*. Paris: International Chamber of Commerce.

15. International Chamber of Commerce (1992). *Uniform Rules for Demand Guarantees ICC Publication N° 458*. Paris: International Chamber of Commerce.

16. _____ (1995). *Uniform Rules for Bank-to-Bank Reimbursement Publication N° 525*. Paris: International Chamber of Commerce.

17. Raymond Jack (1991). *Documentary Credit*. London: Butterworths.

18. Guillermo Jimenez (1997). *ICC Guide to Export-Import Basics*. Paris: International Chamber of Commerce.

19. Abdul Latiff Abdul Rahim (1994). *Guide to Documentary Credit Rules: UCP–500*. Kuala Lumper: Institute of Bankers Malaysia.

20. T. O. Lee (1998). *Banker's L/C Operation Risks Advanced Level Workshop* and newspaper articles in *Hong Kong Economic Journal*, Hong Kong: T. O. Lee Consultants Ltd.

21. K. W. Luk (1995). *Foundations of International Trade Finance*. Hong Kong: Hong Kong Institute of Bankers.

22. Clive M. Schmitthoff (1964). *The Law and Practice of International Trade*. London: Stevens.

23. Paul Todd (1993). *Bills of Lading & Bankers' Documentary Credits*. London: Lloyd's of London Press Ltd.

24. Cowdell/Hyde Watson (1997). *Finance of International Trade 6*[th] Edition. London: Institute of Financial Services, U.K.

25. Wickremeratne, Lakshman Y. and Michael Rowe (1998). *Trade Finance: The Complete Guide to Documentary Credits*. London: The Chartered Institute of Bankers, U.K.

26. Lakshman Y. Wickremeratne (1996). *ICC Guide to Collection Operations*. Paris: International Chamber of Commerce.

About the Author

Kwai Wing LUK, Diploma, AHKIB; Bachelor in Management, MBA, University of Birmingham. He worked in banks of Hong Kong for 10 years from the early 1980s to the early 1990s as a senior officer. Since 1992, he has taught in local universities. Specializing in commercial banking and trade finance, Mr. Luk has trained many banking professionals in Hong Kong and China. He is an examiner and a marker for the banking institute and former brokers' examination. He has also been a script moderator for books and videos used in bank training, and a guest speaker of multinational firms on international trade finance.

His publications include one book and a number of articles on international trade, banking and finance. He is now a lecturer at the Division of Commerce, City University of Hong Kong.

Acknowledgements

I would like to thank the following institutions and persons for their support in my writing of this book, and for the permission to reproduce parts of their publications:

1. Bank of China, Hong Kong (special thanks to Mr. David Yu, General Manger of BOC Group Operation Centre HK)
2. Chinese General Chamber of Commerce
3. Federation of Hong Kong Industries
4. Hong Kong Export Credit Insurance Corporation
5. Hong Kong General Chamber of Commerce
6. Hong Kong Institute of Bankers
7. Hong Kong Trade Development Council (especially to Mr. Y. M. Wong)
8. International Chamber of Commerce, ICC Asia and Paris, France, for their publications:

   ICC Uniform Customs and Practice for Documentary Credits — 1993 Revision, ICC Publication N° 500 — ISBN 92.842.1155.7 (E), published in its official English version by the International Chamber of Commerce, copyright © 1993 — International Chamber of Commerce (ICC), Paris.

   ICC Uniform Rules for Bank-to-Bank Reimbursements, ICC Publication N° 525 — ISBN 92.842.1185.9 (E), published in its official English version by the International Chamber of Commerce, copyright © 1995 — International Chamber of Commerce (ICC), Paris.

   ICC Uniform Rules for Collections, ICC Publication N° 522 — ISBN 92.842.1184.0 (E), published in its official English version by the International Chamber of Commerce, copyright © 1995 — International Chamber of Commerce (ICC), Paris.

351

All available from: *ICC Publishing*, S. A., 38 Cours Albert 1er, 75008 Paris, France; and from *ICC Asia*, Unit B, 7/F, Shun Ho Tower, 24–30 Ice Street House, Central, Hong Kong

9. Indian Chamber of Commerce, Hong Kong
10. Nalco Associates, Malaysia
11. T. O. Lee Consultants Ltd., Canada
12. Trade Department, Hong Kong SAR

Index